What people are s

From 50 to

We found ourselves nodding our heads in acknowledgment of the challenges inherent in founding and growing a business. The authors have hit on many familiar problems and agonizing decisions. Reflective and honest readers will certainly benefit from the insights offered in these pages.

John Nury, Founder of Circle R Safety

David Nury, Leader of Circle R Safety, D&D Leasing, LLC, and Beth's Barricades

Circle R Safety (founded in 1982) was acquired by private equity in 2017.

From 50 to 500 represents a comprehensive, highly functional toolbox for the small business leader. The book is loaded with valuable insight, relevant business cases, and motivation to learn, grow, and succeed. Small businesses function and execute best as a team, and teams are best led by intelligent and adaptive leaders. Leaders willing to learn and evolve. The book's well-thought-out success narrative serves as a blueprint for positive change management. I strongly encourage people considering a new venture, developing a new business, and scaling an early-stage company to buy this book! Once you do, dog-ear the pages, take notes, and enthusiastically apply the tricks and tools the authors generously provide for the reader. If you do, you will achieve new heights, and your employees and customers will thank you!

Marty Strong, Navy SEAL officer (retired). CEO and Chief Strategy Officer at LGS Management Group. Author of *Be Nimble: How the Creative Navy SEAL Mindset Wins on the Battlefield and in Business*

This book should be on the shortlist for anyone at the helm of a business who feels that most leadership content skews too entrepreneurial or too corporate to be in touch with the intricacies of a rapidly budding organization. *From 50 to 500* brings to life the oft-overlooked leadership needs of growing from a small business to a medium enterprise; and does so in a relatable way that encourages self-reflection, awareness, and improvement.

Roy Amin, Managing Partner at REVPAR VENTURES

We see entrepreneurs and small companies build and develop America's downtowns and main streets. How exciting to see a book that speaks to those business leaders! Without doubt, this is the formula for success—how owners of small companies can grow their organizations and build long-lasting companies that drive our economy.

Randy Lewis, Executive Director of Main Street Martinsburg, accredited by National Main Street Center

This book is carefully crafted to reach the management of companies having more than fifty people and on a growth path to increasing that number. The authors set forth for guidance via a High Impact Leadership Model that includes parameters for Business and People Judgment that are the keys to success. Quarterly reviews focusing on the challenges and decisions of two hypothetical business leaders coupled with authors' insights on the quality and impact of their decisions represent a great universal education for every business manager. Since small businesses do not have the funds to hire people like the authors, this is a great alternative.

Paul Dean, Economist, Investment Banker, and Founder of Collateral Guarantee

Although we are technically buying stock in companies, venture capitalists are really investing in human capital—the founders and management. We would rather invest in an "A" leadership team with a "B" plan than a "B" team with an "A" plan. This book should be required reading for leaders of fast-growing startups or small companies and their teams.

Andrew Zulauf, Executive Director of West Virginia Jobs Investment Trust

The authors pretty much challenged every leadership "guru" and said: You don't understand small business leaders; they are not like execs of large companies. The PRG model is unique and makes all the sense in the world—allowing one to think very specifically about their organization's growth potential. What a great perspective. *From 50 to 500*'s leadership model and development tools speak to me as a small business leader and will help readers to dramatically improve their leadership impact.

Ryan S. Chadwick, Founder of Fathom Brands

There are plenty of business books out there, but few that truly get the challenges of what it is like to grow a small organization into a much larger one. The authors have clearly been in those shoes—the case studies and the year in the life of two leaders were profoundly valuable and practical. I would recommend this book to any leader with an ambition to aggressively and sustainably grow their business.

Rich Berens, CEO and Chief Client Fanatic at Root Inc. (an Accenture company)

From 50 to 500

Mastering the Unique Leadership Challenges of Growing Small Companies

From 50 to 500

Mastering the Unique Leadership
Challenges of Growing Small Companies

Jonathan Dapra, Richard Dapra,
Jonas Akerman

BUSINESS
BOOKS

Winchester, UK
Washington, USA

JOHN HUNT PUBLISHING

First published by Business Books, 2023
Business Books is an imprint of John Hunt Publishing Ltd., No. 3 East St., Alresford,
Hampshire SO24 9EE, UK
office@jhpbooks.com
www.johnhuntpublishing.com
www.johnhuntpublishing.com/business-books

For distributor details and how to order please visit the 'Ordering' section on our website.

Text copyright: Jonathan Dapra, Richard Dapra, Jonas Akerman 2021

ISBN: 978 1 78904 743 1
978 1 78904 744 8 (ebook)
Library of Congress Control Number: 2021949889

A CIP catalogue record for this book is available from the British Library.

Design: Matthew Greenfield

UK: Printed and bound by CPI Group (UK) Ltd, Croydon, CR0 4YY
Printed in North America by CPI GPS partners

We operate a distinctive and ethical publishing philosophy in
all areas of our business, from our global network of authors to
production and worldwide distribution.

Contents

Acknowledgments   xv

Introduction   1

Section I. Leading in High Growth Environments   5
    Chapter 1. Size Matters   9
    Chapter 2. High Impact Leadership   25

Section II. Meet the Leaders   45
    Chapter 3. Identifying Leader Motivation   51
    Chapter 4. Exploring Business Decision-Making   62
    Chapter 5. Insights into People Decisions   81

Section III. Leadership in the PRG   93
    Chapter 6. Hard to Say No   101
    Chapter 7. Skyrocketing Benefits   108
    Chapter 8. Third-Party Provider   114
    Chapter 9. To Discount or Not   120
    Chapter 10. Getting Products on the Shelves   128
    Chapter 11. Acquisition Opportunity   134
    Chapter 12. Adding the Last 10 Percent   141
    Chapter 13. Bonus Conundrum   148
    Chapter 14. Salesforce Backlash   156
    Chapter 15. The Ultimatum   164
    Chapter 16. Remote Work   171
    Chapter 17. Watering Rocks   178
    Chapter 18. Diversity Challenge   185
    Chapter 19. Safe or Sorry   192
    Chapter 20. Is Now Really the Time?   199
    Chapter 21. Pricing Model Change   208
    Chapter 22. The Departure   216

Chapter 23. High Performer—Low Values   223
Chapter 24. Feature Creep   231
Chapter 25. Holes in the Cheese   241
Chapter 26. Where's the Beef?   249
Chapter 27. Culture Clash   255
Chapter 28. Social Capital   264
Chapter 29. Coaching Challenge   274
Chapter 30. Tempted by Growth   281
Chapter 31. Change Is Tough   291
Chapter 32. Know Your Customer   298
Chapter 33. Old Dogs, New Tricks   306
Chapter 34. Summary Insights   315
Chapter 35. Leadership Results   333

Section IV. Self-Awareness   343
Chapter 36. Self-Assessment: Looking
    in the Mirror   347
Chapter 37. Development: Taking
    Action to Change   359

Closing Thoughts   380
Partners to the World's Small Businesses   382
About the Authors   384
Work Vessels for Veterans   388

Appendices   391
Appendix A. Self-Assessment Reports   393
Appendix B. Seminal Works in Leadership   406
Appendix C. Development Planning Tool   411

Bibliography   413

Dedicated to Jeannie Dapra
A thoughtful friend, world's best mother, most fun nana, and wonderful wife who inspired her family to embrace life, love one another and "Dream Big"

Acknowledgments

First and foremost, the authors would like to thank our families. Your love and encouragement stoked our creative fire for writing *From 50 to 500*. Thanks for always asking about our progress, feigning interest in the more mundane aspects of our work, and for being the biggest cheerleaders in the room.

A cadre of friends and trusted colleagues inspired and supported our efforts to bring you *From 50 to 500*. We want to acknowledge them.

Denise Hutchins makes us look good—her marketing and PR voice has and will continue to guide us as we talk about this book, ourselves, and our company. We think Taylor Graham is great. Early on, she provided an editor's perspective of our narrative that not only reassured but inspired us to write *From 50 to 500* as we did. She was Terry's interpreter, and whenever she touched our work, the words became better. As first-time authors we reached out to several colleagues and authors including Jim Haudan, Rich Berens, Dave Dowling, Robert Brinkerhoff, Debbie Myers, and Roy Amin. We appreciate the time each took to critique our early chapters and the incredibly insightful feedback they provided.

Each of us would like to express our appreciation to individuals who helped us throughout our respective careers and ultimately led us to where we are today.

Jonathan recognizes it was Jayne Mueller, the President of *Dynamic Graphics,* who plucked me away from *AutoFX* and entrusted a young outsider with significant divisions of her company. This was my first experience leading in a PRG organization—I was motivated to do good things there. Later, Andy Zulauf was the first venture capitalist with whom I worked. He was a constant ally and friend who introduced me to the world of private investment. Mark Pover was the first "big name" to join my company's board. Since then, he has always been an email away to advise and offer support. Finally, Jamie Gaucher, whose work in state and local business development agencies has always inspired me to see the potential in the companies right there in the community.

The concept of distinct small business leadership success factors was first developed and researched under the guidance of Dr. Tom Kemp, my doctoral dissertation chair, one of the smartest and equally kind professors I have ever known. A significant challenge in developing that research was accessing leaders willing to be interviewed and profiled. Each had to allow me to interview their direct reports and key stakeholders. It was Jonathan Hodge, CEO of *Advantage Performance Group,* who encouraged many of his peers to participate in my study. Without his selfless effort, the research would have taken significantly more time to complete.

Finally, Jonathan thanks Professors Roxana Wright and Botao An, my most respected colleagues who gave their time and expertise whenever I came to them with a question. Roxana has been a trusted sounding board. Her capacity to dissect our approaches and provide meaningful feedback helped make this more relevant and accessible to readers.

Richard would like to begin by recognizing Bill Byham, the founder of *Development Dimensions International,* who gave me the opportunity to learn and apply the assessment center method with many great clients. Bill is a role model for pushing innovation and professionalism in the field of assessment and development. He would also like to acknowledge the executive team at *Liberty Mutual,* who were committed to raising the standard for talent identification and development as a key corporate goal. They provided the resources and support for helping me achieve their goal.

Many thanks to my *BTS* assessment practice colleagues, particularly Jurgen Bank and David Bernal, who were the stalwarts of initially building the practice and great colleagues during the early years. Later, Sandra Hartog and her *Fenestra* team joined us, and we achieved and exceeded expectations for the combined practice. I learned a great deal from our work together. Finally, sincere thanks to the BTS leadership team and consultants at all levels who welcomed me and my germ of an idea for what an assessment practice might look like for BTS. You were not just supportive, but your encouragement and courage to introduce me to your clients and work collaboratively was heartwarming and will always be appreciated.

Jonas would like to begin by recognizing his wife, Tina. You were the foundation supporting my success at BTS and the more challenging times when we returned to Sweden. I would not be standing here today without you.

Henrik Ekelund, founder of *BTS Group*. His work building one of the largest and best consulting and leadership development companies in the world taught me much and afforded me the opportunity to lead. He lives the model and regularly exhibits the strongest business acumen of the thousands of leaders we have encountered. A special thanks to the management team and many great people at *BTS USA* who always challenged me as a leader and then were 100 percent behind the decisions—no matter how we arrived at them.

Let me begin by thanking the many amazing colleagues with whom I worked at BTS. Additionally, several clients and colleagues helped me to achieve significant business success. It was Diane Gannon, former head of talent and Art Roberts, head of HR at *Kodak Office Imaging*, who first to dared to engage BTS USA to help develop their executives' business acumen around the Kodak strategy with a focus on improving cash-flow. Vicky Lostetter, who believed in BTS and convinced top executives at both *The Coca-Cola Company* and *Microsoft* that developing their leaders was the only way to successfully grow and execute company strategies.

Jonas would also like to thank several influential professionals, including Borje Ekholm who always took time to help me better understand the ever-changing role of the CEO and how to effectively work with a board of directors. No matter how dire the situation in the construction business, Hans Ekstedt of *Penser Bank* was always there to help find creative financial solutions for us to succeed. Susan Burnett, a former client from *Deloitte* and later a BTS colleague, always shared with me her wisdom and experience developing and growing executives in ways that were uniquely successful.

Finally, Jonas acknowledges Andreas Paulsson, owner of *ICA Stop* in Stockholm, Sweden. He took the time to help us understand the keys to growing a specialty grocery business and his guidance ensured our leader, Terry, was a rich and accurate composite of a grocery business executive.

To all who contributed to and supported the development of *From 50 to 500*, you have our sincere gratitude.

Effective leadership is not about making speeches or being liked; leadership is defined by results not attributes.

Peter Drucker

Introduction

Who Should Read This Book?

From 50 to 500 is for leaders running companies with fifty, one hundred, and as many as five hundred full-time employees interested in maximizing their impact on the success and growth of their organizations. This book is also for small business leaders who aspire to grow their companies to beyond fifty employees. Finally, it is for those interested in what makes leaders of smaller businesses different from executives running large enterprises. *You may be surprised.*

What This Book Is Not

From 50 to 500 is not theoretical. It is not a compilation of the authors' opinions. It is not a passive, lazy read. It is not a pie-in-the-sky treatise or esoteric perspective of leadership—the book is not dull. It is not based on, nor does it delve into complex psychological constructs that might underpin (or undermine) leadership. It is not irrelevant to you, a small business leader.

What Is the Focus of the Book?

Our objective is to enable you to become a more confident leader, someone who positively impacts the full range of results defining organizational success. To achieve this objective, we address the challenges small business leaders face as their companies grow from fifty employees to one hundred and beyond. As a company's size increases, the challenges, opportunities, and obstacles its leader faces become varied and more complex. The nature of their capabilities and decisions changes, as does their impact on company success. As a result, their leadership must adapt and grow stronger.

How Does the Book Achieve Its Objective?

From 50 to 500 is divided into four sections, each building on and reinforcing the other to achieve our objective: Make the reader a stronger, more confident leader who positively impacts their company's results.

Leading in High Growth Environments

This section establishes a foundation critical for the remainder of the book. It ensures everyone understands and agrees on the range of companies categorized as *small*. Not every firm with fewer than five hundred employees is the same. *The Potential for Rapid Growth model* is our approach to segmenting this range of small businesses. You should know where you fit in the span of fifty to five hundred, recognizing what makes companies like yours distinct and understanding your growth potential.

This section also represents insights from our years spent observing and profiling thousands of successful small business leaders as well as our tenures leading small companies of our own. The result is a unique competency model, the *High Impact Leadership model*SM. It is the basis for achieving insights into effective small business leadership within rapid growth environments. We detail the model, explaining how a leader's Motivators, Business Judgment, People Judgment, and Derailer avoidance reliably result in highly effective business and people decisions, having a significant impact on your company's success.

Introductory Interviews

Next, we introduce two fictional small business leaders. Each of them faces challenges comparable to those you encounter every day. Jamie is the founder and president of *e-Dine Corporation*, a software manufacturer specializing in restaurant Point-of-Sale (POS) products. Her company employs sixty-one full-time associates. Terry recently took the helm of his family's three-store organic grocery chain, *Eat Fresh Specialty Markets.* He has ninety-two full- and part-time employees.

The introductory interviews provide a perspective of our leaders' businesses, their aspirations for success, and initial insight into their motivations as well as how they lead. Then, together, we evaluate what we see and hear throughout the discussions and begin developing our pictures of Jamie and Terry as leaders.

A Year in the Life of Two Small Business Leaders

The chapters in this section build on the process we presented during the introductory interviews. We will look at key experiences each leader reports throughout the upcoming operating year. In these interviews, the leaders describe significant events in their company. Each chapter explores the decisions a leader made to address a specific situation, challenge, or opportunity. These rich conversations and resulting behaviors provide a foundation from which we can readily glean and discuss significant insights into Jamie's and Terry's leadership effectiveness. Their effectiveness is documented in a scorecard and tied to their quarterly results across four key categories: *Market, People, Financial,* and *Operations.*

We conclude the business year and this section by profiling each leader relative to the High Impact Leadership model[SM]. We summarize insights into their leadership effectiveness and describe how their leadership impacted their annual results.

Self-Awareness

In this section, we dissect the concept of self-awareness, a critical attribute for small business leaders. Self-awareness is the capacity to recognize one's strengths and limitations, resulting in behavior change. In other words, the willingness to hold a mirror up to yourself and act on what you see.

We introduce a comprehensive self-assessment tool capable

of yielding an in-depth, quantitative perspective of your leadership effectiveness across each component of the High Impact Leadership model℠—Motivators, Business and People Judgment, and Derailers.

The last part of the section continues our focus on self-awareness by discussing the second piece of its definition: taking action to change. There is little value to a leader knowing where one should improve but failing to take action to change. Behavior change focused on performance improvement is typically referred to as development. Our approach to development enables leaders to act on the results of their self-assessment. We explore the three Development Domains available to small business leaders.

What Is the Ultimate Value of Reading This Book?

We hope you not only read *From 50 to 500* but also interact with it. Those interactions will lead to insights relative to our small business leaders and, more importantly, to a personal understanding of your leadership effectiveness. Your insights represent the basis for reinforcing what you do well and strengthening areas in which you would like to increase your effectiveness. In other words, *From 50 to 500* helps you become a more effective leader who positively impacts your people, results, and potential to grow as a company and as a leader.

Section I

Leading in High Growth Environments

This first section establishes a foundation critical for our collective success. Chapter 1 ensures everyone understands how we look at small businesses. This book is written for a unique group of leaders with distinct business challenges and, by all indications, the most significant opportunity to build and grow a company quickly. But unfortunately, the small business leader is not well understood by governments, academics, practitioners, and service providers.

We need to begin by agreeing on the range of companies categorized as *small*. Not every firm with fewer than five hundred employees is the same. *The Potential for Rapid Growth model* is our approach to segmenting this range of small businesses. You should know why and recognize what makes companies like yours, with more than fifty full-time employees but fewer than five hundred, a distinct category. We did not just pull these numbers out of the air. Statistics and trends worldwide indicate that companies in this range are the most likely to experience variable growth rates. There are incredible opportunities for leaders of such companies, but the challenges are equally consequential.

Once we are all on the same page about who you are and the markets in which you operate, we will introduce our leadership model. The framework is intentionally uncomplicated and straightforward; businesspeople can quickly appreciate and understand the variables necessary to effectively lead in the PRG. That does not mean the model lacks an underpinning in science — it does. Our work is competencies-based, a construct pioneered in the early 1970s by psychologist David McClelland of Harvard.

The thirty-second summary of McClelland's work is: If one wants to know what an exceptional policeman, social worker, schoolteacher, or business leader looks like, sit down and watch what the best do every day. High performers in any field demonstrate a set of behaviors — skills, abilities, knowledge, and attitudes that collectively differ from all their peers. One can observe and report those unique behaviors in a *competency* model. The competency model is *predictive*, meaning, if a police officer regularly exhibits the model's behaviors, they are typically an exemplary officer. The same would be true of a high-performing teacher, craftsman, salesperson, or business leader. Why are we emphasizing McClelland's work? Because it is rooted in behavior—what you do or don't do, say or fail to say. A competencies-based approach shows you what effective and ineffective behavior looks like. Most importantly, leaders can learn to review their actions and plan to better model more effective behaviors.

We have invested years profiling you, your business challenges, and opportunities. The result is our unique form of a competency model, the High Impact Leadership model^{SM}. Our model is the basis for achieving insights into effective small business leadership within rapid growth environments. Chapter 2 describes the model, explaining how a combination of Motivators, Business Judgment, People Judgment, and Derailer avoidance reliably results in highly effective leadership decisions. Those decisions have a significant impact on your company's success.

Let's begin with the statement that summarizes our audience and sets the stage for everything we do throughout this book: *size matters*.

Chapter 1

Size Matters

The world is complex. Each day we encounter a limitless assortment of products, services, opinions, lifestyles, and leisure activities. Yet, somehow, most people navigate this cacophony we call life and comfortably make choices. For example:

One expects speed limits to vary, depending on the nature of the road and the population surrounding a street. Traffic signs indicate different speeds for distinct locations. We have yet to encounter a speed sign that reads, "Fast" or "Slow."
Or,
When you reach in to adjust the water temperature of your morning shower, the handle moves incrementally from cold to hot. Most people find a comfortable position within the range of the two extremes. Have you ever seen a shower with only a "hot" and "cold" setting?

Almost everything in life exists within a range of two straightforward and easy-to-understand descriptions, like *black* or *white*. But we are capable of understanding what lies between—*the grays*. Businesses, government, and society provide context and guidelines to help us understand the differences between the extremes.

For as complicated as the world is, human beings appear quite capable of differentiating broad categories of products, services, and settings. What if we told you many do not understand the range of businesses outside the extremes of *small* and *large companies*?

It's true!

We have researched the range of seminal works, explored the

history of small business advocacy in both the US and Europe, and surveyed thousands of businesspeople to find common ground. We thought, *Surely there must be some universal standard for recognizing different types of business as they grow and develop.* There is not. One might wonder if this phenomenon exists because there is no need. Perhaps researchers and practitioners have ignored this space because they believed the nature of business and leadership is relatively the same, regardless of a company's size and structure. We say company size matters because it does. We would argue (and suspect you, as a small business leader, would agree) that professionals must understand the difference between small, mid-sized, and large companies because they are different beasts. These organizations require different approaches to everything, from operations, to planning, and strategy. Without a doubt, leaders of these businesses face distinct challenges as their companies grow and become more formalized. Yet, small to mid-sized companies are unique and ignored by the academic and professional communities. There are few guidelines and practically no research dedicated to building a better understanding and support for these organizations and the men and women who lead them.

Let's take a look at the current landscape of knowledge relating to small and mid-sized businesses. We will let you judge the degree of insight.

An Imperfect System

In the US, since the 1950s, the Small Business Administration (SBA) has set the standard for how we define the size of a company:

> *An organization with 500 or more full-time employees is a large company. Businesses with fewer than 500 employees are small companies.*

That's it. No more questions. Nothing else to consider. Further categorizations do not exist. The European Commission (EC) was discerning enough to break up the range of small business enterprises into three categories: micro, small, and medium. The EC also uses full-time employees to differentiate firms and then adds a minimum revenue variable. This additional effort provides a little more insight into the assortment of organizations that make up the marketplace.

The fact is, throughout the world, we use a binary method to classify business. The "black" and the "white" are defined. Is the approach inaccurate? It would help if you started somewhere, and five hundred full-time employees consistently appears to indicate a company is large. But the range between one employee and 499 is not homogeneous. A company looks different as it grows from five people to fifty, one hundred, or more. We have no guidelines to talk about the "grays." What are the types of businesses within the broad category of a small company? Likely, several distinct groups exist, ranging from sole proprietors or partnerships to mom-and-pops, small companies, and mid-sized companies.

|————— Small Businesses (1-499) —————| Large Businesses

When you say you are the leader of a small business, most people have no concept of your organization's size, scope, or impact. They might think you own a local retail store or restaurant. Some will think you run a mom-and-pop operation or work from an office in your home as a freelancer. Imagine those people's faces when you tell them you employ fifty, one hundred, or even three hundred associates and conduct business worldwide. What do they think when you report your organization earns millions in yearly revenues, and you are growing every year? Now they are thinking,

the twentieth anniversary in 2016), *In Search of Excellence,* is a comprehensive study of how successful companies were created and led. The authors specifically noted they did not include small companies because they did not consider them consequential or influential. Be it lack of meaningful data or a reluctance to see a small company as distinct, most management and leadership works do not provide different insights for the small or mid-sized company leader. A cursory review of the related disciplines is similarly void of small business knowledge.

Thousands of colleges and universities promote undergraduate and graduate programs specializing in small business. The typical curriculum applies general management, operations, accounting, marketing, and finance theory and mixes in classes on entrepreneurship, innovation, and startups or business planning. Little of what we have seen in curricular approaches to small business addresses the needs of a small to mid-sized business leader. When we speak with business professors about growing small companies—that path of going from fifty to seventy-five to one hundred employees, we often are met with alarmed faces. Many have been quick to say, "We may be teaching business too generically and are not speaking to the needs of a significant group of companies and leaders."

Don't get us wrong—some researchers are looking into classifying the range of small companies. But the collective works and knowledge currently available to support business leaders like you are less than complete.

Many Firms—Little Insight

An imperfect system for classifying and understanding small companies, confusion with startups and entrepreneurship, and a lack of business knowledge that genuinely speaks to the distinct nature of small to mid-sized companies—we see a major hole.

Small businesses are a substantial group of companies that people do business with, are employed by, or encounter. In the United States alone, companies the SBA reports as "small businesses" employed over 158.9 million people. Just over 1 percent of the companies across North America and the European Union are considered "large." These are impressive statistics. But inherently, one looks at those numbers and has to wonder: *How does one break that 99 percent of "small companies" into meaningful categories?*

We inevitably arrive back at the SBA's *Rule of 500* and recognize the problem with the black-and-white categorization of small or large businesses. The system uses one variable: the number of full-time employees. Perhaps this is the first problem with the framework. Some want to consider other variables to judge the size of an organization. Researchers have suggested including variables like yearly revenue, number of physical locations, and years in business. We can see how tempting it would be to evaluate other factors. Still, we would argue employee count might be the only reasonably equivalent variable one can compare among the range of small companies spanning thousands of industries. Revenue is relative to industry and products; margin and cost differences immediately make an income variable a poor factor for comparison. Certain businesses may require more physical locations because of their business model, but is a three-store bakery bigger than a sixty-person research firm located in one building? The arguments for most added variables are not compelling. But people as a variable makes a lot of sense.

Size is ultimately about your capacity to serve the market. You need people to advance your operations, and you will bring on more people when you want to grow. We believe defining company size by full-time employees is a pretty easy-to-understand and compelling approach. The more you grow your company, the more structure, management, and leadership are necessary. The challenges to leaders change. As you move from five associates to fifteen, a leader will start to find his view and oversight of the organization more challenging. The day-to-day operations change. Grow to fifty, and you begin to build layers of managers. As you grow, the layers of managers and leaders increase, and the organization will look more and more like a large company (from both the outside and the inside). Leaders often struggle with the concept of "control and oversight" as their companies grow.

The father of management, Peter Drucker, shared this point of view. He is the only noted business researcher to have ever published any theoretical work on differentiating small and large companies. Not surprisingly, Drucker thought the key was people and levels of management. He proposed that leaders have key people, a handful of direct and indirect reports, whose role is to complete their understanding of the organization and current operations. When a leader must go outside those key people to find information, this was likely an indication your company was growing beyond what most people in the 1960s would have thought a small company. Drucker suggested that more levels of management and structure indicate a larger company.

This leaves us in a precarious situation. The system established by the SBA (and later the EC) is a reasonable and relatively accurate approach for determining the broad categories of business size: *small* or *large*. However, what we recognize is the gray area within the category. There is a range of different-sized companies, and no one has thought about the needs of an organization and how varied the leadership challenges become as it grows within the category.

A Meaningful Look at the Range of Small Companies

There are over 63 million firms doing business in the United States, Canada, Mexico, and the European Union. Again, 99 percent of all companies operating in North America and across the European Union are small businesses. Below is a breakdown of establishments in those countries using classifications common to national census databases.

A World of Differently-Sized Firms	North America			
	United States	*Canada*	*Mexico*	**European Union**
Employees				
< 50	32.2 m	1.2 m	4.8 m	24.4 m
50–250	218.4 k	51.2 k	29.1 k	49.1 k
250–500	39.3 k	7.3 k	2.5 k	7.0 k
> 500	58.1 k	2.9 k	7.5 k	22.6 k

Approximated from US Census, Government of Canada, Statistics Mexico, and Eurostat

How does anyone differentiate the types of organizations everyone has lumped into this category of *small companies*?

We would advance a framework for segmenting the range of small companies complete with universally recognizable names and meaningful definitions of the business structure and best practices in the ideal world. Unfortunately, such a system is beyond the collective reach and influence of the authors. And we are not sure anyone could devise a formal system the government could implement that would not be overly complex and produce universally accepted and understood results by businesspeople and consumers. The SBA took over twenty years to come up with the existing system.

We would ask: *When you see the EC terms of micro-firm, small-firm, and mid-sized-firm, do you intuitively understand what each of those companies looks like?* After years of research and our professional experiences as small business leaders and in the executive development practice, we have realized there is no perfect nor universal system for defining the range of small businesses. But there are purposeful, easy-to-understand approaches for segmenting small companies. We have developed a framework in which companies are grouped by employee counts equating to stages of growth. For leader development, we think it is less about the names—small, small to mid-sized, mid-sized—and all about the challenges inherent with the changing structure of a growing company. We will use the term "small business" throughout the book, but our focus is specific to your growth stage and the implications as a leader.

The PRG

One long-term trend in most of the small business data reported across North America and Europe is a small but appreciable percentage of companies classified as "small businesses" grow beyond the fifty full-time employee mark. Firms with more than fifty employees tend to grow rapidly over five years. The data also suggest that most quick-growing small companies slow and often peak around three hundred employees. Thus, a fraction of a percentage of small businesses grow to become large companies. We analyzed this trend and looked at the growth patterns a typical company might demonstrate over time. We reviewed case studies of firms throughout the world that characterized growth and interviewed small business leaders about changes they experience in their organizations. Our analysis led us to believe specific organizations are well-positioned to quickly develop a more significant industry presence, increase market ownership, attract more customers, gain competitive advantage, earn more significant revenue with improved margins, and enhance internal efficiencies as well as associate engagement. There are several stages of growth during which organizational structures and needs will dramatically change, and small business leaders must be well prepared to understand the challenges to grow their companies most effectively. The *Potential for Rapid Growth* model (PRG) is our approach to segmenting the range of small businesses and focusing on a distinct group of companies most frequently misunderstood and underserved by academics and practitioners. As we said earlier: *You look like a big company, but you are not.*

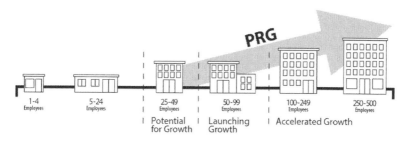

The PRG uses buckets of full-time employees to characterize organizations within the range of companies people call small businesses. When you think about the structure necessary to manage or lead a company within a particular bucket, you can identify the degree of formality and complexity that characterizes the organization. You can also begin to visualize the role a leader must play as they manage through varied stages of rapid growth.

At the low end of all small businesses are companies with less than five employees: the sole proprietors and professional partnerships, contractors, and local service businesses. These companies are likely flat and informally structured. The owner is a *doer* whose productivity is typically the primary driver of company success. Such companies are the backbone of the world's economy, representing almost 55 percent of all small companies. Structurally, the next bucket is closely related. A business employing between five and twenty-four full-time employees is more significant. Still, it probably looks like the companies in the first bucket: flat, informal, and a high degree of owner engagement in the production or service offering. Together, these two buckets represent just over 74 percent of all small companies in North America and the European Union. The PRG does not explicitly target owners of companies within these two buckets. From our perspective, these are the types of companies most people think of as small businesses — the neighborhood stores, the mom-and-pops, and local restaurants, and the like. Although the owners of such companies are hardworking, industrious, and driven, the nature of the business is often not predisposed to growth. One might question our willingness to dismiss such a sizable portion of the small business population, but remember, these are established businesses. If we were evaluating startup companies, we might be inclined to factor a percentage of these companies into our model; the assumption being some would move along the range in the future. But we know most of the firms in these categories have remained around the same employee count for three to five years.

Potential for Growth

The next bucket represents the onramp to the PRG. It includes organizations with twenty-five to forty-nine full-time employees and is the most nebulous grouping.

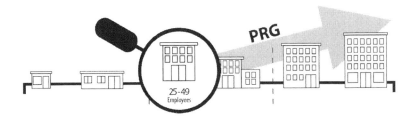

The sample data of companies inside this range often illustrate two types of companies. Some are an extension or the "bleed-over" from the second bucket. The structure remains informal; a level of supervisors has developed to support the owner. An excellent example of this bleed-over might be a family restaurant that became so popular that the owners opened a second location. Again, the nature of the traditional small business is flat, informal, and often local to an area. Some will, over time, experience a degree of growth in staff. However, the basic structure stays the same.

A portion of this group is different from the companies described as bleeding over from the last bucket. Many organizations begin to build a structure as associates grow from twenty to thirty or forty. Some will be organized with supervisory and even executive roles. These are the companies with the potential to grow. Our data indicates about 4.9 million of these firms exist across North America and the European Union. Our analyses suggest a fraction of companies in this bucket increase in size, capacity, or market presence. We speculate the catalyst for future growth lies firmly with the company owner. Many business owners have a scope of impact in their minds. Not everyone is driven by a mission to expand and dominate a market. A portion of these companies are revenue-driven tech and venture-backed startups. A fraction of these firms will advance and quickly become large companies. Some will exit through a merger or acquisition. Many will fail. If you are a company leader with the potential for growth, this book and the leadership model should be inspiring and helpful for your development.

The following three buckets of the PRG describe rapidly growing companies throughout North America and the European Union. As of this writing, nearly half a million firms are experiencing some degree of rapid growth. We see the expanding employee count as the trigger of this growth because the more associates in your organization, the greater the complexity. The company will require additional levels of management. Directors and officers with specialized skills are needed to advance strategy. A leader's role in the company is changing, moving from a doer and manager of people to truly being a leader who must face new challenges and make critical decisions. The buckets represent companies at two crucial stages of organizational size and development: *launching growth* and *accelerated growth*.

Launching Growth

An organization with fifty to ninety-nine employees sits at the start of the PRG, beginning to add people and build greater formality throughout the company. We call this the *launching growth* stage.

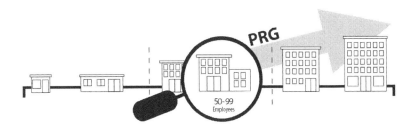

Census and SBA data suggest most companies grow from fifty to one hundred employees in a relatively brief time, typically one to three years. Imagine how different every aspect of the company looks when it almost doubles in size at such an accelerated pace. The company appears established and organized. The leader has a comprehensive view of the day-to-day operations. Likely, the decisions one makes are predictable, and leaders are comfortable making choices. Then growth occurs. The aggressive pursuit of market presence, sales, and influence in the industry changes the company's look, feel, and pace. New employees quickly arrive, and a leader's view of the company changes. They can no longer touch every aspect of the business. Their key people are growing in number and taking on more responsibility and decision-making throughout the company. There are more challenges and day-to-day decisions of consequence to be made. The pace of the growth introduces complexity throughout the company and changes the roles and responsibilities of most leaders.

Accelerated Growth

As a company moves past the initial stage of launching growth, the potential for ongoing, consistent development is maximized. The data suggests that growth beyond one hundred employees also occurs quickly and then begins to taper off for most companies as the employee count exceeds three hundred. As a result, few firms continue to grow and transform into what the SBA would consider a large company (over five hundred full-time employees). In effect, this is the transformation to what many would call a mid-sized company.

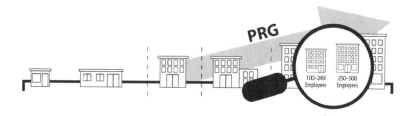

We consider this stage of the PRG as a time of accelerated growth. Again, what might this company look like? As its market presence increases, so too does the size of the organization. People arrive at every level, but a large percentage of new hires are likely to be entry-level support, sales and operations staff, and supervisors. The organization will typically become more formal and organized; additional layers of management appear between the leader, their direct reports, and most associates. The pace of change and the complexity of decision-making will increase. Leaders will inevitably face new and unfamiliar situations they must evaluate and then react to.

The PRG represents organizational growth that propels companies toward more significant opportunities and increased value but simultaneously introduces a series of changes that can challenge even the most capable leaders. Across the broad and homogeneous range of companies with as few as one or two employees and as many as five hundred, the PRG helps one better identify several stages of growth that equate to what people might think of as a small or mid-sized company. We use the buckets to clarify the role a leader plays as their company progresses through the PRG. As growth occurs and organizations become more formalized, leaders must adjust their approaches and develop specific capabilities to be effective decision-makers and impact the company.

Leaders can use the PRG to understand what their company looks like. Call it whatever you like—*small, micro, mid-sized;* the critical takeaway is your recognition of what your company's current size and organizational structure mean for you as a leader. Once you understand this, you can begin to assess your performance and start developing a particular set of capabilities that will make you a better and more effective leader.

Now that we all agree on the types of companies in the PRG, we can look at our model for developing high impact leadership within this rapid growth environment.

Chapter 2

High Impact Leadership

Now that we know about the importance of size in defining the parameters and challenges of small businesses, let's transition to business leadership.

Why is leadership an important concept for us to consider? The answer is obvious to those of you who are company leaders. Strong leadership yields quantifiable financial results—revenue growth, profitability, cash flow, customer satisfaction—and qualitative people results, such as talent attraction and retention and employee engagement, not to mention your personal satisfaction as a leader.

The central question we hope to answer is:

What does great leadership look like?

Leadership has been the focus of a myriad of theories, models, and research. The formal study of management and leadership began in the late 1800s when F. W. Taylor applied scientific methods to management from which evolved the scientific management movement. In the 1940s, the principles of scientific management were challenged by the *human relations movement,* suggesting humans were more than assets. Instead, they were human resources requiring communication, structure, feedback, support, and incentives beyond pay. From this early work grew many studies, theories, and models of leadership and management. Academics often segment these into five categories. Let's briefly talk about each.

Theories dating back to times when those interested in leaders profiled heroic emperors and warriors and sought to classify their characteristics and personalities are known as Great Man theory. Most leadership practitioners have dismissed these theories because they are often exclusionary, but you would be surprised how many people still fall back on this thinking. For example, you or a colleague may have read Walter Isaacson's biography of Steve Jobs. Although a powerful story about the man, his character, and his varied approaches to running Apple, many thought to mimic Jobs' characteristics to be better leaders. Some practitioners and coaches began recommending the book to executives wishing to be more dynamic and innovative. How do you think that worked?

Building on the assumption particular individuals have superior qualities distinguishing them from less successful followers, the trait theorists attempted to identify those qualities. In the 1920s, these researchers identified and defined emotional and physical attributes associated with successful leadership. For a long time, the approach was: *If you are tall, muscular, and speak with a certain tone, you must be a leader.* By this standard, most executives could not develop and become a great leader. There is a bias to these early theories that suggest only a select few have the potential to lead. No one here believes that.

Throughout the 1960s and even today, some professionals like to talk about leadership styles. Leadership style theories are a somewhat limited behavioral approach that suggests, *if your employees do this, you do that.* Approaches like the Management GRID are intuitive and thus are still talked about in leadership classes and seminars. Imagine your job being as easy as deciding how your employees think (for example, they fear you, or they think of you as a friend) and then acting in a prescribed way thought to compliment that employee. We find such a simple management scheme problematic.

The situational and contingency theorists looked at leadership styles and thought those approaches too simple. They proposed leaders should evaluate individuals in different situations and then decide how to work with the employee. Thus, look at the person, the problem, and the outcome you want to achieve. These approaches are popular for introducing new managers to the motivational methods a leader can consider. These frameworks are based on individual employees and discrete situations. Certainly, you must work one-on-one with a range of people, but your job is to influence and inspire people throughout your organization. Your decisions are more complex.

Much of what you see and hear today is a new take on transformational leadership theory, an approach that has remained popular since its introduction in the 1970s. At the center of these approaches is a leader's ability to build relationships across an organization and inspire people to change. Becoming a transformational leader can happen in many ways. You might develop skills to paint a picture of your vision and help people see it. Other transformational leaders seek to unleash transparency and communication as a way of moving toward shared goals. However you look at transformational leadership, you often walk away thinking: *To be great, a leader needs to be engaging and motivating; if they are, then everything will fall into place.* As a small business leader, you know the job is more than a rousing speech at the company meeting. You must constantly evaluate, react, and make decisions, big and small.

Our intent is not to delve into these theories and models but to give you a taste of where leadership development theories have been and point out their limitations. A great deal can be learned about leadership by gaining a more in-depth perspective of the research and theories. If you choose to do so, read with a critical eye by asking questions such as:

How does this apply to me?

How actionable is the model?

How will the model help me strengthen my impact as a leader?

One must recognize that most research, models, and theories have been developed and based on leadership within the context of large organizations. Accordingly, much of the work has limited predictability and application to leaders' day-to-day activities and challenges in the PRG environment described in Chapter 1. Most studies lack *context*. We believe leadership is contextual, so we should go back and modify our initial question to read:

What does leadership look like in the PRG environment?

High Impact Leadership

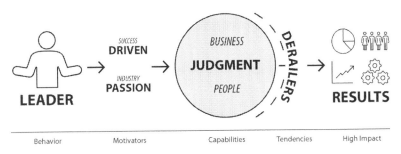

The graphic above represents a comprehensive picture of those elements of leadership required of a PRG leader to be successful. The model is based on our research into the requirements and challenges of leadership in the PRG environment. As a result, it is contextual and relevant to you, the small business leader. The High Impact Leadership model℠. starts with you, the leader.

Our focus throughout the book will be on observing leader behavior—everything you do and say, the actions and words that define you as a leader. Behaviors are observable; it is sometimes what you don't do or communicate under a particular set of conditions. In other words, no behavior is behavior, particularly when you have options to act but fail to do so. Everything you do or say as a leader is observable and impacts your effectiveness as a leader.

To reiterate, the model starts with the leader and the behavior they demonstrate. We have used our research and observations of PRG leaders in various industries and situations to identify effective behaviors most closely associated with a high degree of motivation and highly effective capability leading to strong business results in the PRG environment. We have analyzed and categorized those behaviors, resulting in a simple but powerful model of PRG leadership consisting of three components: *Motivators*, *Capabilities*, and *Derailers*.

Let's take some time to explore each.

Motivators

Leaders are motivated. They demonstrate a drive and desire to succeed from within, but their motivation is also observable to all they interact with, including customers, associates, and stakeholders. In the case of small company leaders, the two Motivators are highly contextual. Let's look at the first Motivator.

Success Driven: You are inspired to build an organization of consequence reflecting who you are as a business leader.

Without the aspiration to build a noteworthy organization that reflects you, the business leader, you will be less than ultimately successful. You must provide the parameters of what an organization of consequence or a noteworthy organization means to you. Then, you need to demonstrate your strong desire to make that organization a reality. Being Success Driven is a Motivator for the leader and motivates those you lead. If you exhibit a drive and enthusiasm to be successful, you will find this enthusiasm positively impacts your associates, customers, and stakeholders.

Being Success Driven reflects confidence that can be contagious and enables you to influence others beyond the content of your words. For example, recruiting the right talent and motivating them to help you build a successful business is critical to your success as a leader in any business environment, especially the PRG. You will not be successful in attracting and retaining strong talent without demonstrating Success Driven behaviors like painting a compelling picture of the future, displaying a willingness to solve difficult problems, and modeling a deep understanding and caring for your fellow associates. To reiterate, Success Driven goes beyond words; it includes the passion and actions required to motivate your customers, associates, and stakeholders to enthusiastically support you as you build your business.

The same two-way motivation applies to the second Motivator.

Industry Passion: You are motivated to develop personal expertise and apply knowledge to build a successful business.

Without the motivation to develop your expertise within your industry and market, you cannot: effectively define the expectations for your organization; use critical industry and market knowledge to set a strategy that distinguishes you from the competition; identify opportunities for growth before they become yesterday's news; nor garner the credibility you as a leader need from your associates, customers, and stakeholders.

Credibility is the operative word here. Expertise and knowledge are the foundations of credibility, particularly industry expertise in the PRG environment. Industry Passion is a Motivator that must be fostered, fed, and demonstrated by the leader. It may be illustrated by taking the initiative to continuously improve one's scope of knowledge, evaluating personal strengths, or continually looking for contacts and establishing mutually beneficial relationships.

Think about the various stakeholders beyond associates and customers with whom PRG leaders need to be successful. They often must establish relationships with community advocates in local government or community organizations such as the Chamber of Commerce or church associations. They frequently associate with industry representatives or union officials. They need to develop strong relationships with key people in their local financial institutions (as well as those organizations or investor groups where they may potentially do business). What banker would be inclined to approve a line of credit or a loan to an executive who had not established a credible relationship based in part on a depth of industry knowledge? A banker becomes an advocate because they believe the leader is extremely well-versed in their industry; the leader knows how to compete and plan to achieve realistic goals. This leader sees how they will achieve their goals and is confident and enthusiastic about their ability to get the job done.

Those who are leaders in the PRG should be able to gauge the degree to which you are Success Driven and have Industry Passion. Later, we will help you do an in-depth assessment of these two Motivators, but for now, think about how strongly you feel and demonstrate each. Although we are far from a "touchy-feely" approach to leadership, you need to feel Success Driven and Industry Passion in your head and gut. You can use the definitions of these Motivators to test the degree to which you are inspired to build an organization that reflects you. You may already, but is it enough? If not, why? The same goes for Industry Passion. Are you spending the time necessary to learn as much as possible about the industry, its future, and your competitors? If not, why not?

Now, let's think about the degree to which you demonstrate the Motivators. This is the translation from your degree of internal motivation to how much and how enthusiastically you show Success Driven and Industry Passion to your associates, customers, and stakeholders. *Demonstration* is how these Motivators begin to define you as a leader because what motivates you, in turn, must be what motivates others associated with the success of your business. Although motivation comes from within, you, as a PRG leader, must demonstrate it by your behavior. What you do and say illustrates your degree of motivation to others.

For now, think of the opportunities you have had to demonstrate how important it is for you to build a business that reflects who you are as a business leader (Success Driven) and your opportunities to show your industry expertise (Industry Passion).

Next, we will describe the capabilities required to demonstrate high-impact Judgment. Remember, the Motivators are the driving forces you need to apply the Judgment and related capabilities that follow.

Capabilities Underlying High Impact Judgment

Our High Impact Leadership model^{SM} for PRG leaders describes two types of Judgment—Business and People. Our focus is on the quality and timeliness of a leader's decisions—thus, Judgment. Decisions are the most visible, high-impact actions a leader can take. Decisions have far-reaching implications and affect every aspect of a business, from financial results to customer satisfaction to associate retention and engagement. Leaders are judged by the quality of their decisions more than any other aspect of their role.

Five capabilities support each type of Judgment. Capabilities are typically a combination of skills, behaviors, mindset, and knowledge applied together to achieve a specific goal and related outcomes. We should consider the five capabilities supporting each type of Judgment as the core capabilities or "dimensions" underlying a leader's ability to effectively demonstrate Business and People Judgment.

Business Judgment

Business Judgment: Decisions leaders make as they develop and execute strategy, overcome obstacles, and recognize opportunities to innovate and grow.

The first type of Judgment leaders can demonstrate is Business

Judgment. *Sound Business Judgment yields good business outcomes.* A good business outcome can be measured in various ways, most of which are quantitative in nature. For example, a good business result could include exceeding your profitability forecast, improved customer retention, or diversifying your revenue to achieve growth. Achieving these outcomes requires any number of business decisions as a prerequisite.

There are five distinct capabilities underlying Business Judgment: *Data Savvy, Strategic Mindset, Customer Focus, Financial Awareness,* and *Balanced Decision-Making.*

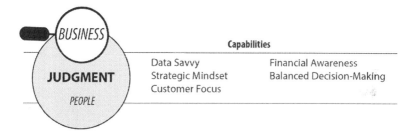

	Capabilities	
	Data Savvy	Financial Awareness
	Strategic Mindset	Balanced Decision-Making
	Customer Focus	

We have researched and identified several behaviors that typify strong performance in each. Let's explore the core capabilities of Business Judgment and help you to see what each looks like in the PRG environment.

We define Data Savvy as a leader's ability to acquire and analyze the right information to help address a complex challenge or problem. A leader demonstrating Data Savvy will reference different types of qualitative and quantitative resources, recognize patterns in seemingly unrelated data to develop actionable insights, use analytical tools to manipulate and visualize information, and ask incisive questions to get to the core issue. They often will seek multiple opinions or interpretations of information. Data does not "tell" you anything—but leaders must interpret information with a confidence that comes from knowing they use reliable data and conduct credible analyses.

A second more broad-scoped capability is Strategic Mindset, defined as a leader's ability to formulate and maintain a well-defined direction for their business using diverse inputs and considering potential disruptors in the industry. A leader who demonstrates Strategic Mindset identifies opportunities and threats by monitoring their environment (government, society, and economic forces of change). They "see" the big picture and can explain how their business plan is likely to play out. Finally, they recognize the organizational core competency necessary to execute strategy.

Next, consider Customer Focus as a critical dimension of Business Judgment. It is defined as seeing the company as a solution provider and demonstrating a deep understanding of customer needs. Exhibiting thorough knowledge of one's products and services, engaging with customers to solve problems and understand their needs, having knowledge of the most important factors/metrics driving success in the client's business, identifying the growth potential (or limitations) of customers—all represent behaviors associated with Customer Focus. A leader demonstrating Customer Focus will also monitor their competitors' actions.

Financial Awareness is foundational to strong Business Judgment. It is more than just understanding financials, it is the ability to apply fiscal knowledge to solve problems. We define Financial Awareness as thinking about the short- and long-term impact of decisions on operational viability and the organization's fiscal health. Leaders in the PRG can demonstrate this capability in several ways, but a key behavior is exhibiting a comprehensive understanding of how the company makes money. Additionally, they define and monitor key financial metrics as the basis for evaluating the financial risks of potential decisions. They should also be confident enough to seek out expert guidance to supplement their financial acumen.

The final capability underlying Business Judgment is Balanced

Decision-Making. There may appear to be an overlap between Business Judgment and Balanced Decision-Making. Business Judgment is the aggregate view of a PRG leader's decisions, which includes the impact of the capabilities discussed above. Balanced Decision-Making focuses on the timeliness and quality of a discrete, day-to-day decision. The capability is defined as: addressing business challenges by quickly generating timely alternative solutions, weighing the implications, and making decisions that balance risk and reward. It can be illustrated by developing "what if" scenarios, recognizing operational capacity and resource implications, or identifying obstacles to achieving quality outcomes and overcoming them with innovation solutions. Highly effective leaders involve appropriate associates in decisions to ensure they have a balanced perspective.

Other capabilities impact the quality of a PRG leader's decisions, but our research and observations tell us these are the core, most relevant capabilities required for strong Business Judgment. If a leader demonstrates strength in these five capabilities, they will consistently make high-quality decisions, positively impacting the success of their organization.

As you think about Business Judgment and its application to you as a PRG leader, recognize interactions and overlaps of the core capabilities we've just explored. For example, your ability to acquire the right data, analyze it and see significant trends and implications (Data Savvy) might be linked to a strategic growth decision, a customer-retention decision, or an investment decision depending on the nature of the data you acquired and analyzed. The key point here is that your effectiveness in demonstrating Data Savvy behavior may impact other capabilities and ultimately the strength of your overall Business Judgment. The interaction among the capabilities and their impact on Business Judgment will be illustrated throughout the book via scenarios encountered by two PRG leaders as they steer their businesses, guided by unique, industry-specific growth strategies.

People Judgment

The second type of Judgment expressed in the High Impact Leadership model℠ is all about your ability to maximize the impact of the most valuable resource: your associates. In contrast to Business Judgment, which leads to good business outcomes, strong People Judgment leads to engaged, highly productive associates who thrive in a team-oriented, collaborative culture while supporting good business outcomes.

People Judgment: Decisions leaders make as they build and lead a team of driven, thoughtful, and company-centric associates.

As was the case with Business Judgment, People Judgment consists of five critical capabilities: *Engagement, Relationship Building, Team Development, Individual Development,* and *Decisiveness.*

	Capabilities	
BUSINESS JUDGMENT PEOPLE	Engagement Relationship Building Team Development	Individual Development Decisiveness

We begin with Engagement, defined as maintaining awareness of and being responsive to the needs of associates at all levels of the organization. An engaged leader is frequently available to associates. They encourage open communication and candid feedback, and employ a direct and honest feedback style. Highly effective PRG leaders also take the time to discuss organizational needs and directions—as a result building alignment with their people. They regularly explain the rationale for decisions which often becomes the basis for further alignment and commitment.

Relationship Building is the next capability and applies to both internal and external interactions. We define it as connecting with people to build lasting collaborative relationships. Behaviors illustrating strength in Relationship Building can include a leader's commitment to regularly communicate with external partners and customers. Internally, they engage associates from all areas of the organization, personalizing their interactions. Regardless of context, the highly effective PRG leader builds professional relationships based on sensitivity, respect, and trust.

The third capability underlying People Judgment is Team Development. The ability to develop support and commitment from colleagues is critical to a PRG leader's success. The definition of Team Development is: fostering an environment in which team members are accountable to each other, build shared goals, and consistently achieve. Encouraging team-generated ideas and accomplishments may be one of the most important and difficult-to-achieve behaviors underlying Team Development. Leaders also illustrate this capability by valuing diversity and promoting respect and relationships within their teams. From a more fundamental management perspective, a PRG leader must set clear individual and team goals as well as coach associates to think beyond personal achievements. Given the complexity represented by individual differences, highly effective Team Development is a challenge for many leaders.

In contrast to Team Development, the Individual Development capability requires a more narrow but equally important focus. We define it as demonstrating the interest and capacity to develop each associate's talent to their maximum potential. First and foremost, leaders must identify and establish processes to select, promote, and develop associates throughout their companies. Additionally, they must ensure their subordinate leaders understand and implement those processes. On an individual basis, leaders need to invest time and energy in the ongoing development of their people—both high performers as well as those with opportunities to improve their performance. From a more fundamental and often overlooked perspective, they must provide regular performance feedback and targeted coaching as well as ensuring their leadership team demonstrates similar skills. The above behaviors are tangible examples of how PRG leaders demonstrate Individual Development.

The last capability underlying People Judgment is Decisiveness—the key people decision-making component. Earlier, we pointed to the perceived overlap between Business Judgment and Balanced Decision-Making. Here, we see a similar intersection of People Judgment and Decisiveness. Again, the Judgments are aggregate views. People Judgment represents the summary impact of multiple decisions on the organization, its culture, and its people. Decisiveness is focused on the quality and timeliness of discrete people decisions. Our definition of this key capability is: addressing people-related issues and problems by making timely, considerate, but resolute decisions resulting in the best outcomes for individuals and the organization. Some key behaviors illustrating this capability include assessing the situation from the viewpoint of the individual and the organization by frequently soliciting others' perspective, considering alternative courses of action and their implications, as well as recognizing the importance of making a timely decision. Highly effective PRG leaders must consider the quality of their decisions and how they are communicated. As a result, leaders must communicate their choices in a thoughtful but firm manner, always sticking to their decision. The resolute nature of this capability can be challenging for leaders but becomes much easier when they are confident in the outcomes and implications of their decisions for both the organization and individuals.

You might be wondering why there is not a specific dimension for effective communication. We do not separate communication because communication underlies every component of People

Judgment—regular, direct, honest communication. As with Business Judgment, there is potential for overlap in the behaviors underlying each of the People Judgment capabilities. For example, the PRG leader cannot be a strong Team Developer unless they demonstrate behaviors associated with Engagement, Relationship Building, and Decisiveness.

It is essential to note the similarity between Balanced Decision-Making in Business Judgment and Decisiveness in People Judgment. Both are directly associated with and measure the quality of a leader's decision; both require timeliness, and both require consideration of options. The ultimate quality of one's business decision is its impact on the success of the business and the achievement of one's business goals as measured by a significant financial, operational, or market metric. The quality of a people decision is the degree to which the individual or individuals believe they have had the opportunity to be heard and treated fairly, and the decision has been communicated with consideration and respect. Regardless of whether the decision favors the individual or the organization, those basic tenets are the basis for one's ability to build a team of thoughtful, committed associates.

Although there is a simple, transparent logic associated with the capabilities underlying strong People Judgment, many PRG leaders take the effectiveness in this area for granted. For example, some leaders may say, "I'm great with my people; they love me." But what does that mean? Do they "love you" because you wave as you go by, you have few performance standards, and you pay well? Or do they love you because you provide regular feedback, coach them on achieving realistic career and performance goals, and respect dissenting opinions? Understanding and analyzing your behavior relative to the five capabilities underlying People Judgment can be one of the most fruitful exercises you can have as a PRG leader. It will help better focus your behavior and increase your effectiveness to lead more highly engaged, team-oriented associates.

Derailers

In our movement through the model, we discussed the Motivators and Judgment required for successful, high-impact PRG leadership. Motivators and Judgment are the foundations of effective leadership. The more you increase your motivation and strengthen your decision-making capabilities, the more successful you will be as a leader. On the other hand, Derailers get in the way of a leader's progress, inhibiting them from reaching their potential. Derailers typically lead to the quick demise and failure of a leader.

As has been the case with most leadership research, the study of Derailers has been conducted in large organizations. For example, Jon Bentz pioneered the concept of derailment in the late 1970s. He researched hundreds of failed managers at Sears. Bentz's work was followed by Morgan McCall and Michael Lombardo of the Center for Creative Leadership throughout the 1980s. Their approach to executive derailment focused on successful career executives who did not live up to their potential in the organization's eyes. Their research identified Ten Fatal Flaws:

- Specific performance problems
- Insensitivity to others
- Cold, aloof, arrogant
- Betrayal of trust
- Over-managing
- Overly ambitious
- Failing to staff effectively
- Inability to think strategically
- Unable to adapt to a boss with a different style
- Overdependence on a mentor or an advocate

The McCall and Lombardo research named a mix of capability and trait-based flaws. For example, failing to staff effectively is caused by a lack of talent identification and organizational know-how. Being cold, aloof, and arrogant are trait-based behavioral tendencies and psychologically hard-wired. This distinction is important because capability-based flaws can be remedied through training, coaching, and other developmental activities. Trait-based flaws are more difficult to change and require more focused self-awareness and targeted coaching.

More recently, research has focused on the taxonomy of derailment. The classification defining derailment is predominantly trait-based. These traits are the subjects of several psychological tests designed to identify propensities or tendencies for derailment. Depending on the researcher or test developer, the Derailer traits vary in number and title.

Common examples we identified as frequently occurring in leaders at all levels:

- *Eccentric*: Disdainful of practical matters, prone to generate fanciful ideas, unconventional
- *Mistrustful*: Cynical, guarded, impatient, intolerant, and difficulty forming mutually supportive relationships
- *Volatile*: Lacking frustration tolerance and social restraint, temperamental, unpredictable
- *Undisciplined*: Not bound by organizational rules and regulations; inattentive to detail
- *Detached*: Distant, aloof, socially inhibited, dislikes teamwork
- *Rigid*: Lacks flexibility, wedded to existing regulations and procedures
- *Manipulative*: Political, questions others' motives, or reluctant to deal with people in an open, direct manner
- *Arrogant*: Prone to "play to the gallery," show off, inclined to dominate discussions

41

The detrimental impact of these Derailers is evident in how the demonstration of the behavior associated with these traits could hinder potential and result in failure as a leader. These traits may be difficult to change. As was the case with McCall and Lombardo's trait-based flaws, these Derailers tend to be hard-wired in the leader's personality. Modifying the behavior associated with trait-based Derailers requires an openness to feedback and a significant amount of self-reflection. Coaching and mentoring are the primary vehicles used to change derailing behavior.

Although the research on Derailers was based on executives and managers in large organizations, we think it fair to generalize their applicability to our PRG environment. The lesson is to be cognizant of the existence of the Derailers identified in the large organization research above and hold a mirror to yourself to ensure you are not demonstrating behaviors that may be detrimental to your success as a leader.

Our research has identified derailing behavior in the PRG environment. We discovered the following four derailers unique to small business leaders:

- *Formality-Structure Disconnect*: Minimizes the importance of structure, process, and performance standards within the company
- *In the Weeds*: Becomes immersed in day-to-day activities resulting in a sharp decline in personal productivity and company performance
- *Informal Influencers*: Routinely consults a group of advisors or confidants who are not direct reports but whose opinions may be less informed and overly weighted
- *Over-Simplified Decision-Making*: Rushes to make complex decisions while relying on incomplete information and gut feelings

These Derailers can limit your potential as a leader or impact your day-to-day and long-term effectiveness as a leader, but they do not appear to be as hard-wired as some of the trait-based Derailers discussed above. Our Derailers represent behavior tendencies you may have learned over your tenure as a small business leader. As a result, you can quickly identify these tendencies and do something to improve—you won't need a mentor, a coach, psychologist, or therapist.

We'll take a much deeper dive into the small business Derailers later in the book as part of an in-depth self-assessment. Until then, we will look for Derailer tendencies in our protagonist leaders as they confront various business challenges throughout the year.

Summing Up Our Approach

We started this chapter with a brief review of the leadership theories and models purported by authors for many years. We critiqued them and pointed out their shortcomings. To avoid the pitfalls of the large organization-based theories and models, we developed the High Impact Leadership modelSM. to reflect the following principles:

- *Simple*—avoiding complex language
- *Focused on* what is critical to success
- *Relevant* to small business leaders and those who aspire to those roles
- *Actionable—impactful*—leaders can use the model to assess, develop, and refine their capabilities

Hopefully, the model has met these criteria. Use them as a "check" as we move forward in applying it to our hypothetical leaders and their challenges.

The above narrative has focused on answering:

What does high-impact leadership look like in the PRG environment?

The next critical question is:

How can you, the PRG leader, use the High Impact model to further develop and refine your leadership behaviors to exceed expectations for your business?

Please note that we intentionally use the words "further develop and refine." We know you are motivated, or you would not be reading this book. We know you have capabilities, or your business would not be as successful as it is. Finally, we know you are likely aware of Derailers, or you would already be derailed. We also know everyone can improve; small improvements in leadership performance can yield tremendous results. The remainder of the book is devoted to helping you to refine your capabilities to meet the challenges small business leaders face.

You will meet two PRG leaders who will soon feel very real to you. You will become familiar with their backgrounds, the impetus for starting their respective businesses, the status of their companies, and their visions for growth. Most importantly, you will walk with them as they confront many situations and challenges that require strong leadership. You will observe their behavior and see the implications of their decisions. You will assess the degree of motivation and capability they demonstrate as they confront challenges that may appear eerily like those you are facing or will encounter. Essentially, you will see two PRG leaders applying the High Impact Leadership model^{SM} — sometimes effectively, and, at other times, not so much. We will discuss what they did, how they did it, whom they involved, and what they could have done differently to yield a better business outcome. You will be their observer and coach. More importantly, you will see how the model applies to you and how you can refine your behavior to make yourself a stronger, high-impact leader.

Section II

Meet the Leaders

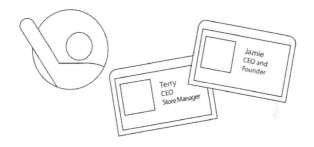

Meet the Leaders

We have now determined that size truly matters and how companies can be readily categorized across segments of the PRG environment. A view of highly effective small business leadership via the High Impact Leadership model℠ and its components was described along with its implications for generating results. Now, let's experience the model in action.

Allow us to introduce two fictional small business leaders facing challenges comparable to those you encounter every day. What follows are brief biographies and an overview of how they organized their companies. Take a few minutes to get to know them and their organizations. Jamie and Terry have different backgrounds and experiences, but both lead businesses experiencing growth and can maximize their impact on the company, their people, clients, community, and respective industries.

Jamie: e-Dine Corporation

Jamie is the founder and president of e-Dine Corporation, a software manufacturer specializing in restaurant point-of-sale (POS) products. She grew up working in her family's restaurant and was inspired to create technology to make restaurant operations better and improve dining experiences. Jamie started e-Dine six years ago with a handful of employees. Since the launch of its first POS system, e-Dine has quickly become a popular solution provider for independent restaurant owners. The company is currently enjoying regional success on the West Coast. Under Jamie's leadership, e-Dine has grown from five to sixty-one full-time employees, most in the software development and sales departments. E-Dine POS sales have more than doubled in the past two years. Jamie believes *the time is now*; e-Dine is poised to increase market share and expand its reach to new regions. She recognizes the organization requires new associates to support her strategy.

Jamie organized the company much like the larger organizations where she previously worked. E-Dine is centralized, and most of the decision-making occurs at headquarters, where many of her key leaders, the technology, and customer support staffs are located. There are two satellite offices in major regional hubs from which salespeople and field support associates work. The following organizational chart should help you to visualize the operations better.

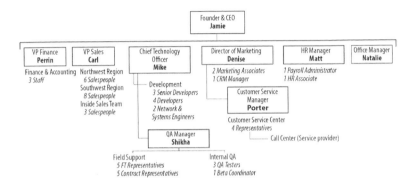

Terry: Eat Fresh Specialty Markets

Terry recently took the helm of his family's organic grocery chain, Eat Fresh Specialty Markets. The Eat Fresh name is popular in the three local communities (none more than twenty miles apart) where his stores have served customers for over twenty years. Terry wants to expand. He believes customer interest in healthy eating is growing. Although the grocery industry is incredibly competitive, Terry knows Eat Fresh represents something different—an experience health-conscious clients and sophisticated shoppers embrace. He is considering several options for launching new stores in other regions.

Terry is a hands-on leader, spending a portion of each day at every location. The Eat Fresh stores employ ninety-two full- and part-time associates. A central operations team of nineteen professionals is responsible for vendors, logistics, finances, and human resources. Each store has an assistant store manager, all of whom report to Terry. He sees a bright future for Eat Fresh, where his specialty grocery stores are a weekly stop for customers in more and more areas throughout the region. The following organization chart illustrates the relatively flat organization Terry has built.

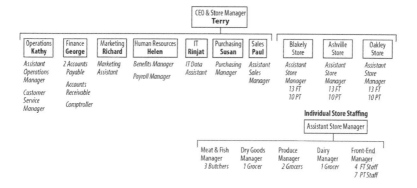

Introductory Interviews

Now that you have met Jamie and Terry, let's get to know them a bit better through a series of introductory interviews. We will spend the following few chapters focusing on each one's behaviors relative to the three major components of the High Impact Leadership model[SM]: Motivators, Business Judgment, and People Judgment.

Our goal throughout these interviews is to begin developing an initial perspective of each leader. These conversations help us better understand the motivations and capabilities these leaders regularly demonstrate. Understanding the methods and approaches Jamie and Terry use to evaluate and learn from their decisions is of great interest. Why? Because ultimately, what one learns from the implications and impact of their decisions affects the quality of future decisions.

The interviewing process is a lot like watching one of those old-fashioned Polaroid photos develop. Remember holding that card-like picture in your hand and seeing the image slowly develop? The snapshot starts blurry, but you have a reasonable idea of the image. Over time, more detail comes into focus. You begin to understand the picture better. A fully processed photo provides a clear view of your subject matter.

This is much like what we will do with Jamie and Terry throughout the book. Our first interviews are an early view of their Polaroids. We begin to see patterns in behavior across the various components of the High Impact Leadership model[SM] that bring both leaders into focus. After these introductory interviews, we should have a reasonable idea of the degree to which each is motivated, as well as some insight into their Business and People Judgment.

Let's start our interviews and discuss what we see at e-Dine and Eat Fresh.

Chapter 3

Identifying Leader Motivation

Let's begin by applying the High Impact Leadership model™ in the same way as it was developed—by listening to and observing PRG leaders. We will be interviewing Jamie and Terry. The first part of the interview will focus on the Motivators component of the model.

What will we be listening for? Our focus is on two Motivators: *Success Driven* and *Industry Passion*.

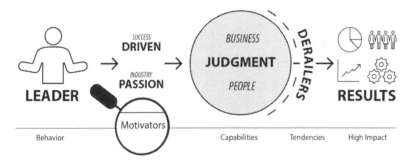

Although motivation comes from within, we do not know it is there until we see it. In other words, behavior demonstrates a leader's motivation. To understand the degree to which a leader is Success Driven, we will be looking for behavior showing the degree to which a leader feels inspired to build strong organizations that reflect their values.

As a guide to help you assess this type of motivation, let's think in terms of three "buckets" of behavior to look for that illustrate Success Driven:

- Builds a Culture: Communicates personal values and encourages a high degree of autonomy and commitment
- Impact and Influence: Paints a vision and gains

commitment to company goals and strategy by regular communication and discussion

- Enterprising: Focuses continually on possibilities within the marketplace that could provide solutions to new and unmet customer needs

During this first section of the interview, we will also look for behaviors associated with Industry Passion, motivation to develop personal expertise, and apply it to building a successful business. Look and listen for two "buckets" of behavior relative to Industry Passion:

- Self-Directed Learning: Takes initiative to continuously improve knowledge associated with building a successful business in a specific industry
- Network Building: Develops and maintains relationships with a diverse group of individuals who may help advance the business

As you read each leader interview, look for behaviors associated with being a highly motivated business leader. Think about what it means to be driven to succeed and have a passion for an industry. Use the "buckets" to help identify behaviors associated with the Motivators. This is not an exact science but an important process that can help you to evaluate our leaders and yourself, your associates, and new hires.

Opening Interview: Jamie

Jamie, thank you for spending time with us today. We are eager to get to know you better and hear about what inspired you to start your company and what continues to drive you as a leader.
What inspired or motivated you to start your software company?

I grew up in a restaurant family. My great-great-grandfather opened The Pilgram in 1902, and our restaurant has hosted weekend dinners, family get-togethers, and special events for everyone throughout the community. I love the business, but I have no culinary skills. I always had a passion for computers and software, and I was intrigued by the power computers brought to the workplaces throughout the late nineties. I went to school for business and then joined a large software company specializing in office solutions. I sold the products and later was promoted into product development. After several years, I decided to go back to school and get an MBA. I thought I could take my skills and join a company like Microsoft or work for a consulting firm.

During graduate school, I worked at my family's restaurant. Honestly, I thought this would be an easy way to earn money and focus on my studies. But a funny thing happened when I went back to the restaurant: I saw our business as a case study in business productivity. Everywhere I looked, I saw how we had been doing the same things for a *hundred years*. I regularly saw inefficiencies a software solution could address. The business could be better managed, employee responsibilities streamlined and expanded, and customer experiences improved. I used problems I saw at our restaurant as examples in my MBA classes. When it was time to graduate, I knew what I needed to do next; I had to build a software company focusing on improving how a restaurateur can run and manage their business.

How important is it for you as a leader to demonstrate your motivation to succeed to your associates? Why?

We only succeed when everyone in the organization comes to work with a commitment and the energy to pursue great solutions for our customers. For me, it is critical. I started this company to be a partner with restaurant owners—these folks have incredibly challenging jobs. They come to us and, more importantly, stay with us because we genuinely want to help them to manage their business. The moment we lose that sincerity and passion, e-Dine becomes nothing but a bunch of hucksters trying to sell you a bunch of bells and whistles.

Why this industry? What makes the markets, customers, and challenges so appealing?

Software is so cool because you can have ideas and "see" a unique and technologically masterful solution, but what you envision is often not yet possible by today's standards. We created an awesome POS system that helps our customers to run their restaurants better, but that is just the beginning. We see our product becoming infinitely more valuable as we integrate and innovate technologies. For example, soon, machine intelligence will become commonplace. When it does, our software could predict what people will order, when to start firing a meal, and more. I will not geek out on you, but let's just say our product will get better and better each year as we integrate new technology.

How does your industry expertise impact your effectiveness as a leader?

Speaking for this company, I cannot imagine being successful out of the gate without the insights I brought to the party. The whole idea came from my software development side debating the restaurant side of my head. I think we achieved acceptance in the market and can grow because I know how to build software *and* intimately understand the restaurant industry. I sometimes think, *What would happen if something happened to me tomorrow?* Right now, everyone I work with is a specialist. They are great at what they do, but no one has a broad understanding of the two pieces that drive this business: software development and the day-to-day operations of a restaurant.

Authors' Insights

Jamie's enthusiasm, energy, and commitment to the company's success are readily apparent from her interview responses. She is clearly inspired to build an organization of consequence and is focused on the possibilities reflected in the marketplace. She has a vision for the organization based on her in-depth perspective of the industry.

Jamie began her immersion into the industry during her MBA studies, where she demonstrated a strong motivation to develop her expertise and apply it to building a successful business. She is well-read and up-to-date on the state of the industry, software development, and related technology.

We are already beginning to see a potential pattern of behavior for Jamie—enthusiasm, energy, technical know-how, industry savvy, and maybe some tech-geek tendencies. The question is, does Jamie leverage her enthusiasm and expertise with her associates? Although she recognizes her associates are "specialists," she did not indicate the need to develop and broaden their perspectives and skill sets to help her achieve the high level of success to which she aspires. Also, she stated she wants "everyone in the organization to come to work with a commitment and the energy to pursue great solutions for our customers" but did not mention any leadership actions on her part to generate that commitment and energy. We need to keep these behaviors in mind as we proceed through the interview to see if they are, in fact, trends or premature observations that will be mitigated by more appropriate behavior.

Opening Interview: Terry

Terry, thanks for taking the time to talk about Eat Fresh and how you came to lead this popular healthy eating grocery store. What inspired or motivated you to start your grocery business?

My parents started the business shortly after they were married. It began as a fruits and vegetables market and grew to more of a local specialty grocery store. My uncle, who lives abroad, also manages a similar grocery store in his town. As a youngster, I worked in both my parents' and my uncle's stores. I helped in every part of the business. It was a great way to learn all the ins and outs of the operation. When my parents decided they wanted to slow down, I was ready to shift from working in the corporate world. I decided it would be interesting to build on my parents' initial idea. The business they made was popular in our area. I felt it would be rewarding to use what they had built as a foundation for something bigger. I wanted to see if I could make a robust set of healthy food stores with a strong brand.

How has that motivation changed as you've built the business?

Initially, I wanted to gradually take the idea that my parents started to more communities around us. As I learned how much people appreciated the original idea of fresh and local products and the impact eating right had on people's well-being, I wanted to offer our products to more people. It became a passion—to ensure that people ate the best possible food for their health. I saw how the big chains were focused on large packing and price while the general health in the country was declining due to what we eat. I felt it was a great market opportunity. We could be one of the companies to lead a lifestyle and grocery buying change. So, now my goal is to open at least one store a year for the next five years.

How important is it for you as a leader to demonstrate your motivation to succeed to your associates?

Whether it is employees, suppliers, or customers, people always look to the leader to see if they are inspired. If I am not motivated, why should my employees be? I want people to come to work not only for a paycheck but to make a difference. It all starts with me. For example, I check in each day with the fish department in one of the stores and visit our fish suppliers once a month. I care, and it shows others how important I feel it is that we have the freshest fish available. In the past, I tried to implement things that might have sounded good, but I didn't value or care that much about them. People see right through that, and it never works out well. You must be genuinely engaged and enthusiastic. Otherwise, it would be best if you do something else.

What excites you about the industry?

Food is something every person depends on. It has an enormous impact on people. Think about it: every person eats through the good times and the not-so-great times. Food has a tremendous effect on our health and well-being. Healthy people tend to be happier. That impacts our healthcare costs. Also, by using local and organic foods, we improve sustainability, which is important if we want to leave something behind for future generations.

How have you developed your industry expertise since you initially started the business?

Once you get into the grocery business, it's a lot more than great fresh food. We need to deliver consistently new, healthy products to our customers while remaining a profitable, growing business. With increased competition, the need for sustainability, rapidly changing technology, and social norms driving organic shopping, I need to understand how all these will impact our business today and in the future.

Take technology, for example. It allows you to offer new

services and operate more efficiently, but at what cost? How does different tech best serve my suppliers, customers, and employees? To stay on top of all the changes in my industry, I must do a lot more research. In the past, I could visit other stores, talk to suppliers, and read the industry press. Now, I do all that and attend trade shows and events that parallel my industry, visit companies great in logistics, read books, spend time online in industry groups—you name it. I need to stay on top of how things are changing.

How does your industry expertise impact your effectiveness as a leader?

First, we must be confident in our goals for the near term and future. What will we invest most of our time and money in to make sure we deliver on our promise to stakeholders and continue to be the grocery store of choice? I need to have a pretty good idea of what the future holds for organic foods and retail groceries. If I don't, it will impact us all. Knowing the industry builds enormous trust among your employees and suppliers. If they believe that you understand and know what you're doing, that builds confidence. They will listen to and follow your lead.

Authors' Insights

Terry appears to also be highly motivated to succeed, but his definition of success seems more reputation and service-driven than financially driven. By service-driven, we mean he has a strong desire to serve his customers with high-quality food and develop a reputation for being concerned with the ultimate health of his customers. He demonstrates a genuine passion for ensuring people have an opportunity to purchase the healthiest food possible and conveys a confidence that "we could be one of the companies to lead the change."

Terry tries to instill his passion for quality and motivation for success in his associates by modeling the behavior he wants them to demonstrate. He believes actions speak louder than words, and as a result, focuses his behavior on illustrating his passion for quality and freshness. However, his examples of checking on the fish department and suppliers daily could easily be construed as standard management monitoring practices.

Terry definitely demonstrates a focus on developing a depth of industry knowledge that will aid him in building a successful organization. He provided several examples of taking the initiative and time to develop his industry expertise via attendance at trade shows, visiting competitors, and looking at companies outside the industry that illustrate expertise that might make his business more competitive. Also, he recognizes his industry acumen is important to demonstrate to his employees and will aid him in making good decisions. He did not, however, indicate the importance of developing industry expertise in his associates. He also indicated a tendency we should look for as we move forward in the interview—his propensity to potentially spread himself too thin.

Comparing Jamie and Terry

Terry and Jamie represent interesting similarities and contrasts as it relates to their motivations. Both appear to be highly motived to succeed, and both are heavily engaged in and recognize the importance of developing their industry expertise. Jamie demonstrates a high degree of energy and enthusiasm for building a commercially successful company, while success for Terry is predicated on the health of his customers and helping to reduce healthcare costs.

Both appear to be high energy, enthusiastic and driven by the opportunities they've identified in their respective industries. Both give considerable lip service to the importance of their associates, but neither has taken overt action to illustrate to their associates how vital their expertise and talents are to the organization's success beyond their prescribed roles.

Identifying how these two leaders, who are motivated differently, ultimately demonstrate a unique and effective set of capabilities to run their business and influence their associates successfully will be our challenge as we move forward.

Quantitative Assessment of the Dimensions of Motivation

After hearing Terry's and Jamie's responses to our questions and summarizing our insights above, we put our heads together and took a first pass at evaluating the degree of impact each demonstrated relative to the dimensions of both Success Driven and Industry Passion. We emphasize "tried" because we realize a short interview will not give us the range of information or the complete view one needs to make a definitive assessment, particularly as it relates to Motivators, which need to be observed over time. Nevertheless, we thought it would be worth the effort to see what types of tendencies each leader was illustrating and what we should be looking for as we observe them on a day-to-day basis throughout the coming year.

Before we dive into the assessments, let's talk about our approach to rating each dimension. We use a simple three-point scale:

We always assume the bucket is "half-full," meaning we think Jamie or Terry demonstrate a reasonable degree of capability unless they show us differently. They may show us they are highly effective by consistently demonstrating behaviors associated with a given capability—filling the bucket with behavior. Similarly, if a leader exhibits little or any behavior related to the dimensions, we consider a lower rating. Hopefully, this will become clearer as we discuss ratings.

As our insights above indicate, Enterprising and Self-Directed Learning are areas where Jamie and Terry demonstrate strengths. Their respective businesses would not be as successful as they currently are if they were not continually focusing on the marketplace and looking for innovative ways to leverage opportunities. Their initiative to develop their market expertise was obvious. It is important to note the leader carries the burden for being Enterprising and showing Self-Directed Learning as an individual. These are individually driven and do not require the support of or reaction from others to be successful. The remaining dimensions require interaction, communication, and acceptance by others. Let's be sure to observe whether either of our leaders can motivate their associates to the degree necessary to achieve their goals.

Scorecard

Motivators			
Jamie		Terry	
Builds Unique Culture	3	Builds Unique Culture	2
Impact and Influence	2	Impact and Influence	2
Enterprising	3	Enterprising	2
Self-Directed Learning	3	Self-Directed Learning	3
Network Building	2	Network Building	2

Consider how you would rate Jamie's and Terry's motivation. Feel free to deviate from our rating, but as you do so, make a note of how you arrived at your rating.

Chapter 4

Exploring Business Decision-Making

Now that we have our initial impressions of what motivates Jamie and Terry and how they instill their motivations in their associates, let's move into the next component of our model, which focuses on Business Judgment.

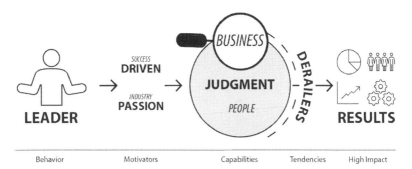

| Behavior | Motivators | Capabilities | Tendencies | High Impact |

Business Judgment is about decisions leaders make as they develop and execute strategy, overcome obstacles, and recognize opportunities to invest and grow—the daily decisions made to ensure a business is successful. Business Judgment is one of the most critical elements of a leader's success. It is so broad that it must be viewed as the interaction and summation of five associated capabilities:

- Data Savvy: Acquires and analyzes the right information to help address a complex challenge or problem
- Strategic Mindset: Formulates and maintains a well-defined direction for the business
- Customer Focus: Sees the company as a solution provider and demonstrates a deep understanding of customer needs

- Financial Awareness: Thinks about the short- and long-term impact of decisions on operational viability and the organization's fiscal health
- Balanced Decision-Making: Addresses business changes and challenges by generating timely alternative solutions, weighing the implications, and making a decision that balances risk and reward

We will continue our initial interviews with Jamie and Terry, now focusing on Business Judgment. These interviews provide a macro view of the behaviors Jamie and Terry demonstrated relative to Business Judgment. Consider this chapter a continued introduction to our leaders. At the end of our conversations, we will provide thoughts on their level of capability in this area. A more in-depth analysis, on a dimension by dimension basis, will come in Section 2, when we interview the leaders quarterly for a year.

Business Judgment Interview: Jamie

Jamie, we would like to shift gears and talk more about e-Dine and how specifically you are leading the company toward the mission and vision we spoke about earlier. Tell us about your long-range planning process.

I started this company to help restaurant owners better run their businesses. *This is what we do,* and the future should reflect this vision. We repeatedly ask three guiding questions to ensure we understand where we are going:

1. How well are our customers managing their businesses with our support?
2. How will things change for those customers, and are we ready to address those changes?

3. What will the future dining experiences look like so we can plot where our knowledge and technology might best be deployed in the future?

These questions guide our business planning. The answers form our long-term roadmap.

What information do you use as the basis for your planning?

As I look at our long-term future, I try to understand how things will change for our customers and the software industry. There are plenty of trade associations and journals for both the restaurant and software industries, so I have access to reasonably priced and detailed data. I also rely on the insights of customers and partners and closely monitoring our competitors. In addition, our associates often bring distinct perspectives that help me better understand what we are doing in the marketplace.

I read a lot, not just about the restaurant and software industries. I try to look at industries and markets that look and feel like ours to have a big picture of the trends suggesting opportunities or things that could compromise our growth and success.

Whom do you involve in the process? Why?

Everyone. If you work here, you regularly consider our three guiding questions, especially the first question regarding how well customers manage their businesses with our support. If you recognize our customers' restaurants could be running more efficiently and making more money, you speak up. If you regularly see a customer problem we are well-suited to solve, point it out. Idea-sharing is a big part of our corporate DNA, and I will do everything possible to cultivate that culture. We also have quarterly meetings, where everyone in the company meets to discuss current plans, share concerns and ideas, and celebrate successes.

How do you monitor your plan? Frequency?

I look at day-to-day performance and spend a day each week with our VP of finance to ensure we are on track. I talk to my key leaders every week to ensure we are achieving our goals. Once a quarter, the executive team devotes an entire day for a deep dive into the current plan and performance. We also revisit the long-term plan. Things change quickly. Our strategic plan is a framework we need to refine continually. We are confident in our long-term plan but recognize potential opportunities or market changers we must be ready to jump on.

What are the key financial metrics you monitor to evaluate the financial health of your business?

I regularly think about our burn rate, the monthly expenses and fixed costs I know we need to meet each month. I also focus on our sales targets. We have a sizable chunk of subscription revenue, so I am a bit hawkish on that churn rate. When I want to focus on the bottom line, I immediately look at earnings before income, taxes, depreciation, and amortization (EBITDA) because that is the daily profit. The accountants and VP of finance can always play with the numbers after that, but EBITDA is pure and easy to understand.

How often do you monitor them?

Once a week, I sit down with Perrin, our VP of finance, and we spend three or four hours in a comprehensive review of our performance to plan. She is great. She knows I will occasionally ask her to clarify the financial impact of something I might be thinking about. I need her expertise to counsel me on why a particular outcome might be more or less appreciated.

Give me an example of how monitoring those metrics enabled you to identify a potential problem and address it before becoming significant.

Just last quarter, I was looking at our end-of-quarter sales results. At first glance, I was happy; sales revenue was almost 45 percent above projection. We had a significant uptick in new software sales. Here's the thing—we sell POS software that carries a one-time fee, but our support is sold per-incident or as a subscription. The premium support is billed monthly and represents a sizable stream of revenue.

When I looked at the sales numbers more closely, the premium service sales revenue was on target with the quota but not significantly higher and in proportion to the new software sales. I quickly recognized our salespeople sold more software but failed to secure the premium support. I checked with Perrin, who confirmed this was going on. We discussed the implications. Our current plan assumes a quarter of all new sales include the service subscription. That revenue isolates the company from software upgrade cycle slumps. Our commission structure did not incentivize this. As soon as our salespeople met their monthly quota, we saw a shift in their sales focus. Most emphasized lower acquisition costs by selling the software and suggesting the per-incident support was always available if a problem arose. Our VP of sales confirmed this was true for many reps because it took more time and effort to sell the software and support.

We caught it early and quickly addressed the issue. The next quarter, we introduced an enhanced commission plan that emphasized the necessary ratio of service contracts and heavily rewarded software and premium service sales.

Give me an example of how you've established and maintained a relationship with one of your customers.

I know many of our customers, especially those who first started with our high-value clients and us. Pat Stephens comes to mind. Pat was initially a problem client. Pat owns four high-end restaurants and clubs in the city and first came to us as we were moving from our version 1 product to the new, feature-rich FOH Dine V2. Pat was interested in several of the new features, but the software was in beta. We were only a month into the beta and at least three months until the market release. Pat's restaurants were soft-launching in three months, and the official openings were expected to follow one to two months later. We wanted the business, and Pat needed several planned new features, so we agreed to sell the first version and make Pat's restaurants' beta sites. As you can imagine, beta software and a four-location restaurant doing a soft-launch—what could go wrong?

Despite the assistance of our premium support team and a QA representative we assigned to work exclusively on-site for two months, there were some quirks one must expect in beta software. Pat was under the stress of the launch, and whenever a bug surfaced, he would become almost bombastic. The sales, QA, and service reps were rightly intimidated when Pat complained.

I decided to get on a plane and spend two days on-site. This was the best thing I ever did. Over those two days, I divided my time between our team working on the install and being a casual advisor to Pat, who appreciated our commitment to his business. Everything came together after that; both Pat and our latest version of the POS were a success. Pat remains one of our best customers and is someone I regularly go to with questions about the industry, our service, and even our competitors. Pat is prominently featured in one of our customer testimonials videos and has been our guest at several company meetings. Pat's restaurants regularly participate in our alpha and beta programs. I would say we've developed a real give-and-take relationship. This is the kind of connection I always envisioned e-Dine could build with customers.

What about competitors? How do you monitor competitive activity and its impact on your customers?

I work with our VP of marketing to collect information about our competitors and potential competitors. You would be amazed at how much you can gather by checking your competitors' sites and regularly searching the web for keywords. We also ask our customers. When I am in the field, I will ask people, "How are we doing? What's our competitor showing you these days you think we should be aware of and should consider doing (or not doing)?" We work with several industry hardware suppliers who often have valuable insights into changes coming into the market.

I'm a big believer in competitive intelligence. We spend time attempting to understand other strategies and business models. This information helps us better recognize what our customers are looking for and what drives their purchase decisions. You also must look at companies not currently in the space but those that could suddenly show up and be a threat.

Tell me about a complex challenge or problem you've confronted recently that required you to get information or data you typically don't have available.

Last year, we thought there might be an opportunity to leverage our existing products into a growing foodservice industry segment. We wanted to pull our ordering component and Wi-Fi functionality to make products for food trucks.

Food truck customers are different from our typical high-end restaurant clients. We knew the food truck segment was rapidly growing, especially in urban areas. If we had relied solely on this anecdotal data, we might have jumped to build software for them. But as we gathered more information and did our diligence, a complete picture developed. We were not well-positioned to compete in this arena.

Content aggregation services have allowed access to data that would previously be within the reach of only the biggest companies with equally large research budgets. We purchased an industry report from one of these research companies. That report was a comprehensive overview of the industry, potential customer profiles, key competitors, and the long-term outlook. This was a credible view of the market.

We also needed to understand how potential customers in the food truck industry would perceive our offerings. This is not our typical customer. We were able to buy respondents from a survey panel company offering access to people within different jobs and industries. For $750, we were able to survey two hundred food truck operators and gauge their reaction to everything from product features to cost sensitivity.

We supplemented this data with information from the trades, partner feedback, and various articles in which industry experts and enthusiasts talked about food truck trends. In a few weeks, we had what we thought was a complete and believable picture of the food truck industry, and we knew we could not be competitive in the space.

Give me an example of how you've used the financial metrics you described as the basis for helping make a critical decision.

I told you I think about the monthly burn rate all the time. In the last quarter, we were behind on a maintenance release. We incurred 120 hours of contract developer overtime at $125 an hour. There were multiple charges from the device manufacturers for expedited reviews of our apps. We spent an unexpected $18,000 to simply maintain a component of our product.

Our Chief Technology Officer told me he never anticipated the updates to take so long. Even worse, we were putting some of our best people on it even though they were overqualified. The cost of their efforts far exceeded what we would typically pay for this type of work. Senior developers identify and fix critical issues in the system code. Once they do that, lower-level developers package the updated software and app releases. We were using our best people to push out a maintenance release. I suggested that we contract a part-time developer to deliver our bug fixes and update releases.

We looked at some local talent who could be put on retainer and then billed at fifty dollars an hour as needed. Most updates would take a junior developer no more than eight hours to complete. We also considered a proposition from a staffing group specializing in contract developers from India. An experienced Indian app developer was twelve dollars an hour with a guarantee of eighty service hours in a year. The recruiter informed us that the developer assigned to each engagement was likely to be different, but all were well-versed in app coding. Our CTO had positive experiences working with the recruiter at his previous job. He observed that the Indian developers always delivered but often required more guidance. An update would likely take the foreign contractor two days to complete the work. We chose to bring on a local contractor. Although the cost was more, that developer could commit to a long-term contract and became the point-person for the update process. We know he can work independently to turn around a new build quickly. Our update process is efficient. Plus, I think we are grooming a developer who could easily transition to a full-time role as we grow.

Authors' Insights

Jamie appears to have a strong Strategic Mindset, as evidenced by the comprehensiveness of her planning activities, her use of data, and her knowledge of industry trends. In particular, her focus on creating a comprehensive strategy, monitoring its execution, and updating the process's plans was a primary focus as a leader. She emphasized involving her associates in developing the business direction by continually asking three key questions; however, she did not reference opportunities to collect the insights gained from asking those questions, nor did she give an example of her associates influencing the strategic direction of the business. This tendency to do things independently is consistent with what we began to see in the motivation section of the interview.

The importance of identifying and monitoring key financial metrics driving e-Dine is always on Jamie's mind. She is capable of defining their relationship to business success. She uses key metrics to make decisions. For example, she used "burn rate" and compensation data to arrive at an operational decision regarding the use of developer resources. However, we may be seeing a tendency for Jamie to be transactional in her use of financial metrics, given her focus on measures such as burn rate and sales goals. By "transactional," we mean she may be relying too much on a set of metrics that indicate short-term results and misses broader, more impactful measures that contribute to a healthy long-term profit and loss (P&L). Also, Jamie may be representing more awareness of the meaning and importance of financial metrics versus having in-depth financial acumen, as demonstrated by her need to meet with the VP of finance weekly.

Finally, Jamie has built the business on a high degree of Customer Focus. Her approach to resolving the issues related to the software beta test with a long-term customer illustrated her initiative to jump in and be a key factor in ensuring all problems were resolved. This inclination at this point in the company's evolution and this particular customer may have been appropriate. As we observe Jamie in the future, does she develop her associates to address complex customer issues and empower them to deal with those issues relatively independently? We will get some insight into Jamie's leadership style and how to develop her associates in the next section.

Business Judgment Interview: Terry

Tell me about your long-range planning process.

We have a vision, mission, and values that guide us and our strategy. Our vision recently changed to being the most recognized fresh food specialty grocery store in the northern part of the region. Our mission remains the same: enable the people and the environment we impact to have the best possible long-term outcome. With the change in our vision, we are now looking to grow the number of stores in the local region and expand to other nearby regions. This came about in our annual strategy meeting, where we gather to decide the long- and short-term focus for the business.

To reach our long-term goals—growth, profitability, employee engagement, customer satisfaction, and environmental impact—we set medium- and short-term goals driven by key focus areas. For the focus areas, we have separate focus groups that work with implementing and measuring the focus areas.

What information do you use as the basis for your planning?

There are a few things we look at. The most important one is our same-store sales compared to last year. This tells us what sold last year during a holiday, event, or certain promotion. That, along with inventory turns and waste, is critical if we want to be recognized for having fresh food while still maintaining profits. We do quarterly surveys in all our stores as well as annual employee engagement surveys. Naturally, we look at a series of financial metrics to ensure they are on track to reach the goals and see possible business trends. We also look at what the big supermarket chains do and talk to our suppliers to understand what they see and need.

Who is "we"?

The management team, head of finance, head of operations, head of human resources, and assistant store managers are all involved. I am the manager of all three stores. On some things, we involve the employees, especially when it is important to get their input and buy-in.

How do you monitor your plan?

I think it is important to have different information at different times. We have tried to think through the most important metrics. We look at a host of information and report-outs from the stores. Daily, we look at things like same-store sales, revenue, etc. Every month we look more at things impacted by our initiatives, such as basket size and inventory turns. Naturally, we have quarterly and yearly numbers.

Give me an example of when you recognized an opportunity to impact your growth significantly.

We have had grab-and-go salads for a long time. We continued to see steady growth in the pre-made salads. So, we gathered the management team and asked ourselves, based on this trend, how could we leverage it and grow faster? Since all our stores had wonderful produce departments, we decided to leverage the produce and create build-your-own salads.

How did you recognize the opportunity for in-store salad bars?

When something starts to differ from the normal numbers, whether it is up or down, we ask ourselves why. In this case, it was a combination of seeing the steady increase in grab-and-go salads and hearing and reading the discussions of health trends in our country.

What did you do?

Initially, we took many items from our produce department, grilled chicken and cold cuts, and created a salad bar. It was popular, but people asked for other ingredients to put in their salad, like tuna, eggs, and shrimp. So we expanded the salad bar to a full-fledged entry where you can make almost any salad you can think of. There are over eighty different ingredients available.

What kind of results did the introduction of the salad bar generate?

I would say it has gone well, but it hasn't been without its challenges. Our customers have made the salad bar a regular stop. We have increased sales of almost every fresh item featured on the bar. But the best part is that customers are coming in more often. Many customers originally came in just to pick up a salad, but they always ended up buying a lot more. The hardest part has been that we have had to staff a complete kitchen to make many of the salad bar things. Not only are more people and equipment needed, but the rules of how you prepare and serve food are strict. We needed to invest in a lot of training upfront, and we learned some lessons in the first few months relating to efficiency and waste. Now we do it well. Those salad bars contribute a lot to our success.

What are the key financial metrics you monitor to evaluate the financial health of your business?

As I mentioned earlier, we monitor financial and other business metrics at various times throughout the year, all with a slightly different purpose.

We monitor specific performance metrics daily, like same-store sales. Comparing any day's sales to the previous year helps us judge if it was a good day or a relatively lousy day. We can quickly evaluate unique or unusual events that might help us understand performance differences. Every week we look for early trends and success in our store planning. Every month we are mostly focused on the P&L. We start comparing performance across seasons and the previous year, especially on revenue and average basket size, which indicates the number of people in our typical customers' households.

Each quarter, we evaluate a variety of key metrics and the three primary financial statements, not only to tell us what has happened but, more importantly, to tell us if something is changing or trending that requires us to make changes. So you could say we use the financial statements not only as taillights but also headlights.

Given the diversity of people who represent your customer base, how do you identify and stay in touch with their needs, tastes, and budget, their buying habits?

With today's enormous amount of data you can get on your customers' buying habits and profiles and the amount of available data on the industry and competitors, it's much easier than ever before. The challenge is to ensure you are looking at the most relevant data that tells you something of value. For example, we started a membership club last year. It's of great benefit to our customers and helps us gather information about our customers' preferences. We see shopping patterns and can dissect by gender, age, income areas, etc.

What information do you typically have at your fingertips relative to your customers?

We look at all kinds of variables, including seasons, weather, holidays, and ongoing events, to be prepared to have what our customers are looking for. Then, we make sure we have plenty of those items in stock and they are easy to find.

How do you use that information to identify growth potential?

If we were to take a holiday where a certain type of food is expected to be served, naturally, we make sure to have plenty of that in stock and on display and everything else that usually accompanies the meal. We added a free, in-store cooking class that showcases recipes for a few of the key meals often prepared for that holiday. This allows the customer to enhance the possibility of having a great-tasting dinner and include all the things that "should" be available during that holiday. By having the cooking classes in the store, we increase the number and size of baskets for that holiday. It also helps us predict how much we need to stock in the stores.

What about competitors—how do you monitor competitive activity and its impact on your customers?

We try to stay on top of competitors' discount campaigns. The internet is certainly helpful for that. We try not to get into a price war because that erodes profitability. We also visit both local and large chains to see what they are doing. At conventions and even with competitors, we talk about what they see as the future of our industry. The large chains are often forthcoming as they see little threat from us. Overall, we see that competition is increasing in the organic and specialized food areas.

Tell me about a complex challenge or problem you've confronted recently that required you to get information and data you typically don't have available.

We implemented a customer loyalty program. It allowed our customers to get exclusive discounts, advance notice to upcoming sales items, and they earn reward points to use toward future purchases. For us, it increased the likelihood of them coming to our stores, and we could get a better understanding of their preferences and buying habits. I worried that implementing the system sounded more straightforward than it probably was, so I wanted to do my research.

Where and how did you get the information you needed?

I decided to dig into understanding loyalty programs, especially the systems behind them. I attended more conferences and trade shows to understand what they were using and learn more about the technology itself. I read articles and met with town officials and legal people. I spent time on the internet looking at other companies' loyalty programs and not just in our industry. I checked out everything from airlines and hotels to pharmacy chains.

What analysis was required?

We were most concerned with privacy—balancing how much customer information we needed against what most people would feel was reasonable to share with a merchant. We began by collecting all the terms and conditions statements our competitors used in their programs. We also looked at how reward programs are typically structured within the industry. We used several resources from national retail grocer trade magazines. As we began to get a better idea of the types of data we wanted to collect, we consulted an attorney to get their reaction. He did not see any red flags.

What solution did you arrive at after your analysis?

We identified the critical personal data we needed to effectively manage a loyalty program. We found we didn't need a lot of personal data—the transactional and internally generated information are what really drive the program's analytical insights. We were able to launch a great new customer affinity tool and turn our approach into a socially conscious decision.

Authors' Insights

Who would have guessed after hearing Terry's responses to the motivation questions and our assessment of his service-driven motivation for success that he would demonstrate such strong Business Judgment? He indicated a focus on execution as measured by several sophisticated, industry-specific performance metrics and a comprehensive set of financial metrics. He was able to describe his performance metrics and illustrate how he uses them to solve problems.

Terry's Financial Awareness and insight into the numbers are highly-related to his interest in soliciting the right information from which to make decisions and his ability to act on what the data analysis tells him. Terry's use of IT data relative to customer loyalty programs is a good example of his focus on obtaining the correct data and making a quality decision.

Terry continues to show a mixed set of behaviors relative to employee involvement and engagement. He described soliciting perspectives from associates at various levels as he worked to change the vision. However, he did all the data collection and analysis relative to the decision on the customer loyalty program on his own, a process highly amenable to delegation. The latter example reinforces our earlier observation of Terry's tendency to spread himself too thin. His role as the store manager for all three stores also validates that tendency.

Comparison of Business Judgments

After listening to the responses to our questions relating to Business Judgment, we put our heads together and took the first pass at evaluating the degree of effectiveness each of our leaders demonstrated. We emphasize "tried" because we recognize that a short interview will not give us the range of information or the complete view needed to make a definitive assessment of each dimension. We thought it would be worth the effort to see what types of tendencies each leader was illustrating and what we should be looking for as we observe them daily throughout the coming year.

Both Jamie and Terry were thought effective in acquiring the right data and using it as the basis for making decisions (Data Savvy). Still, neither provided examples beyond what we would expect of business heads with their levels of education and experience. By the same token, we saw Jamie as highly effective in her Strategic Mindset due to the time and focus she and her colleagues gave the development and monitoring of their strategy. Terry, on the other hand, focused on his vision for the company but did not discuss or emphasize the development of his company strategy in any of his responses.

Terry showed strength in Customer Focus through his many examples of soliciting customer input and using customer data effectively. Jamie demonstrated an adequate level of Customer Focus based on the frequency and strength of the illustrations she provided. Financial Awareness represents an interesting contrast in the capability levels of Jamie and Terry. Jamie tended to focus on a few transactional financial metrics, while Terry defined and monitored an impressive number of metrics. We also reacted to the amount of time Jamie spent with her VP of finance. Our initial assessment: She might not be filling the Financial Awareness bucket. Both appeared effective relative to Balanced Decision-Making. We will have the opportunity to observe this dimension in more depth in the chapters to come.

Again, this assessment represents our initial evaluation based on a limited retrospective interview—this is the primary picture coming into focus in our Polaroid. We will continue this process based on many more in-depth observations resulting from specific on-the-job scenarios in subsequent chapters.

Chapter 5

Insights into People Decisions

While a successful business is predicated on talented, committed people, one does not hire people with those characteristics fully developed. Hopefully, you select well and hire people with the potential to develop into high-performing associates, but it is the critical role of the business leader to create such a workforce of associates. This is what People Judgement is all about—making decisions and communicating effectively, resulting in a team of thoughtful, empowered, and company-centric associates.

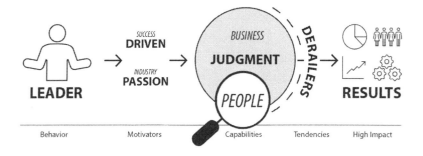

| Behavior | Motivators | | Capabilities | Tendencies | High Impact |

People Judgment is a critical but complex capability that must be viewed, developed, and demonstrated in five subordinate capabilities or dimensions:

- Engagement: Maintains awareness of and responsiveness to the needs of associates at all levels of the organization
- Relationship Building: Connects with people (internally and externally) to build lasting collaborative relationships
- Team Development: Fosters an environment where team members are accountable to each other, build shared goals, and consistently achieve
- Individual Development: Demonstrates the capability

and interest in developing each associate's talent to their maximum potential

- Decisiveness: Addresses people-related issues and problems by making timely, considerate but resolute decisions that result in the best outcomes for individuals and the organization

As was the case with Business Judgment, these interviews provide an initial view of Jamie and Terry. We will gain crucial insights into their overall level of People Judgment but not a perspective of the supporting dimensions.

People Judgment Interview: Jamie

We talked about you, your plans for the company, and several business events you have encountered during your tenure with e-Dine. Jamie, we'd like to wrap up this initial interview by talking about the people in your organization. Talk to us about the importance of building relationships with your associates.

I want everyone in this company to recognize they are part of the e-Dine team. We have a common goal, and I hope we believe in what we are doing. We must come ready to play—to contribute our best because our accomplishments are critical to the team's successes. Team members need to know and respect each other; we must be comfortable that everyone is bringing their unique skills to the game, and we win and lose together. I think professional and amiable relationships are crucial for our success.

What do you do regularly to ensure you have a strong, positive relationship with your associates?

When I started the company, I interviewed every new associate, regardless of their position. I wanted to look every person in the eye and tell them what we are all about and ensure everyone could see and commit to that future. I genuinely believe the best teams are built when people feel they can be open, where their opinions are respected and necessary for company success. This was easy to do when I had a company of twenty-five, but this approach was not tenable as we began to welcome new people to our team each month. We transitioned to a monthly welcome lunch—just me and new associates from all company areas, spending an hour in the conference room with a box lunch, getting to know each other, better understanding what brought them to us.

I have known many of our associates since their first day on the job. We have worked to make e-Dine what it is today. I try not to lose that connection as the company develops, even as our day-to-day interactions have dramatically changed. I don't ever want to be the person who comes in and sits in her office with the door closed. As we have grown, the scope of my audience has narrowed. I have found ways to keep connected, reaching out and acknowledging individual successes and contributions. For example, each week, as I look through the flash reports, I might notice an exception sale and simply circle the item and write a quick note: "Thanks for the effort—you made us a little better today." I fold that sheet in half and throw it into an inter-office envelope for the rep.

Similarly, I ask the leadership team to be aware of the "little wins" and not only recognize them within their groups but pass some of the best on to me. I usually put an hour aside each week to draft brief emails to associates throughout the company whose efforts I have heard of. Similarly, I will try to bring up someone's contributions when I am with any of our groups.

How important is teamwork in your business? Why?

I think much of our success has been due to a culture where teamwork is the mantra. No one can do it on their own. We have big plans, and everyone at e-Dine understands what we want to accomplish as a company. More importantly, we all are passionate believers that together, we are changing the restaurant business to serve our customers better. For example, the first place we continually look for feedback on software functionality is within the company. Our CTO runs an online forum where associates share stories they have heard from customers relating to *ease of use* and intuitiveness. He regularly summarizes the findings and then communicates with our salespeople, internal testers, and key partners. This collaboration has helped us respond quickly to changing user needs.

How do you foster teamwork among your associates?

We have talked a lot about how we win as a team, but the best teams celebrate the successes of their members. I think we have built such a phenomenal team at e-Dine because we are rooting for each other. At every level of the organization, we recognize achievement and reward performance. Our associates know they are valued and well-compensated for excellence. Building healthy competition is equally as important because individual successes motivate our peers to bring their best game.

How do you ensure you acquire, develop, and retain the level of talent you need to meet and exceed your business goals?

We invest heavily in our people. We have developed what we think is a comprehensive hiring process to ensure we attract and identify the best people. Our job descriptions clearly illustrate what responsibilities and contributions we expect. Prospective candidates will speak with our HR manager. If they appear promising, they will have video interviews with their potential manager. We then invite top candidates in for several hours to allow everyone to get to know each other better. We regularly promote from within whenever possible. We structure bonuses, commissions, and company-wide incentives to ensure people are well-compensated for outstanding performance.

Once an associate commits to us, we commit to their professional success. Every manager here has a mandate: how can you help your associates become better than they thought they could be? We invest in supplementary training and education and look to mentor people. Most of our managers and senior leaders are homegrown.

How do you model and encourage open communication and discussion regarding the needs and direction of your business?

The best teams communicate. We are collectively pursuing success in the market, which takes the combined efforts, insights, and feedback of every member. I always remind our associates that everyone talks about the importance of communication, but open and truthful communication is hard work. We must be able to talk about what is working and what is not working. Peers owe it to each other to applaud successes and insist on their best performance each day. Everyone in the organization should understand where we are going as a company and be aware of our collective progress.

My approach has always been to be open about our plans, our successes, and any potential obstacles we face. Yes, differing degrees of detail are necessary for people at various levels of the organization. Still, I want well-informed and engaged associates throughout the company. We have quarterly all-employee meetings with every department and function: customer service, development, sales, accounting, maintenance—everyone on the team. We share current performance, challenges, new approaches, anything going on at e-Dine. At least half of that meeting is a discussion. My team and I will take questions from everyone. In many ways, it is like a town hall meeting.

Although most of these meetings have been fun and productive, some become tense as we uncover a concern or criticism. But in the end, we are better as an organization because we have identified an issue and take steps to adjust.

In a related area, how do you make yourself available to associates and encourage the feedback and insights you need to stay abreast of what's happening in your organization?

I try to be out of my office and in other areas of the building every day. On busy days, I want at least a half-hour to stop by one of the departments or visit the snack room to chat with whoever might be around. I like to be a part of group and department meetings throughout the week to hear how people execute and offer any insight or support. This is also how I stay more intimately attached to them and informed.

Authors' Insights

Jamie recognizes the importance of building relationships and establishing communications with the associates of e-Dine. Initially, Jamie interviewed every new associate. As the company grew, she transitioned to monthly onboarding lunches. She also spends time in the various operational functions, talks with associates, and finds ways to communicate regularly. She appears committed to building a culture of communication and teamwork.

Jamie advocates strong talent development as a key to both business success and her success as a leader. She has established consistent processes to ensure effective selection, development, and retention of talent. Teamwork appears to be another vital area of focus for Jamie. She stated: "Much of our success has been due to a culture where teamwork is the mantra. No one can do it on their own." Although enthusiastic in her zeal to create a culture of teamwork, we did not hear specific examples of what Jamie does to promote teamwork from a leadership perspective—particularly with her leadership team. Suffice it to say, our introduction to Jamie via our one-on-one interview has evidenced a highly articulate, enthusiastic, and tech-savvy business leader; however, the pattern of behavior indicating a lack of planned, overt action to get her associates involved and prepared to participate in higher-level planning and being empowered to address significant challenges needs further investigation.

People Judgment Interview: Terry

Terry, let's talk about your associates and the importance of building relationships.

Turnover is a huge challenge in the grocery business, even at the assistant store manager level. It is difficult—no, it is simply impossible—to build a relationship with every employee. I have identified the most critical roles in the organization and those tough to replace. I spend more time with those people to ensure they feel they know what is going on and know what they want. Building relationships with people in the business can really influence the culture and values of the company. Plus, when people feel valued, the result is often extra effort and a reluctance to leave.

What do you do regularly to ensure you have a strong positive relationship with your associates?

I take several formal and informal approaches. The formal ones are important because they create structure and help people set goals and see their progress. I try to have weekly or monthly sit-downs with my leadership team. I also try to have brief and informal conversations with everyone in a management role. It can be as simple as working with someone for thirty minutes a few times a year. It shows that I want to understand what they do and where their challenges lie. During this time, I always try to bring up things we discussed the last time we worked together. It doesn't always have to be work-related. I am not trying to become their friend, but I want them to know I listen to the things they say, and I am invested in them. I congratulate people on their birthdays and special occasions; if someone has a milestone birthday or work anniversary, I make sure they get a nice gift with a handwritten card from me.

How important is teamwork in your business? Why?

I think teamwork is critical to any business. It is just kind of obvious to me that you cannot be successful if you are only in it for yourself and not willing to support your coworkers. In a store, you never know what will happen, and people must be able to jump in and help, even if it is not their primary area. Also, when people work together, there's a collective knowledge versus an individual perspective. For example, say a long summer weekend is coming. People typically grill out. Well, maybe the butcher in one of our stores did not make the connection; the weekend ahead was a long one. That Wednesday morning, he planned to stock the regular supply of hamburgers and sausages for our deli. The bakeshop manager might notice that and casually remind him, "I doubled my bun orders for the weekend; do you think the meats match that forecast?" The butcher will likely recognize he has to get back into the shop and grind more prime chuck. That is what teamwork gets you. People look out for each other. When you feel like you are part of a team, you like coming to work and are happier because everyone wants the feeling of belonging to something.

How do you foster teamwork among your associates?

We ask people to bring up some of their biggest challenges during our weekly or monthly store and department meetings at the store level. I always look to the group and say, "How can we help our teammates?" You would be surprised how many people from different departments and roles jump in with ideas. We solve many problems this way. Equally as important, our associates recognize the value each person brings to our team. I think a lot of camaraderie happens through these exchanges.

How do you ensure you acquire, develop, and retain the level of talent you need to meet and exceed your business goals?

Well, a brand isn't just for customers. It's also for employees. If people feel pride in the company, they stay longer and help you recruit. We get most of our people through employee referrals. A good brand attracts good people—they want to work here. For me, a brand is not just products and services; it's about values, including how a company treats its associates. I think the whole of a brand attracts talent.

People stay when they feel respected, engaged, and challenged. I want Eat Fresh associates to always feel they are learning and adding value. I believe it is important to mix up the day-to-day job with some stretch assignments now and then. I am almost always surprised to see how people step up to a new challenge if given a chance. For example, we always make sure our associates receive training on an individual level to do their job better and contribute to their long-term growth within the company.

One of the most important things you can do in an organization is ensure that people understand where we are heading, how we make money, and where they fit within that process. When people truly feel connected with the plan, they will make it happen. I am always amazed at the things people will do to help the company reach its goals.

How do you model and encourage open communication and discussion regarding the needs and direction of your business?

Encouraging open communication throughout the company is essential, especially in the age of social media, portable devices, and real-time communication. We share our key goals with all employees and update them regularly so everyone knows where we stand. I also spend time each quarter making sure everyone understands why we chose specific goals and my thinking behind them. People may not always agree with our decisions or what we are doing, which is okay. Business never has a right or wrong answer. It's always a judgment call. If the people here at Eat Fresh understand the why and how of a decision, they are part of the process. I believe they are more apt to commit to whatever we attempt to do.

Communication is necessary for everyone to win. It's not just the leadership team communicating honestly with associates. Every employee needs to recognize that we are at our best when we are open and honest. We encourage employees to talk with their peers, their supervisors, and the leadership team. If you have a meaningful idea, a concern, or even a compliment, share it. We promote unbiased critiques and praise as a process for making everyone more successful.

In a related area, how do you make yourself available to associates and encourage the feedback and insights you need to stay abreast of what's happening in your organization?

Part of it is what I said earlier about building relationships. It's about spending time in the stores and departments, listening and talking to the people. I very much believe in leading from the front. When you do, people feel they can come to you because they know you. Also, my door is always open, and I mean literally. The only time it is closed is during a confidential discussion. I point out that my door is open, and I want them always to feel they can stop in.

Authors' Insights

Terry recognizes the importance of people and creates a culture where associates identify with and maintain the brand. He demonstrates a strong awareness of the basics in dealing with people—listening, recognizing small achievements, working with associates, and maintaining regular communication with individuals and the entire organization. Terry's communication style appears to be open and straightforward, without a lot of hype. He makes himself available to his associates. We must observe how his communication style may need to change given his growth plans.

Comparison of Jamie's and Terry's People Judgment

Both Terry and Jamie are articulate and enthusiastic about the importance of ongoing communication, relationships, and people. Engagement appears to be a strength for both. Relationship Building is a dimension in which they appear to be effective, given what we've heard thus far, but certainly not a strength.

Team Development and Individual Development are the two dimensions of People Judgment in which our leaders evidenced potential problems. Jamie talks about the "team" and gives some examples of team input, but the strength of those examples is limited. The same is true for Individual Development. She did not provide any examples, nor could she articulate the importance of developing each associate's talent to its potential.

Terry did not mention the importance of team or individual coaching or performance feedback. His lack of examples led us to question his degree of effectiveness in Team or Individual Development. We should be on the lookout for a correlation of Terry spreading himself too thin concerning performance in several of the dimensions of People Judgment.

We will end with this reminder: these insights are our initial evaluations based on retrospective interviews that provided limited views of the leaders. We are just getting to know Jamie and Terry. This is an incomplete picture. The view will become clearer and more focused in the chapters ahead.

What's Next?

Next, we will follow our leaders for a year as they face market challenges and opportunities, experience workplace incidents, and execute strategies. We will interview them at the end of each quarter to discuss the critical challenges and decisions they made. With each scenario, we will continue to build and clarify our leader profiles.

Section III
Leadership in the PRG

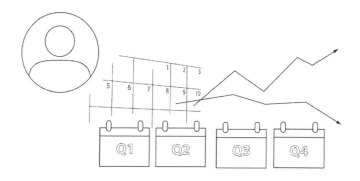

We learned quite a bit about our leaders from the initial interviews. After a brief conversation, we already have a reasonably good understanding of their motivations and can make an initial appraisal of their respective capabilities. Notice we did not say *strengths and weaknesses*. At this point, we have seen and heard some positive behaviors as well as indicators of less-than-effective leadership. However, we need to see a lot more of these leaders across a variety of challenging situations to make a definitive assessment.

Think about the Polaroid photo. From the time you snap the picture to the end of the development process, the image becomes more detailed; you confirm many things you thought you saw and spot new, sometimes striking, pieces of the portrait.

We need time for the details to come into focus within our pictures of Jamie and Terry. Those details manifest in the critical business decisions and significant people issues each leader addresses over a year leading through the PRG.

Our approach to supplementing, enhancing, and clarifying Jamie's and Terry's leadership pictures builds on the process we introduced during the first interviews. We will look at the key experiences each leader reported throughout the upcoming operating year. Each quarter, the leaders will sit down with us to report what has happened in their company. We have broken this section into four interview periods: Q1, Q2, Q3, and Q4, followed by an end-of-year summary. Within the quarter, we will highlight critical incidents Jamie and Terry reported as stand-alone chapters. Each chapter explores the decisions a leader made to address situations, events, or opportunities. These rich conversations and resulting behaviors will provide a foundation from which we can readily glean significant insights into Jamie's and Terry's leadership effectiveness.

In Chapter 3, we introduced a simple scorecard in which we rated the various dimension of the Motivators. We will use a version of that scorecard throughout the interviews.

Business Judgment		People Judgment	
①————②——▼——③		①——▼——②————③	
Data Savvy	3	Engagement	NO
Strategic Mindset	2	Relationship Building	2
Customer Focus	1	Team Development	1
Financial Awareness	NO	Individual Development	3
Balanced Decision-Making	1	Decisiveness	1

The scorecard indicates our assessment of each leader across the various dimensions of Business or People Judgment. We can also begin to summarize how those dimensions collectively represent a degree of effectiveness in these two components of the High Impact Leadership model[SM]. Not every situation represents an opportunity for a leader to demonstrate each dimension of the Judgments. When we encounter a scenario in which one or more of the dimensions were not observed, the scorecard will reflect this absence as "NO."

Leadership Behavior and Results

Our next series of interviews will assess our leaders' performance and highlight the impact of their actions and decisions on the organization. The scorecard is now expanded, becoming more of a dashboard. We will rate leadership capabilities and monitor four broad categories of key performance outcomes:

1. *Market*: Exceeding sales quotas, penetrating a segment with greater intensity than competitors, or being recognized as one of the leaders in the marketplace are all results leaders work to achieve in this category.

2. *People*: Of critical importance to any long-term business success is a workforce of highly motivated and dedicated associates who believe in the company's mission and vision. How is company morale? What does turnover look like? Do people grow within the organization?

3. *Financial*: Outcomes that directly contribute to the fiscal

health and value of the company. This category could include metrics such as revenue, product margins, cash flow, profitable income, and cash reserves. In a specific scenario, the fiscal impact might be a significantly lowered contribution margin, savings in healthcare and benefits costs, or more quickly servicing debt.

4. *Operations*: When a company recognizes optimization or gains new expertise that results in parity or competitive advantage, this is an example of improved operational performance. Implementing a new logistics system or outsourcing a labor and cost-intensive function might also be considered a positive operating result. A shift of packaging from a manual production line to a robotic-assisted line represents yet another positive operational yield.

The expanded scorecard provides a quick and easy-to-understand summary of a leader's impact on results in each scenario—an arrow indicates the impact is *positive* (up), *negative* (down) or *neutral* (side arrows).

Why the emphasis on the results data? When someone says an executive is a "good leader," we typically ask, "Why?" From there, we hear everything from being inspirational to a hard worker or showing financial wizardry or market genius. From our perspective, there is no such thing as a *good* or *bad* leader; it is more about one's degree of effectiveness.

We are comfortable saying most small business leaders are effective. Effective leadership results in solid revenue gains, profits, and incremental growth. This is important to understand. *Effective is the norm.* If the results you achieve meet expectations, that's okay. Statistically, every population falls into the middle of a bell curve. The two ends of the curve are most interesting to us when assessing performance.

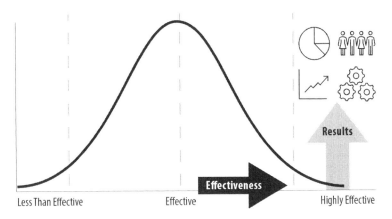

It is probably reasonable to say that no leader will last long if they consistently fall under the tail of less than effective. The other side of the curve is where we all should aspire to perform—always to be a highly effective leader who can impact profitability, growth, and meaningful change across their organizations. The more effective the leader, the more likely their organizational results will improve.

As we collectively look at our leaders and reflect on their behaviors, we will begin to see the degree of effectiveness each demonstrates and the results achieved in their organizations. Neither is likely to do everything perfectly. Leaders continually develop and refine their skills. What is important to recognize is how the most incremental improvements to one's leadership capabilities can exponentially impact results across an organization. The better Jamie or Terry fills up the buckets of behavior representing the dimensions of the High Impact Leadership model℠, the higher the likelihood their decisions will lead to better results—they *move the mean* across the various results categories defining company success.

Okay, enough with the setup. Let's settle in and spend a year with Jamie and Terry. Together, we will experience their leadership approaches across a range of situations. We will see the impact of their actions and decisions on organizational results. Additionally, we will summarize our insights relative to their respective strengths and areas in which they may want to improve—moving the mean of their performance. Finally, we will do a deep dive into the performance metrics that define success within their organizations to gauge their leadership impact.

Q1: Jamie

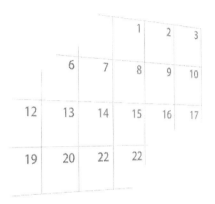

Chapter 6

Hard to Say No

The new year began with an unsolicited call and surprising offer for e-Dine to customize and license a version of its POS product—and the customer was willing to make a substantial payment for this license. How will Jamie react? Can she afford to pass up an opportunity? More importantly, are she and her team capable of executing the current strategic plan and accommodating this new initiative?

Jamie, tell us about a specific business challenge or opportunity you faced this past quarter.

My year began with an opportunity that was quite a challenge. The first week of the new year, I received a call from an executive at *CinemaCo*, a national theater chain with headquarters right down the road. He needed a new POS system for their concessions, which had become more like a casual dining restaurant inside the chain's 2,500 theaters. Rather than building its own software, he thought they could license a customized version of our product. The guy loved e-Dine's software and knew precisely what components of our POS they could leverage, as well as the new features the theaters would need. He was prepared to pay a multi-million-dollar fee for development and licensing.

What was your reaction?

Soon after I hung up the phone, I looked at our CTO, Mike, and Perrin, our VP of finance, and said: "Did the weather forecast call for showers of money?" Out of nowhere, we had an opportunity to leverage our technology into a lateral but certainly not competitive market, build some new intellectual property (IP), and generate a significant chunk of revenue. This was not a market in which we were interested, so the opportunity was surprising. My mind immediately went back to my enterprise software days. I remembered the easiest and most profitable sales were customizations of existing products. I was excited to explore the potential deal.

What did you do next?

We put together a tiger team, including me, Mike, Perrin, and Porter, our customer service manager. We agreed to start by simply looking at the feasibility: Could we do it? How much time? The development cost. The rollout—in other words, how many people would we need to hire and train, and could we create a new support model wherein we trained CinemaCo managers, so they represented the first level of support? I reached out to my network and found a friend who happened to have a colleague in the theater business. He connected us, and we hired him to provide some industry diligence. As this team worked to understand the project approach, Carl, our VP of sales, and I flew out and met with the CinemaCo team to learn more and handle the initial negotiations. During these early discussions, we constantly exchanged information between the two groups, ensuring we had almost real-time data for planning and positioning ourselves with the client.

Why did you choose those people? Who led each team?

I led both. It seemed to make sense for me to run point on the feasibility and the negotiations. I have the most comprehensive view of our resources and capabilities. A deal this significant and unique to our company required me to be a part of the negotiations and planning from the outset.

What did your feasibility study tell you?

We quickly came to see there were no significant technology roadblocks to developing this theater-specific POS. The project was going to take a lot of time. We could repurpose 80 percent of our code. We update and enhance our IP significantly more than this for most new versions. But everything about this project was busywork and represented six to nine months in mundane things like changing the user interface to reflect the client's branding and ensuring the new user experience (UX) made sense for someone taking orders at the concession stand versus a waiter at a diner's table. We were looking at a lot of field testing.

The team had two concerns. The first was related to our experience in the industry. Our CTO was adamant that our insights into the service industry were transferable, especially with access to our consultant and a liaison from CinemaCo working with us throughout the process. I agreed, the variable being how engaged the CinemaCo contact was in the process. A more pressing concern was installation and support. Our total installed base of clients in the restaurant industry is just under 19,500, and we built that over six years. How would we install and support what would have to be a simultaneous rollout to all the chains? We would have to hire and train upward of thirty contractors for six months, then develop a plan to transfer a portion of them into the full-time ranks of our outbound support team.

What was the value of this opportunity?

Financially, the CinemaCo deal represented a short-term financial windfall. We projected we would net almost three million dollars in the first year if we used our current development and QA teams.

Even with the costly investment in a temporary installation and support team, we would be well ahead of the game. The long-term merits of the deal were not as clear.

Why?

CinemaCo wanted to buy a customized copy of our system, what we call a "code snapshot," which means they own that code and can adjust it in the future. Now, they cannot use it to sell to others or become a POS vendor, but if you think about it, we are giving them tens of millions of dollars of our code for a single fee. There is a reasonable chance they will not come back to us for new coding of features, enhancements, and the like. We do not receive a royalty because it is custom work. We might not see another dollar after the initial transaction, which means we got a significant payment and have some new IP for a related industry, but likely one in which we are not interested in competing. This was a tough decision.

What did you decide to do?

If this deal came to us when we were a bit more established, I would have jumped all over it, but we could not afford to lose our focus at this point in our strategic development. I decided to pass.

Why?

We had to. The moment you stop looking at the chunk of money they were offering, you get your focus back on what's really important: e-Dine. If we took this contract, the upcoming year's entire operation would have been all about CinemaCo. Our developers and QA people would be tied up in their system, not working to make ours the best in the industry. We looked at options for hiring more developers or using outside contractors, but both were inefficient, and honestly, we did not think we could do it without people who knew our code well.

At the end of the year, CinemaCo would no longer be in the picture. They would have their system, and there was a reasonable chance we would not hear from them again. In the meantime, we would be at least eight months behind on our software roadmap, and that simply cannot happen at this stage of our growth. We need to be innovating regularly to ensure our existing customers are thrilled, and our soon-to-be customers recognize we are consistently delivering the solutions that make their businesses a success.

It is hard to walk away from the proverbial gift horse. But no matter how you dissect the situation, the project was tangential to our strategy, and we would have been misusing our resources for a short-term win.

Authors' Insights

As a PRG leader, the biggest takeaway from this scenario is: *Do not be distracted from sticking to your strategy.* Jamie demonstrated Strategic Mindset by thoroughly analyzing a potential windfall and recognizing it for what it was: A one-time financially lucrative opportunity that would inordinately utilize resources, distract the organization from its core competency, and potentially misdirect e-Dine from identifying innovative solutions that could positively impact its success in the marketplace. Michael Porter famously said, "The essence of strategy is choosing what *not* to do." Jamie chose well. One might ask if Jamie could have achieved a different outcome had she negotiated another type of deal. The one-time payment, although significant, offered no long-term affinity to e-Dine. Would Jamie's choices have looked different if the agreement captured less money upfront but included an ongoing royalty payment and gave e-Dine the right of first refusal for opportunities to update the code?

Jamie also demonstrated significant Balanced Decision-Making behavior in addressing this situation. In particular, she considered short-term and long-term rewards and risks while recognizing the operational capacity and resource implications of taking on the CinemaCo project. Finally, she maintained a high degree of Financial Awareness relative to accepting or rejecting the project. As a result, we see Jamie demonstrated significant Business Judgment. Short term, her choice did not result in a financial windfall, but her decision precluded taking the organization off-course and damaging e-Dine's long-term success in its core market.

In addition to her Business Judgment, Jamie used her people well. She put together a diverse team of suitable operational heads to analyze and assess the viability and impact of the potential project. One might question whether she should have led the negotiations team, and the team evaluating the project viability. We think that in this situation, we should give her the benefit of the doubt. This opportunity arose out of nowhere, and the timeline to react and decide was relatively short. Jamie built the company and knew e-Dine better than anyone. Plus, this was a huge financial and strategic decision for which she ultimately had to take accountability. Her Engagement, being regularly available to her team, discussing the company's needs, and explaining to all the rationale for choosing to reject the offer, positively affected the team and ensured the company's long-term strategy. Jamie demonstrated excellent People Judgment.

The notable impact of Jamie's leadership on organizational results is primarily in the people category—her team avoided any potential deviation from planned timelines, and progress toward the next version of the software remains on track. We suspect her leadership team is also pleased to see the company is being recognized as an innovative solution provider. In the short term, the impact of her decisions was neutral in terms of market and operations. Similarly, there was no negative financial impact. Yes, e-Dine's rejection of the CinemaCo deal represented millions of unrecognized dollars in the current year. But no one was expecting the windfall, and the decision was made because every analysis indicated the project would detract from the primary revenue generated by the POS.

Scorecard

Business Judgment		People Judgment	
①————②——▼——③		①————②——▼——③	
Data Savvy	NO	Engagement	3
Strategic Mindset	3	Relationship Building	NO
Customer Focus	NO	Team Development	3
Financial Awareness	2	Individual Development	NO
Balanced Decision-Making	3	Decisiveness	NO
Results			
↔	↑	↔	↔
Market	People	Financial	Operations

How did you assess Jamie's leadership in this situation? Where do we agree? How do we differ? Why?

PRG leaders must evaluate opportunities and sometimes make difficult choices. Have you been in a situation like Jamie's?

What happened?

What would you do differently?

Chapter 7

Skyrocketing Benefits

E-Dine has always provided company-paid healthcare and a sundry of benefits for its employees. But Jamie's HR manager has come to her with some important news. Skyrocketing premiums and the projected growth in associates suggest the company can no longer absorb the entire cost of such a robust benefits program.

Tell me about your recent issue involving the employee benefits program.

Our program renews at the start of the second quarter, so Matt, our HR manager, had been working with our providers to negotiate fees and services. When we started the company, I was committed to providing healthcare to all associates at no cost. I believed this was our responsibility to the people who were taking a chance to come to build e-Dine. I thought this was a compelling benefit too.

Matt was supposed to meet with me to explain his progress and give me an idea of the changes and costs we could expect for the new year. He has done an excellent job of maintaining plan costs for the past few years. He negotiates well and has been smart about tailoring the less critical secondary services within the package. We had budgeted a rate-up of 7 percent. Well, I should have known there was a problem by the look on his face. Our current benefits package would increase by 31 percent per employee.

What was your reaction to the news?

My first question was: What did Perrin, our VP of finance, say when you showed her the numbers? Matt shared Perrin's budget forecast and notes. The bottom line was, continuing to absorb the benefits at this rate would reduce our forecasted profits by at least $150,000, possibly $300,000, if we added the number of associates projected in our best-case forecast.

What did you do?

I was looking at a decision that had implications for the bottom line and this organization. I knew we likely had several choices. The first would be to shop for other benefit providers and put together an equivalent package in the next two months. I asked Matt how practical this would be, and he said it would be a challenge. Still, he could likely build a similar package, but he doubted we would get anywhere below a 15 percent rate. We would have to put together an entirely new rollout, learn how new providers worked, and our associates would have to familiarize themselves with a host of new providers. Plus, our costs would still go up beyond what we budgeted. I quickly decided this was not a reasonable approach—too much turmoil to introduce when we have so many other things we are pushing to do. We were going to stick with the benefits plan we had.

So, the debate I had to have with myself was how to deal with the cost increase.

What were your choices?

Well, I could simply say our commitment to employee healthcare is tantamount to who we are. We would have to adjust our financial expectations to ensure we meet our responsibility. I also started to recognize that things change, and rising healthcare costs impact businesses large and small. Maybe growth has to include some change and some sharing of responsibility. I could explain this to our employees and say that we will continue to pay the majority of the premium, but the rate-up would be shared.

What did you decide?

I decided we had to share the burden of the increasing costs, but I wanted to be sure we did right by our associates. I talked with Perrin about the impact of different cost splits. We agreed we had already budgeted a 7 percent increase. Perrin wanted to pass the additional 24 percent on to our associates, thus ensuring our current financials would remain relatively the same. I thought this was not in the spirit of burden-sharing. More importantly, I was concerned that without a candid approach to an increase and a sincere effort demonstrating we were all sacrificing, people would be affected. I could see this being a significant challenge to motivation. I suggested we pay what we budgeted, and we split the remaining increase equally. Our projected profits would go down, but now our loss would be between $86,000 to well under $110,000. This option was acceptable to me, especially when I knew we could continue to offer a premium set of benefits for an extremely competitive rate.

How was your decision received?

Very well. We had little pushback.

Why do you think the change was so well-received?

Because we were upfront, honest, and fair. I had a virtual meeting with all associates and laid out the facts. I talked about our commitment to the best of benefits and the realization that the changing market made it impossible to deliver the quality package to which we all had grown accustomed. I walked through the options for less costly and comprehensive packages. I shared the rates and showed the various ways we could have passed on the cost, explaining how we were sharing the costs equally. We talked a bit about how benefits are the "hidden paycheck" of any employee's compensation and how much we paid for insurance each month. Many associates said they had no idea e-Dine had been that generous for so long and were okay contributing. The average costs were less than $58 per pay period.

How would you rate your results?

Good. We continue to have great benefits. Our associates recognize the cost, and although no one ever wants to spend more money, most understand they pay a fraction of the bill.

Authors' Insights

Sometimes a decision appears to be all about money. You might expect Jamie would be using many Business Judgment capabilities. But what you see here is that much of what drove the successful outcomes was Jamie's People Judgment. Remember, the two types of Judgment seldom exist in a vacuum; leaders demonstrate dimensions of both types of Judgment in most decisions.

Jamie faced what we are sure is a situation familiar to many readers. A key initiative, deliverable, or project suddenly exceeds your cost expectations. What do you do? In this case, the costs were related to the company benefits program. Although there are significant implications for the year's bottom-line profitability, the rate change primarily impacts people. Associates would now have a less comprehensive set of benefits or suddenly find themselves paying for a benefit that was always fully paid for by the company.

When we looked at Jamie's Business Judgment, we saw

robust action investigating, addressing, and deciding how to overcome this obstacle. She demonstrated Balanced Decision-Making. One would say she was cognizant of the financial implications of her decision; thus, we thought she used sound Financial Awareness.

On the People Judgment side, we observed several highly effective behaviors. If you think back to the Motivators, we recognized high-impact leaders build unique cultures, believing in the company values and commitments. Jamie was not likely to offer lesser-quality benefits, nor would she shift the financial burden to her employees. But she knew growth and market changes simply would not allow her to carry the entire financial burden. Jamie could have passed on a significant portion of the rate-up and ensured her bottom line was not affected. But she recognized the impact this could have on her people. She chose to share the costs, and she communicated the change via an impromptu all-company meeting. The thoughtful and honest approach was an example of Decisiveness. We were surprised by how little pushback Jamie received from long-term employees. Change is never easy. In our experience, few changes in benefits stories are so well-received. The key to leading change is to do much of what Jamie did, but don't be alarmed if you hear a few grumbles.

What were the results? Jamie's leadership impact in the people category is down. Associates never like change, and when that change includes having to pay more for something they previously received for free—the immediate reaction is pushback. Jamie's efforts to explain the shared burden will help to alleviate the issue over time. There will be a financial loss because of the increased administration in handling the new rates. Still, the overall impact of her decision is neutral, as is financial and operational.

Scorecard

Business Judgment		People Judgment	
Data Savvy	NO	Engagement	2
Strategic Mindset	NO	Relationship Building	NO
Customer Focus	NO	Team Development	NO
Financial Awareness	2	Individual Development	NO
Balanced Decision-Making	2	Decisiveness	3

Business Judgment: ① ——— ② ——— ③ (arrow at 2)
People Judgment: ① ——— ② ——— ③ (arrow between 2 and 3)

Results

Market	People	Financial	Operations
↔	↓	↔	↔

How did you assess Jamie's leadership in this situation? Where do we agree? How do we differ? Why?

How do you approach benefits? Have you had to address skyrocketing benefit in your company?

What happened?

What would you do differently?

Chapter 8

Third-Party Provider

E-Dine's office manager has traditionally overseen the computer and hardware needs of company employees. The CTO and his developers frequently troubleshoot technical support issues. As the company has grown, this responsibility has taken on a life of its own. Jamie's office manager has negotiated a contract with a computer systems and support provider to centralize purchasing, installation, and support for computers throughout the company—a significant change in how hardware and support have been handled.

Jamie, tell me about an operational challenge you addressed this quarter.

There have been several, but I didn't want to end our discussion without talking with you about our switch to *WratchTech*, our new hardware procurement management and support service.

Why did this come to mind as a critical event?

I guess because of the way it all came about. I recognized that growth throws all kinds of unplanned needs at you and changes your routines. I need to empower my people to keep an eye out for these challenges and encourage them to make choices or bring solutions to the table.

Some big insights. Tell me what happened.

Natalie is our office manager. She was one of the first ten hires here at e-Dine—she is smart and she's invested. In one way or another, Nat has had her hand in so many projects over the years. One of the things she is currently responsible for is overseeing computer equipment for our people. I am talking about everything from the laptops we give the reps, the desktops in the various departments, the machines our developers code on, and the devices my team and I use. This whole process began rather informally—we would hire someone, our CTO, Mike, would say, "They are going to need a laptop," or, "That new guy will need a desktop like the others in the outbound group." Natalie would purchase what was needed. As we have grown, each department has a general idea of their needs, and Nat has us set up with a business account at one of the national computer retailers. The whole operation was kind of a black box to me. I never really thought about it because Natalie is so efficient.

You know what? No process here should be that opaque to me. She was overwhelmed, and the whole procedure was inefficient. Had she not taken the initiative to explain what we were doing and seek outside providers, she would have collapsed under the weight of our growth.

Let me digress. Natalie sent me a somewhat cryptic email saying: we must speak immediately about computer acquisition and support before heading over a cliff. I think I wrote back and told her I would clear time that same day. When we met that afternoon, she began by telling me, "I don't want you to think I am overstepping my boundaries, but I know how we got where we are today and where we want to go. If we don't address this, I am going to fail you and the company."

I chuckled and assured her nothing could be that bad. I asked her to walk me through what was going on. As I said, I was blind to all this. She managed over a hundred machines using an ad-hoc system of a spreadsheet and a combination of paid take-in repair at the local computer store, machine warranty services, and troubleshooting support from most of our developers. As soon as she walked me through her system,

I saw the implications. I apologized for being so blind to the responsibilities placed on her. Natalie stopped me mid-sentence, saying, "Hey, I am here to get this done. I am at the point where I'm doing a bad job, which costs us more than it should. Plus, we're getting too big to do things this unprofessionally."

Before I could reply, Natalie pulled out several presentation pages highlighting the problems. She hit on inefficiency, a lack of standards, poor device management, costly repairs, and long downtimes. You don't know her, but Nat is straightforward. She pulled out her next page prefacing by saying, "And this may not be my business, but I think the developers have better things to do with their time than fix frozen computers." Her sheet was a rough count of requests she had made to our developer team for support in the past six months. By her estimate, she was calling on them almost six hours a week. Then she showed me the final sheet, a proposal to contract our computer services to a small but national firm called WratchTech. She had spoken with two of their reps and negotiated the first round of an impressive contract. She felt we would save at least 10–15 percent on any hardware purchase. The monthly support was less than we paid in warranties, retail repairs, and replacements. Plus, with WratchTech managing the process, she would be free to work on more notable projects.

What did you do?

My natural inclination would be to take something like this and work with the associate to flesh out the details and make it happen. But in Natalie's case, I decided to ask a few questions to make sure we had the same goals and let her run with them. I suggested she talk with Carl and his group to get their input and sell them on the time they were getting back to focus on building our products. I also asked that she think carefully about the transition. Natalie told me she was thinking about that and was going to go back to them and try to bargain for free management of the existing hardware as we grandfather the devices out. That was a great idea. I didn't think she would get it. Guess what? She did.

What kind of results did you get?

We brought WratchTech on midway through this quarter. I do not know the long-term financials, but the last four laptops we purchased were $700 less than the same machines we bought when managing the process on our own. I can also tell you we closed more open bugs in the codebase this past quarter, which we can attribute to one thing: our developer team had more time to debug and focus on the product. I also think we are more efficient and professional. When we hire someone, a new machine is sitting there waiting for them, and a twenty-four-hour tech agent is standing by. In the field, our reps and QA team will have the same equipment. I like that consistency. For me, though, seeing Natalie identify this problem and single-handedly fix it is a big win. She is rightfully proud of what she did. That confidence is just going to motivate her to excel with whatever she does next. Now that she has more bandwidth, I have several things I would like her to do.

Authors' Insights

What a pleasing and somewhat surprising way to end our first round of interviews with Jamie. We have seen much strategic thinking and intensity when it comes to Jamie's understanding of business and growth. We often wonder if she shares her Industry Passion to develop others. Natalie's story told us a lot, and we think it may have opened Jamie's eyes to some of her strengths and development areas.

Jamie's experience with Natalie reflects a common issue we see when companies grow and formalize—internal processes suddenly become very inefficient. Many small businesses find growth introduces a need for greater formality than the systems previously handled in a more relaxed way among early team members. As we looked and listened for the dimensions of Business Judgment, we were surprised Jamie, who often exhibits a strong Strategic Mindset, had not considered the implication of growth on internal operations and competencies. We think we can comfortably assume this was a rare blind spot and not a lack of awareness of the daily operations. Jamie clearly "clicked" and knew the repercussions of continued inefficiency in this area when presented with the problem. We are quite sure Jamie started thinking about what the wasted hours of prime developer time meant for the product. She demonstrated a degree of Balanced Decision-Making in recognizing the issue and how she chose to delegate.

Let's look at People Judgment. She has built a relationship with Natalie. She knows and trusts her after years of working together. We could tell by the way she talked about Natalie's time at e-Dine that Jamie had developed a personal relationship that allowed her to communicate effectively with her associate. She gave Natalie a high degree of autonomy to move forward and make this deal happen, which showed Decisiveness. We thought Jamie's openness to Natalie's initial email was laudable and an example of Engagement. However, we did wonder if she presents this degree of approachability to all e-Dine associates.

The impact of Jamie's leadership capabilities on company results was clear, immediate, and appears significant. We do not see any correlation to market factors. Financially, e-Dine is already saving money on its hardware and support. What can you say about people? Natalie is racking up achievements and confidence. We suspect the visibility of Natalie's success inspires others throughout the organization. The e-Dine corporation is also experiencing improved operations, from the quick and easy hardware acquisition to the consistency of products and support received across the company. We do not want to sound like every result is ideal or perfect. Natalie will likely experience a learning curve working with WratchTech. She will also have to develop her approach for managing a key vendor to ensure organizational expectations are consistently met.

Scorecard

Business Judgment		People Judgment	
①————②————③		①————②————③	
Data Savvy	NO	Engagement	2
Strategic Mindset	NO	Relationship Building	2
Customer Focus	NO	Team Development	NO
Financial Awareness	2	Individual Development	NO
Balanced Decision-Making	2	Decisiveness	2
Results			
↔	↑	↑	↑
Market	People	Financial	Operations

How would you assess Jamie's leadership in this situation? Where do we agree? How do we differ? Why?

Have you made the switch to a once tightly held process? What were the results of your decision?

Have you recently given oversight of an initiative to an associate? How did they do?

In both cases, what would you do differently?

Chapter 9

To Discount or Not

A long-time e-Dine customer has told his sales representative he soon might not renew his service subscription. The customer is considering transitioning to a competitor's POS priced considerably less than the e-Dine solution. He wants a significant discount on his service agreement and a free upgrade to the next release of the e-Dine POS software. How much is a customer worth to Jamie?

You mentioned you recently were forced to make a difficult choice regarding a major customer.

Well, they are no longer our customer. I hear about it from everyone in the sales and marketing groups, and we are feeling it in our numbers. But there was no way to keep the customer and his restaurants on board and maintain our commitment to fair pricing.

Tell us more about this situation.

I didn't mean to be abrupt. Let me back up. I believe that our POS and customer field support are valuable. They directly contribute to our customers' efficiency and profitability. We invested years of time, money, and research in building this system, and it's priced accordingly. Every member of my team, certainly every salesperson, has heard my speech about selling value. We are premium-priced because we are exceptional at the things we do. If you know the value a product brings to the market, why would you accept anything less? Variable or negotiated pricing tells customers you do not believe in your value proposition. The price you see is the price everyone pays; we do not discount.

Okay. We understand your position. What happened?

Jocko Evangeline owns Che Jacques restaurants. He was one of our first big wins in the market; Che Jacques has fifty-six locations. All use our POS. Jocko is a premium service subscriber who has been most generous in evangelizing our product. We use his testimonials in the field and feature footage of his locations in several of our promotional materials. After three years with us, he suddenly told his account rep, Roxana, he has been approached by several POS systems willing to give him a great deal and a much lower-priced service.

Roxana is our most senior sales rep. She brought Jocko to e-Dine and works hard to maintain a close relationship with him. I am disappointed in Roxana because she moved away from our core tenet: value. At the first mention of competitors and cost, Roxana immediately suggested she bring Carl, our VP of sales, to discuss finding some discounts for such an important client. She planted the seed in Jocko's head. By the time she and Carl met with him a week later, Jocko had a list of expectations he wanted for being a special customer. He wanted us to discount his monthly service fee by 25 percent and insisted that the next upgrade cycle be free. Carl did his best to mitigate the situation. He worked to reestablish how important twenty-four-hour phone and field support is to a restaurant operation. He reminded Jocko of the nights our people were on-site, enabling the restaurant to get up and running in less than two hours. But Jocko was singularly focused on receiving a discount because he was a good customer.

Within an hour of this meeting, Carl and Roxana were on a video call with me. They stressed how important it was to make the customer happy.

What happened during that call?

I was so angry I am not sure I thoroughly listened to their arguments. Carl argued we could not lose the revenue. Our reputation would suffer because of how often our salespeople used Jocko's restaurants as a testimonial. He and Roxana wanted to give him a 10 percent discount on the subscription and offer the next version of the software at no charge. I told them this was not worth it. I tried to reiterate the importance of value. I also told them this discount would be industry news within a month, and soon every client would want a discount. Carl started to see the problem with discounting the subscription. He countered by suggesting we offer Jocko a 50 percent discount on the next version of the software. He reasoned, "They buy almost twice as many licenses as our next biggest customers."

What did you think could happen?

I knew Jocko's business was significant. If he left us, we would lose over $100,000 a year in just the monthly support subscription revenue. We would also lose his regular upgrades for those fifty-six restaurants—that's about $84,000 every eighteen to twenty-four months. This is significant. The sales team would need to find new customers to replace those licenses and hit our aggressive quarterly new sales goals. Most of our customers manage less than three locations. I knew we could expect to miss some targets this quarter.

Carl's concerns about Che Jacques' publicity value were more than valid. In the northwest region, this chain is well known. We got a lot of mileage out of those testimonials and promo videos. I thought the loss could have a short-term effect on our ability to bring in new clients, especially multi-site restaurants. I also thought about switching costs. I wondered if Jocko would eventually realize the expense of switching out equipment, installing new software, and training his staff would not be worth it. And I'll be honest, the products Jocko was suggesting he might switch to were inferior. If Carl went back and did some handholding, he might back down.

What did you decide to do?

I felt the most important thing was to maintain our approach to pricing. So, I told Carl to do what he could to appease Jocko, but the price was not changing.

What happened after you chose to stick to your pricing approach and said no?

Jocko said he understood but felt he should be rewarded for years of early and mass adoption. He began looking for a new POS. Just last week, he told Roxana he had signed a deal with a lesser-known competitor. The transition will take time. We would keep his subscription for at least four months, but the changeover would free him up to drop the support after that. The sales group is less than happy and struggles with how this exit looks to current and potential customers. I asked marketing to work with our existing customers to create new promotional materials. Now is the time we need to dig in and limit the loss. Jocko's departure is regrettable. We will get over the loss. I think we will be fine in the long run.

Authors' Insights

Jamie's experience with Jocko brings an age-old dilemma to light: The impact of discounting and allowing customers to dictate exclusive deals. There is never a right or wrong answer. In our experience, the decision is often painful and driven by a leader's philosophy. We worked with an industry-leading advertising company that regularly offered customers free or highly discounted ads in complementary media and markets. On the founder's retirement, the new CEO began his tenure by fundamentally changing the way they did business. At his first all-company meeting, he shared his philosophy: We sell something with immense value, and the price fairly reflects its worth. When we offer a product for less, we tell our customers it isn't worth what we say. He added: When you give away free things, people never find value in them. The CEO announced that the days of discounts and freebies ended right then. He asked everyone to shift their mindset and recognize they delivered great products worth every penny they cost. He was prepared to lose some customers but was not a bit concerned for the future because they would build mutually beneficial relationships with many existing customers and many new ones. Associates attending that meeting left thinking they were about to experience the swift decline of the company. Business boomed. Initially, some customers balked and left, but this was the shakeup. By the end of the year, existing clients were buying more ads, and new customer sales had increased dramatically.

Your approach to pricing depends heavily on both strategy and your understanding of the marketplace—To whom are you selling, and how elastic are these customers when it comes to pricing? Jamie's motivation (Success Driven) is clear: She wants the company culture to focus on value. Jamie's Business Judgment receives mixed reviews. She believes a differentiation pricing plan is critical to e-Dine's long-term success and is comfortable that plenty of customers will pay a premium price for a premium product. This approach is an example of Strategic Mindset.

We questioned Jamie's Financial Awareness; was her decision-making rooted firmly in understanding the financial implications of losing a customer with over fifty installations? Can e-Dine, a company heavily reliant on subscription revenue and bi-yearly upgrades, afford to lose what looks like one of its most significant customers? She has compromised her short-term income and lost a major testimonial that will likely impact sales for more than a quarter. This looks like blindness to short- and mid-term fiscal outcomes. Her Customer Focus appeared missing in her decision-making process. Jamie did not directly engage with Jocko to find a solution to keep him and his restaurants on board. What would her result have looked like if she was committed to keeping this customer? Did she have options besides discounting? What if she had worked to explain e-Dine's inability to provide the exceptional service Jocko had experienced at a lower price? Could she have recognized his value and offered him a financial enticement beyond a discount? Might Jocko have stayed with e-Dine if Jamie had awarded his affinity? She might have expressed how much she appreciated his business and acknowledged how important Che Jacques was to the company. So much so that e-Dine might like to provide him with several complimentary upgrades. Yes, that would be a form of discount, but she would not be setting a standard.

Jamie's People Judgment was equally less than effective. Yes, she was readily available to them and transparent in her thought process, but that does not make for Engagement. What were the implications for Carl, Roxana, and the salesforce in general? We thought her dismissiveness of the sales team's collective concerns was poor Decisiveness that would negatively impact morale. She also demonstrated a good deal of rigidity (a derailing tendency), not wanting to hear or consider how a large client's loss would compromise a winning sales pitch. Now she is scrambling. Carl's people must find over fifty new customers to replace the Che Jacques sites. Marketing is working to create and distribute new promotional materials. No one knows if e-Dine can replace the power of Jocko's varied testimonials. As a result, this scenario represents a lose-lose situation for all involved. Jamie lost credibility with her team and a good customer; the company lost money; the sales team potentially loses commission by their inability to make up for the lost installations—there were not many positive outcomes.

When we look at the impact of Jamie's leadership on company results, we can immediately see there is some disagreement and reaction from all levels of the sales organization (including her VP). The people results are down as expected; an example of associates needing time to recognize a decision that, right now, looks like it impacts their wallets. But as time goes by, if Jamie's rationale is accurate, the salespeople will be earning maximum commissions on every sale. Jamie's choice to let the customer go has an immediate impact on financial variables and operations—e-Dine has staff and support allocated to Jocko's many restaurants. Similarly, the market impact will be felt right away. E-Dine competitors will be sure to get the word out that one of its biggest customers is leaving.

Scorecard

Business Judgment		People Judgment	
1 — 2 — 3		1 — 2 — 3	
Data Savvy	NO	Engagement	1
Strategic Mindset	2	Relationship Building	NO
Customer Focus	1	Team Development	NO
Financial Awareness	1	Individual Development	NO
Balanced Decision-Making	NO	Decisiveness	1
Results			
↓ Market	↓ People	↓ Financial	↓ Operations

How did you assess the situation? Where do we agree? Where do we differ? Why?

How do you approach pricing? Are you more or less rigid than Jamie? How well does your approach serve your fiscal position?

How have you dealt with customer pressure for special pricing considerations?

What would you do differently?

Q1: Terry

			1	2	3
	6	7	8	9	10
12	13	14	15	16	17
19	20	22	22		

Chapter 10

Getting Products on the Shelves

Eat Fresh's delivery and the warehousing of products is inefficient. An internal team proposed two distinctly different solutions to the problem. How will Terry decide? Will his decision send more products flying onto the shelves and into customers' baskets?

Let's talk about a business challenge you experienced this quarter.

Okay. Let me tell you how we discovered the issue. Cash flow is critical to supporting operations and fueling our growth plans. Knowing this, we set a goal for this year to improve cash flow across our operations. I created an internal workgroup with the assistant store managers and a few of the department heads. Their focus was to identify processes and routines in the stores that tied up the most cash, and to think of changes that would free up cash. Everyone was excited, and they came up with many great alternatives.

What did they find?

The group identified several areas that were not optimizing cash flow, but one stood out dramatically—product receiving and off-loading.

Most product deliveries arrive at the stores' loading docks in the early morning. Staff help unload the trucks and place the goods in various staging areas from where it then goes directly into the store or is put into refrigerated or dry storage. As our stores have grown in volume, the physical size of both the delivery trucks and our orders have increased. This has resulted in longer off-loading times. We have limited space to accommodate big trucks and it takes more time for us to unload some larger orders. The receiving bay limitations cause drivers to wait in lines, or they push our deliveries to the end of the day when there is less traffic. This creates a logistical challenge. We've begun to receive complaints from shippers whose drivers' routes are slowed down by the lack of delivery bays.

Food that sits on a truck instead of coming into our warehouse and then onto the shelves is food that can't be sold. The longer it takes a product to reach the store shelf, the lower the inventory turns, which means more cash is tied up in the company.

What alternatives did you consider to address this issue?

The focus group came up with several ideas. After an initial analysis, they recommended two potential solutions. The first was to expand the loading bays' size to accommodate more trucks. All three stores had the space to expand the physical size of the loading bays' area. It would take about four to six months to complete the expansions. This would require a significant capital investment that we could finance with loans from our local bank. We could easily add crew to the morning shift to accommodate the additional off-loading.

The other idea was to install a new logistics system that could "talk" to our suppliers' ordering systems and schedule deliveries throughout the day. This logistics system optimized deliveries—it selected days and times to avoid traffic backlogs. The product's developer estimated six months before it would be fully integrated. We would have to operate using our current procedures alongside the logistics system to allow for data input and analysis. The installation was not expensive, and the monthly subscription was quite reasonable.

How did you make a decision?

I thanked the group for their efforts and let them know I would decide soon. I made a strengths and weaknesses list for the two alternatives and considered both the short- and long-term implications. I asked George, my head of finance, to determine the fiscal impact of the two ideas. He confirmed both were reasonable and financially viable. Then I was ready to decide.

What did you choose to do, and why?

I decided the new logistics system was the way to go. The software will make every store more efficient and I can see its value as we begin adding new stores to the chain. Even though I liked the idea of the bigger loading bay area, it felt more like a quick fix to the problem versus a long-term solution.

How has the system impacted company operations and cash flow?

My key objective in implementing the software was to free up cash. It is too early to know. The system will enable us to become more efficient in the months ahead and scale that efficiency as we grow. But right now, things are a bit chaotic. The system is buggier than I expected. I knew, for a time, we were going to have to run two systems simultaneously, but it looks like it will be almost twice the time the vendor said it would take to implement. People are a bit frustrated. I think they are waiting for the new system to be the magic bullet for all problems. I have to remind them that we have a process that is not the most efficient, but it works. We need to work hard to optimize deliveries throughout the day. We cannot get sloppy as we wait for this better solution to launch.

Authors' Insights

Terry recognized that cash flow was key to supporting his operations and future growth plans. He brought together a team to discover areas within the store that were inefficient and likely impacting Eat Fresh's cash flow. This led to the identification of a major operational issue—the limited receiving space at the stores was causing late deliveries and inventory stockpiles that slowed product placement on shelves. Although Terry's attention to cash flow (Financial Awareness) was the catalyst for discovering this business challenge, much of this scenario illustrated other capabilities of Business and People Judgment.

Let's look at his approach to solving his product delivery issue. He encouraged teamwork and was transparent about the company's direction by establishing the workgroup. However, he may have lost the positive impact of creating the group by taking their final recommendations and ultimately making the decision himself without sharing his analysis or seeking different perspectives or reactions from the group. This was not exemplary Team Development behavior.

Terry decided to implement the logistics system versus expanding the bays because of the lower cost and long-term implications—both seemingly sound rationale for the decision. Terry failed to check the accuracy of the vendor's four- to six-month installation estimate. He did not seek out testimonials or talk with the vendor's customers about their experiences implementing the software. Perhaps he could have gleaned some insight into the time, cost overruns, and ease of implementation. In our experiences building software or integrating major systems into our organizations, one should always consider costs and time related to overruns—because they always happen with new systems. This lack of in-depth analysis relative to implementation resulted in the system taking more time to launch and optimize in the Eat Fresh environment. Thus, cash flow gains for most of the year were minimal. Terry's associates were frustrated because he did not prepare them for the potential difficulties of the implementation. From a long-term perspective, he is forecasting significant improvements in inventory turns for next year. The question remains: Could he have chosen the bay expansion option and been in a better cash flow position at the end of the year? We do not know because the degree of analysis for the bay expansion option appears relatively shallow, outweighed by the low adoption costs and long-term advantages of the logistics system. Terry gave no indication he considered the long-term advantages of bay expansions. The short-term issue was access for vendors in the morning. Perhaps the added space in the current stores would provide a roadmap for efficiency in new stores.

To summarize Terry's effectiveness in meeting his cash flow challenge, we have to give him a mixed evaluation for Business Judgment. He knows how vital cash flow is to an expanding business. Still, his depth of analysis in weighing the options and ultimately implementing the logistics system option was less than optimal. From a People Judgment perspective, he also gets a mixed review. Although he used the focus group to develop teamwork and have his associates help execute the expansion initiative, he did not let them finish the job. Instead, he took over, did the analysis, and made the decision without their further involvement. This was ineffective Decisiveness. Terry's rush to make the decision had a negative impact on the morale of the group. Also, his lack of insight into the requirements, obstacles, and timing of the logistics system's implementation hurt associate morale. He had a significant opportunity to communicate the company direction, the importance of cash flow, and the operational challenges of the new system—he never mentioned doing so. Such actions would have indicated a fairly high degree of Engagement. Finally, his decision process did not achieve the short-term positive cash flow impact he was looking to achieve.

The immediately recognizable results of Terry's cash flow plan were dismal financially and operationally. The extended time and costs were not what he was expecting. Once the system is up and running, we expect the impact on the financial and operational aspects of Eat Fresh will be more notable. We are too early to know how logistics improve the market position and customer experience. Still, we can all agree that the approach to implementing the logistics software was at least frustrating to many associates whose daily work (running two systems in parallel) became confusing and more complex for the quarter.

Scorecard

Business Judgment		People Judgment	
①———▼②———③		▼ ①———②———③	
Data Savvy	2	Engagement	1
Strategic Mindset	1	Relationship Building	2
Customer Focus	NO	Team Development	2
Financial Awareness	3	Individual Development	NO
Balanced Decision-Making	2	Decisiveness	1
Results			
↔	↓	↓	↓
Market	People	Financial	Operations

How did you assess Terry's leadership in this situation? Where do we agree? How do we differ? Why?

What do you do to monitor and maximize cash flow for operations, investing, and financing?

How effective was your most recent effort to improve operational efficiency?

What would you do differently?

Chapter 11

Acquisition Opportunity

Terry has discovered an opportunity — the owner of a nearby chain of organic grocery shops is thinking about retiring. If Eat Fresh could acquire some or all of its stores, Terry's company could quickly expand. Can Terry make a deal? Will he adjust his business strategy in pursuit of more rapid growth?

Terry, tell us why this acquisition interested you.

I have been clear that I want to grow Eat Fresh, and an acquisition was one avenue for our growth. When Susan on my advisory board told me that Organic Dangle's owner was retiring and wanted to sell his three stores, I thought it might be something for us to explore, even though it was bigger growth than I had been planning. Also, we had good profits and revenue growth, so I was fairly confident I had or could secure the capital for an acquisition — even one of this size.

I thought Organic Dangle was similar to Eat Fresh in many ways. Like us, they have medium-sized stores, and their customer commitment is to sell food that improves people's well-being. Their customers also value organic and healthy foods. Although in a different region, their stores are somewhat close to where we had discussed opening new locations. Organic Dangle might allow us to quickly expand into a new geographic area. At first initial glance, it seemed like a great opportunity. It was also quite exciting to think we could almost double our business in one swoop.

What were the alternatives to pursuing a merger?

We have been planning to open a new store at the end of the

year. We identified the building we want to lease, and we planned to start the remodeling in the second quarter. If the Organic Dangle deal didn't happen, we can go forward with this store's opening.

What kind of analysis did you do to evaluate the opportunity?

I reached out to Bob, the Organic Dangle owner, and said we would be interested in taking a closer look. Bob knew of Eat Fresh and had a positive impression of our brand and stores. I believed he and I had similar visions for our companies. I told him this would be a large acquisition for us, so I wanted to understand them and the stores better to make sure this was worth pursuing. I didn't want either of our businesses to get bogged down in diligence if it didn't make sense for us to pursue an acquisition.

We agreed on a simple non-disclosure agreement (NDA) that allowed us to ask detailed questions and share information without them worrying that their financial and operational details would go beyond our leadership team and a small internal working group. I used only a small team of people from Eat Fresh to do the analysis, as I didn't want to take away too much focus on running the current business.

George, our head of finance, and one of his people were tasked with analyzing the business. Helen, our head of human resources, plus one of her associates and I focused on organization and people to see how we would integrate the two businesses.

What did your team find?

George and the finance team got Organic Dangle's financial statements as well as the key financial dashboards and reports they rely on to measure their business. Of course, many financial metrics both companies looked at are similar, but there were other things we don't tend to monitor or emphasize that they do. For example, they were more focused on waste and daily customer traffic, whereas we are more focused on inventory turns and basket size.

The human resources team and I spent time attempting to understand their company and getting a feel for their values. An organization chart is relatively straightforward, though it doesn't tell you how good people are in their roles. Getting a feel for the culture is more difficult, and we could only get anecdotal stories of how they handled internal problems or worked to address company-wide goals and initiatives.

What were your impressions after this initial investigation and analysis?

Even though we may look at different business metrics, it seemed things were more alike than different. The finance team thought a changeover of Organic Dangle stores to Eat Fresh stores would not be major. The only thing that stuck out was that they operated at somewhat lower margins than us. The team was fairly convinced that if we changed some internal procedures and streamlined vendors at Organic Dangle, we could get the same margins at Eat Fresh.

After the human resources team and I understood their organization and who does exactly what, we made a draft of what a merged organization might look like. I found that between the two organizations, plenty of good people would be able to handle running the business. We also saw a good cultural fit between us.

Anything that concerned you?

At this stage, not really. I felt comfortable that this was a big opportunity well worth the time and money to do the full due diligence. It wasn't like we're saying, "Let's do this," but rather, it was worth looking closer.

What did the leadership team think?

Most everyone was on board. The only person against this was Kathy, our head of operations. She thought it would be much better to put all our energy into establishing and building the one store. She thought doubling the size of our entire company and getting our processes to work well across all the stores would completely bury us.

Also, Helen thought it might be more challenging to change the ways things were being done in Organic Dangle. She said people are more averse to change than one may think.

You chose to proceed?

Yes, we moved forward with the due diligence.

How did you address Kathy's and Helen's concerns?

I told Kathy I understood her concerns, but a deal like this doesn't come around too often. She was probably right that there would be more challenges than we expected, but both businesses have good people to overcome the operational challenges. It would be a lot of work, but I didn't think it insurmountable.

As for the other store, we can delay that six to possibly twelve months. We'd probably have to pay a few months' rent, but it should not have a significant impact. Either we can do that store after the acquisition, should we decide to go forward with it, or should we choose not to make the acquisition, we would only lose a few months in opening the store.

With regards to Helen, I agree people are more difficult to change. However, the way we do things at Eat Fresh, I believe, is not radically different than how they are done at Organic

Dangle. So, it wouldn't be that dramatic. Also, just about all of the processes and approaches we use at Eat Fresh were developed together with the stores' employees. Hopefully, this means it should be easier for the Organic Dangle people to accept our ways since they didn't necessarily come from management.

Authors' Insights

Suffice it to say that Terry quickly became excited about the opportunity Organic Dangle represented. We had a difficult time evaluating Terry's leadership impact and effectiveness in this situation. His response to our questions lacked the specificity and quantification needed to make a confident assessment at this early stage in the process. Plus, we do not know how comprehensive his due diligence process may be, nor the conclusions he drew from that diligence. We need to compare those results to Terry's initial evaluations—we will make that comparison in the next quarter. In the meantime, we can look at the methods and variables Terry weighed as he considered moving ahead with the acquisition. Let's try to figure out whether he dove as deeply as may have been prudent, even at this stage of the game.

On the Business Judgment side of the ledger, the first factor Terry considered in his fast-moving initial review was his ability to acquire the capital to make the purchase. His response to his question was a degree of confidence based on "good profits and growth." Of course, profits and growth are not the only variables financial institutions weigh in these decisions. At this point, all we seem to know about the size of the acquisition is that, as Terry says, "it is a big acquisition for us." Terry may have wanted to dig a little more deeply here, exploring other sources before he convinced himself he could get the capital.

As George and his team looked at the financials, they realized Organic Dangle used different metrics to measure performance. Terry gave no indication his team tried to convert Organic Dangle's metrics to those most used within Eat Fresh, such as market basket size or inventory turns. Such conversions would have allowed for a more relevant comparison of performance variables. George and his group did find Organic Dangle operated at "somewhat lower" margins, but they were convinced some changes in "how things were done" could move the margins. Again, we do not know the order of magnitude of the margin differences, nor what kinds of changes would be required to align them. Did Terry go more deeply than he indicated in the interview? We do not know but suspect he did not. Typically, Terry is much more detailed in his responses, particularly with financial information. Our tentative evaluation based on the above is that the depth of his Financial Awareness was lower than it should be, even at this early stage. As a result, his decision-making strength and, ultimately, his overall Business Judgment would be low.

On the operations side, Kathy believed they would be "buried" trying to incorporate Eat Fresh's process across three new stores. Terry told her, "A deal like this doesn't come around too often," and good people would overcome the operational challenges. This was another business decision Terry seemed to have talked himself into without more in-depth analysis. We will see if his assumptions change as a result of the diligence process.

Looking to People Judgment, his HR team looked at values, culture, and the current staff talent levels. Indeed, these are the correct variables to be evaluating. However, Terry did not indicate how the HR team came to their conclusions that the cultures were similar and there were "plenty of good people to handle running the business." Terry's assumptions here may have been impacted by the fact he was on the HR team—an interesting choice for the CEO. Also, the rosy people picture was contradicted by his HR manager's concern with associate reluctance to change. Terry's reaction to Helen's concern was not so dramatic. He indicated that so much of what is done at Eat Fresh is associate supported, so it would be easy for the

Organic Dangle employees to get on board.

As we said above, we are too early in the process to make a definitive evaluation of the dimensions of Business and People Judgment at this point. The scorecard reflects our initial reaction to Terry's decisions relating to this acquisition. Terry's enthusiasm for this unique opportunity may be impacting his judgment. He appears to minimize the impact of critical factors, which would indicate the ultimate success or failure of the acquisition. We will look at this situation again to see if Terry's reactions and decisions change based on the more comprehensive due diligence data and analyses. Will he continue to rationalize his perspective by minimizing any negative information? Or, will he look at the data and metrics objectively and make a well-reasoned, effective decision? More to come!

Scorecard

Business Judgment		People Judgment	
① ▼ ② ③		① ▼ ② ③	
Data Savvy	2	Engagement	NO
Strategic Mindset	2	Relationship Building	NO
Customer Focus	NO	Team Development	2
Financial Awareness	1	Individual Development	NO
Balanced Decision-Making	1	Decisiveness	NO
Results			
⟷	⟷	⟷	⟷
Market	People	Financial	Operations

How did you assess Terry's leadership in this situation? Where do we agree? How do we differ? Why?

What growth opportunities have you encountered and evaluated?

What happened?

What would you do differently?

Chapter 12

Adding the Last 10 Percent

Recently, the head of produce from one of the Eat Fresh stores came to Terry with a new approach for product placement and improved profitability in the stores. The associate had invested her time and energy into an idea from which she believed Eat Fresh would benefit, and Terry saw the potential. Perhaps he saw more. Might he need to add that last 10 percent?

Terry, tell us about a people challenge you faced this quarter.

In one of our stores, Gracie, the head of produce, came to me with an intriguing idea to improve store profitability. She knew people came into our produce department many times a week to buy certain items. Therefore, we typically place produce and other frequently purchased items in the back of the store. Using this approach, we encourage customers to travel through merchandizing aisles and see our sample pop-ups, hoping our seasonal displays tempt them. Gracie had identified the products in the produce department with a reasonable turn rate and high profit margin. She said these items should be placed in prime placement areas in the produce department, for example, at eye level. Right now, many of these prime spots were occupied with lower-margin products. If she was correct, not only should we rearrange the produce section but also the entire store. So, when the customers walked through the store, they would be more likely to impulse-buy products with high-margin versus low-margin.

What was your reaction to her plan?

I was super impressed that one of our department managers had taken so much time and interest to think of ways to make the company more successful. That is the first thing I told her. I asked her if she would sit down and walk me through everything—from the spark of the idea to the "how and why" that we needed to think about in making this happen. We met that same week. She came ready to make the sale.

Gracie had the data, had designed several professional layouts for the department, and developed a sales forecast illustrating varying degrees of success. Her energy and knowledge of the store and her insights into maximizing profitability were impressive.

What did you do?

I thanked her and told her how impressive her effort was. I asked her to give me some time to digest what she had shown me, and we would talk again by the end of the week. I was already pretty sold. I wanted to dive into the plan more to make sure I knew exactly what she was proposing and how fiscally and operationally feasible it would be to implement.

The concept and most numbers made sense. I thought her projections were more than believable. This was innovative, which impressed me because I have always felt we were creative grocers. I got caught up in one aspect of Gracie's plan. Her sales forecast included several important variables. But I noticed she had not accounted for what we call slotting fees. Part of any store layout is based on the shelf space for which distributors are willing to pay. Manufacturers pay for two kinds of placements: display and slotting. A significant portion of paid placement is display when manufacturers pay to have products featured on endcaps or unique exhibits with flashy signage. Slotting fees are different. Manufacturers pay a premium simply to have their products on a store shelf in a specific spot. Maybe Gracie was less familiar with slotting because she was from produce, where slotting is not a significant part of the layout. Most other departments are organized by plan-o-grams driven in part by slotting fees. Although less critical in produce, it does have an impact on the profitability of the product.

How did you address the changes you thought necessary?

I thought about adding in the slotting fees, taking it back to Gracie, and letting her know we would move forward with her plan. I decided this was one of those times when I could share my experience and knowledge to help her learn her plan better and then let her do the work, including slotting fees.

When I met with Gracie, I said several store managers and members of the home office had read her work, and all were of the same mindset—this was a great idea that could increase profitability. I brought up the one hole I saw, suggesting she rework her plan to address the slotting fees. Gracie quickly agreed she had not given them much thought because manufacturers do not heavily control produce. Gracie said she would tweak the plan for the produce department to include slotting fees.

What happened?

We kicked off this quarter by completing the redesign of the produce department in our Oakley store. The entire process took two weeks. I asked Gracie to lead the project. She oversaw that job with care and attention; it was her baby, and she had ownership. In the first two months, we have seen a clear increase in produce profitability. Customers are buying more products with higher margins. We have decided as a next step to rearrange the product placement in several more departments, placing the higher-margin products in prime spots.

Oh, and by the way, my concern about slotting fees might have been unwarranted for the produce department. In the end, it didn't change the placement of a lot of products from Gracie's original plan.

Have you involved Gracie in the continued implementation of her plan?

Gracie will be working with the produce department managers of our other two stores to roll out the redesign over the next two quarters. If she performs as well as I expect, she has earned herself a place on the shortlist for our next store manager position.

Authors' Insights

Terry's story of Gracie and the new produce department plan illustrates an all-too-common challenge small business leaders face, especially as they attempt to navigate strategy in the PRG. Part of the task is knowing when to let go and trust the people to whom you delegate. The other test is recognizing when you are bringing value to your associates and the company by inserting your ideas and adding *that extra 10 percent*. Sometimes, the financial or operational disparity the "extra 10 percent" represents is negligible. Allowing an individual or whole group autonomy might mean the difference between "engaged and motivated" versus associates who feel marginalized and become disengaged because you, as a leader, feel you have to add value.

As we deconstruct Terry's approach to Gracie's product plan, we see a high degree of People Judgment. From the moment she approached him with her ideas, he was responsive and open to her ideas. He not only listened to her plans, but he also carried on a conversation, asking questions and becoming involved in the initiative. Terry took the time to consider the plan. In doing so, he discovered the hole the slotting fees represented. When

Terry took the idea to various senior team members, he was highly transparent and explained the idea came from Gracie. He ensured all began to take notice of this associate. He displayed excellent Engagement.

Terry demonstrated a high degree of Decisiveness by addressing Gracie's idea from her perspective and organization. He was quick to decide to use Gracie's idea, gave her credit for it as he tested it with his staff, and gave her the responsibility for implementing it in her department and the produce departments of the other stores. He also saw this situation as an opportunity to develop an employee. Instead of adding the slotting information himself, he had Gracie do it, which added to her knowledge and ability to adjust a plan based on new information. Terry further enabled her development by having her lead the implementation of her idea in other stores.

Leaders who excel at developing individuals often evaluate the merits of an employee's work "as is" versus any value they might add. They find ways to create learning moments to inspire associates. Terry thought about the implications of the slotting fees and decided they needed addressing. Terry was not mindful of how inserting his insights into the plan might affect Gracie's motivation, engagement, and development.

Terry's Business Judgment continues to be driven by his strong Financial Awareness. He saw the good in Gracie's plan and recognized a potential loss of existing income. His ability to make a quick and credible decision to adopt the strategy showed a reasonable degree of agility. We were surprised that Terry made such a dramatic move in a major department without some input from current customers. He was recreating the shopping experience without buyers' feedback data. He might have at least surveyed regular customers of the Oakley store where the redesign would launch (Customer Focus). Similarly, he might have spent time searching the grocery trades to see if this type of merchandising approach was on trend (Data Savvy). Terry,

Gracie, and the Eat Fresh team were lucky customer perception was favorable.

Let's look at the impact of Terry's leadership on results. We can see the correlation between the degree of effective decision-making and organizational results in Terry's story. Early customer feedback is positive. Buyers perceive the layout as convenient and different from most competitors; thus, market factors were positively affected. Eat Fresh has discovered and is developing what looks like a high performer. The new layout is making money, allowing Terry to see improved profits (higher-margin products in the cart) in this quarter. A quick implementation was a win operationally and looks to be the model for similarly speedy rollouts at other Eat Fresh locations.

Scorecard

Business Judgment		People Judgment	
(1)———▼———(2)———(3)		(1)———(2)———▼———(3)	
Data Savvy	1	Engagement	3
Strategic Mindset	NO	Relationship Building	2
Customer Focus	1	Team Development	NO
Financial Awareness	3	Individual Development	3
Balanced Decision-Making	NO	Decisiveness	3
Results			
↑ Market	↑ People	↑ Financial	↑ Operations

How did you assess Terry's leadership in this situation? Where do we agree? How do we differ? Why?

How do you develop your associates or encourage them to bring ideas to life?

How have you attempted to add value to an employee's idea?

How did your involvement affect the employee's engagement?

What would you do differently?

Q2: Jamie

			1	2	3
6	7		8	9	10
12	13	14	15	16	17
19	20	22	22		

Chapter 13

Bonus Conundrum

Jamie's review of e-Dine's financial position reveals she is more cash-strapped this quarter than any of her team had anticipated. Subsequent discussions with her VP of finance suggest company cash flow might be jeopardized if she proceeds with the annual company bonus payouts.

Tell me about a critical business challenge you experienced this quarter.

I recently struggled with the company bonus plan—what an ordeal. When I started e-Dine, I wanted to build a culture of success; when the company wins, so should our team. In that spirit, all e-Dine employees receive an annual profit-sharing bonus when we meet or exceed our profitability goals for the year.

Were you profitable?

On paper, we were.

What was the problem?

We share year-end results during the first quarter and highlight our accomplishments and shortcomings with all e-Dine associates. Our performance highlights include financials. Everyone looks at the company's profitable earnings because we base the yearly bonus on how profitable the company has been. We had a solid year. We achieved 115 percent of our annual profit goal. Everyone here was excited and looked forward to their bonus. We typically pay the bonus at the start of this quarter. Imagine my surprise when Perrin, our VP of finance, emailed to say we have an issue.

Perrin and I met, and she explained we hit our numbers. However, this first quarter was the worst since our founding in collecting accounts receivables. Our most significant AR is the monthly premium service subscription. It represents about 40 percent of our monthly operating cash flow. Converting that AR into cash for operations has typically been less than thirty days. But that time gap had increased exponentially—a significant chunk of our AR was between forty-five and sixty days. A number were approaching ninety days. We looked great on paper, but our operating cash was taking a big hit. I am preparing to pay a company-wide bonus, and realized those payments would significantly impact our cash flow. For the next six months, our ability to invest in new staff, programs, or promotions would be compromised. The bonus payment was going to tie our hands fiscally. Perrin and I were uncomfortable with the cash flow implications.

What did you do?

There was no way I was going to put us into a six-month cash crunch at this time. We needed to find a way to minimize the bonus' impact and simultaneously address the AR issue. Perrin recommended we pay the bonus over time, splitting the payments over the next two or three quarters. This approach would minimize the impact on our operating capacity. Another method she suggested was that we pay the bonuses as planned while prioritizing collecting subscriptions net-45 and beyond. If we acted quickly to get those accounts under control, we might minimize our operational exposure to forty-five to sixty days. I could not get comfortable with either of those approaches.

What were your choices?

Well, first, I thought an aggressive collection effort was an overly optimistic approach. We allowed almost 10 percent of our customers to get this far behind already. Could we reasonably expect to quickly turn them around and, at the same time, keep all our other subscription payments within that target fifteen-day time gap? I did not see this happening. The situation was a red flag that indicated a need for more staff. Perrin's team could no longer effectively manage our AR because we are growing.

I thought about what delaying the bonuses would say to associates about our success. Our people are invested in e-Dine's performance in large part because of that bonus. The truth is that many would not understand the financial implications. They would see we hit all our sales goals and did everything right to control costs internally and wonder why the hell they aren't getting paid. Not paying the bonus on time would be demoralizing.

What did you do?

The bonus payment was the most urgent issue. I believed any delay would affect morale throughout the organization. I couldn't have that. We are well-positioned to grow into a bigger and more successful company this year; even the smallest decline in associate enthusiasm could destroy that growth. I looked at the total liability and recognized something. The bonus is paid as a percentage of each associate's salary. Nearly 40 percent of the money would be paid to the five leadership team members and me. If we went ahead and paid all associates and Natalie, our office manager, the impact on our operating cash for the rest of the year would be effectively cut in half. I could defer the payment to the leadership team until year-end. If our efforts to recoup the post-forty-day accounts were successful, we might even be able to pay installments over the second half of the year. I expected my team to understand the cash flow impact and recognize our short-term sacrifice ensured we could continue executing our plans.

Decreasing the amount of bonus money paid at the start of Q2 would keep our operating financial position where it needs to be. This company must be flexible and able to support our growth—that requires cash.

What happened as a result of that decision?

I cannot prove this, but I am comfortable the company was best served by paying the associates as promised. The staff, salespeople, and developers received the bonus they deserved and are motivated to continue succeeding. I genuinely believe any delay in paying that bonus would have wreaked havoc throughout the ranks.

Most of my team understood the reason for my decision. Although several would have preferred to receive their money right now, they recognize the short-term sacrifice ensures we can continue to pursue our goals to build this company and become a national player in the restaurant industry.

You said, "Several of the team."

There is always someone. When I took this plan to our weekly leadership meeting, there were some harsh reactions and loud debates. Carl, my VP of sales, was vocally opposed to the decision. He felt he and his team had delivered the goods and thought Perrin's team was the reason we were short on cash. But we talked about the fact that the bonus is based on company growth and profit, not individual KPOs. He was not thrilled, but he was on board. He became more engaged in the process and problem. He suggested Perrin's team develop an early warning system to identify customers who hit the thirty-day mark and share the information with our sales team. Carl thought we might minimize some of the delinquent payments by having the sales rep touch base with their clients to gently remind them of their current contract status.

Our HR manager, Matt, was problematic. Although Matt is part of the leadership team, he is not responsible for a major functional area, and his salary is not comparable to the other VPs and directors. When the group discussed the plan, Matt was relatively quiet. He tacitly agreed with the others. The next day Matt came to my office and told me he could not live with this decision. Unlike others on the team, he relied on that bonus and could not go the year without that income. We talked and he would not budge. I thought he made a reasonable argument that the deferred executive payments were disproportionally affecting him. I was concerned he might seriously lose focus, or worse, he would leave us. I decided to pay his bonus as promised. He should have been excluded from the deferred pay like our office manager. I asked him to keep our agreement between us because I did not want to discuss it with the leadership team.

How did your decision impact e-Dine?

Financially, deferring the leadership team's bonus kept us liquid. It ensured we could continue with several short-term initiatives, including a successful trade-show promotion booth at the National Restaurateurs Conference. That event increased our visibility and has helped us target regions where we plan to grow. We also were able to hire a new AR person for Perrin's team. We needed another associate to manage those accounts. In hindsight, our short staffing of AR was what created this whole issue in the first place.

I already expressed my belief that paying the bonus ensured that our associates remained engaged and driven. I regret not excluding Matt from the original group of direct reports I asked to defer their pay. Even though paying his bonus was the right thing to do, I have received quite a bit of pushback from several leaders. When Perrin saw I authorized Matt's payment, she was not just surprised; she was ticked off.

Authors' Insights

Jamie's second quarter began with an all-too-common challenge just about every leader faces as their organization grows— ensuring you have the necessary funds to support operations. Alan Milt, the founder of Cash Flow Story, is known for saying, "Revenue is vanity, profit is sanity, and cash is king." *Catchy and wise.* In our experiences with PRG companies, cash flow is critically tied to operational agility and success. We were surprised Jamie did not consider the potential increase in AR. E-Dine is focused on expanding its user base. A sizable portion (65 percent) of those customers pay a monthly service fee. As the number of customers increases, one should expect a growing percentage of delinquent accounts. That said, the shift of almost 15 percent of the AR from payment within thirty days to over sixty days was identified within a quarter. When Jamie identified the trend, she recognized the effect these delinquent accounts had on cash flow and immediately addressed the short-term cash crunch. But she also took steps to ensure the company could manage AR to less than thirty days in the future.

From a Business Judgment perspective, we saw a solid performance. Always focused on her strategic growth plans, Jamie quickly recognized e-Dine could not continue adding new staff and investing in planned (or new) initiatives if the bonuses were paid at the start of the quarter. She was adamant that e-Dine would not be cash-strapped for the remainder of the year. Her VP of finance suggested a reasonable but consequential approach: defer the bonuses until the end of the year. A riskier option was to postpone the bonus for a quarter and make a concerted effort to collect past-due accounts. Jamie demonstrated highly effective Financial Awareness and Balanced Decision-Making when she chose to pay most associates and defer paying the leadership group until year-end. She also invested in new AR staff. This decision improved cash flow for the remainder of the quarter, ensuring continued growth. Her choice to adjust liabilities allowed the company to take advantage of new opportunities, including showcasing the company at a national restaurant convention.

Jamie demonstrated a mixed bag of capabilities when reviewing her People Judgment. She was convinced the bonus was more than just a transaction. It was a part of the e-Dine culture, recognizing that people throughout the company were personally responsible for successfully growing the company. She believed any change to the payment would irreparably damage the culture and affect employee motivation. She would not allow this.

The authors had differing views of her choice to pay many e-Dine associates at the start of the quarter. Richard thought Jamie's approach demonstrated highly effective People Judgment and an equally high degree of Engagement in asking key reports to defer their bonuses. In his assessment, the leadership team should understand the fiscal implications and recognize this approach kept the company on its growth trajectory. Jonathan and Jonas disagreed. Jonathan thought Jamie's plan would result in decreased motivation at the executive level—often, people, regardless of their position, react negatively to a change in compensation. This was less-than-effective Team Development. Jonas thought Jamie was quick to discount paying the executive team and wondered why she did not consider a staggered payment to those direct reports. We all agreed Jamie demonstrated little transparency and a complete lack of Decisiveness when she chose to pay Matt his bonus and ask him to keep the arrangement between them.

Most e-Dine associates were happy and engaged when they received their bonuses as expected. Jamie reported her team was disappointed but understood the need to defer their bonus. If this is an accurate appraisal, her leadership resulted in some solid people results. But what if the lack of bonuses at the top level triggered apathy or disengaged her team?

As we end, let's once again look at how Jamie's leadership decisions impacted results across the company. For now, the people category is down because some within the leadership are unhappy about the payment while others are bothered by Jamie's hushed deal with Matt. Operational results improved because the people and processes for managing HR are being addressed. We saw no short-term impacts on market or financial results.

Scorecard

Business Judgment		People Judgment	
Data Savvy	NO	Engagement	2
Strategic Mindset	2	Relationship Building	NO
Customer Focus	NO	Team Development	1
Financial Awareness	3	Individual Development	NO
Balanced Decision-Making	3	Decisiveness	1

Business Judgment scale: (1)———(2)—▼—(3)
People Judgment scale: (1)—▼—(2)———(3)

Results			
↔	↓	↔	↑
Market	People	Financial	Operations

How did you assess Jamie's leadership in this situation? Where do we agree? How do we differ? Why?

How do you prioritize cash flow for operations, investment, and financing?

How effective is your approach?

What can you do to improve your cash flow?

Chapter 14

Salesforce Backlash

Jamie has been pushing to use more predictive analytics by collecting and mining data across the company. Despite usage throughout e-Dine, she was not prepared for the pushback she received from the VP of sales when plans for tracking details about daily field activity were introduced.

Tell us about your recent initiative to collect data in the sales division.

It was quite an ordeal. I wanted to expand our sources of data to help improve our sales results. It's important because we need every competitive advantage we can create to continue penetrating this market.

Since early on, we have been using data analytics to improve our efficiency and gain an edge on sales, customer satisfaction, and productivity. Perhaps the one area where we had significant opportunities to collect more meaningful data and understand better how to be successful was in our outside sales group. Every department bases its targets and justifies budgets, at least partly on predictive analyses developed from company data—except the sales group. Despite having some of the richest data about our customers through our CRM, they have limited information on how the sales function performs. Our sales forecasts are highly speculative—here is what we did for the past three years; we have considered the top prospect lists and looked at the competitors' growth; here's what we are planning to do. This approach doesn't work anymore.

We need a thorough understanding of what goes on in the field. I should have insisted on a complete analysis and justification from the start. However, when we began, I was the only salesperson. Then we hired a few sales reps. Then a few more. At what point do you start taking these hotshot salespeople who are out hitting all kinds of targets for you and ask, "Are they making the best use of their day?" We now have eighteen outside reps and expect to hire at least five more in the next year.

How did you introduce your plan?

During our monthly strategic planning meeting, I asked the vice presidents of finance and sales to begin planning and implement the collection of new data relating to the daily activity of our outside sales representatives. I wanted to start using data analytics to better plan and forecast, direct our training, and guide our commission plan. We needed to make the most effective use of our time in the field. I got nothing but pushback from my VP of sales, Carl.

What were his objections?

Carl was immediately defensive. He looked right at me and said, "What, my word and experience isn't good enough for you anymore?" I was surprised because we have an inside sales team of ten representatives who make outbound calls and set appointments for the outside team. We already track every detail of their workday. We know the number of calls they make, the length of each call, the number of follow-ups, and the demographics of the potential clients to whom our associates successfully make an appointment. We have built our training, our compensation plans, and our lead projections on this data. Heck, Carl pats these associates on the back toward the end of the day and reminds them, "We all know success looks like a hundred calls a day, so take a breath and make the 101st call."

He kept stressing the nature of salespeople; they want to be let go to sell and earn as much as possible. They don't like being controlled. Carl said the group would feel as if we were treating them like children, or this was becoming a "Big Brother" company where they would not want to work.

What did you think would happen without Carl's buy-in?

My initial thought was there is no way he will continue to lead the sales team. We are data-driven. It's a fundamental approach to how we think about our business. I needed to quickly figure out how to get Carl on board or ask for his resignation. His departure would result in some uncertainty and chaos throughout the company, especially among the sales team. I would have to start a search for a new VP because we do not have anyone inside capable of stepping into that role. This was the year I was planning to add two regional sales directors under Carl to manage the growing salesforce better.

I also thought how quickly our salespeople could become disenchanted if we began implementing this approach and Carl was not its most vocal advocate. This would be a substantial change in how we do business and the metrics by which we measure performance. Our people will naturally be uneasy. If the reps perceived Carl was less than 100 percent on board, their motivation would swiftly decrease. I could see us bleeding several of our best salespeople. A major change in our field presence would impact new sales for at least a quarter, if not half the year.

What did you do?

I needed Carl's buy-in. After the meeting, when I asked Carl to co-lead the project, I pulled him aside and said, "You and I have to see how we can get on the same page." I suggested we have dinner that same evening.

Tell us about that dinner.

I began by emphasizing how much I valued Carl's contributions. A good deal of our success is due to his ability to build and motivate this sales team. I told him I was committed to implementing the data analytics program and would be happy to talk about all the reasons why, addressing any and every concern. We could talk as much as he wanted, but I needed us to be on the same page when we were done.

We talked for several hours. Carl felt we would get pushback from several senior salespeople, and they would leave. He did not think it was worth losing them. He was also concerned the entire sales group would feel as though we did not trust them, causing morale to decline. We agreed that all those things could happen. I reminded him we have always used data analytics to our advantage throughout the company, especially for the inside sales group. That data had made our lead generation five times more efficient than when we were blindly cold-calling restaurants. Imagine the insights we would have into the prospective clients and ways to close the sale. Eventually, Carl agreed he would achieve better results with this kind of information. Nevertheless, he did not think the salespeople would feel the same way.

I suggested we needed to do three things. First, he had to be the evangelist for this project, more than me or any other member of the leadership team. Next, we had to be honest about our process and involve influential salespeople in the project planning and implementation. Lastly, we needed to continually talk about the benefits of this project to the company's success and each sales rep's career.

When we finished dinner, I was comfortable that Carl and

I saw the same things. Late that night, he sent me an email confirming this and saying he no longer thought of this as a challenge as much as an opportunity to make our salesforce one of the best in the industry.

What results have you recognized since implementing the data collection program?

Carl has been the biggest cheerleader. That week, he sent an email to the sales team explaining our plans. He had one-on-ones with our two senior sales reps and brought them into the planning group. We made sure everyone knew the data we were collecting and why. More importantly, we have been incredibly open about sharing the insights gleaned from the analytics.

The data has already helped us see ways to work the market better. For example, we noticed our reps have little chance of selling to a client they visit more than two times. It's a lot easier for a sales rep to look at their day and schedule ninety minutes of cold calls instead of seeing a prospect they have been handholding for five or six visits. At the end of this last quarter, we exceeded our sales quota by almost 4 percent. I attribute this increase to improved efficiency in the field.

I wanted to implement this into our budget and planning process in ninety days. It is going to take us six months, mostly because of the time we spent including different stakeholders in the planning committee. We likely would have had similar results if we came to the group with our plan, talked about the benefits, and committed to regularly sharing the insights we discovered.

Authors' Insights

Jamie continues demonstrating what we have come to expect from her—a high degree of Data Savvy and a Strategic Mindset. At Oracle OpenWorld 2004, Hewlett-Packard president Carly

Fiorina stressed the growing need to exhaustively collect diverse data for business decision-making. Jamie's pursuit of data might have been inspired by Fiorina's rallying call that "the goal is to turn data into information and information into insight." Jamie is focused on growth and comfortable letting data analytics guide the company to greater sales and efficiencies. For this reason, she came to the table with an urgency to identify and collect data generated by the outside salespeople. Jamie knew this is a wealth of information waiting for e-Dine to tap into that can positively impact revenue. Jamie's Business Judgment drove the plan for mining extensive field data to enhance the sales cycle.

Jamie faced significant resistance at the outset from Carl. To make this program a success, she needed to demonstrate a high degree of People Judgment. How did she do? From our perspective, Jamie was less-than-effective in her rollout of the project with Carl. Yes, we see e-Dine is an organization driven by data, including portions of Carl's department. But surely Jamie had to recognize that a significant extension of data collection and analytics into sales would be disruptive. One wonders why she did not bring Carl in on this well before the rollout at the executive meeting. Jamie could have brought him on board, and that day, Carl would have been the cheerleader, introducing the next big growth plan for the company. Such an approach would have alleviated her concerns about salesforce defection as the two would likely have created a message and method for communicating with the sales team. Her failure to discuss organizational needs or explain the rationale for choosing to fast-track collecting data from the sales team were examples of poor Engagement.

Jamie's abrupt introduction of the plan caused a key employee to react. Imagine your top sales leader asking you if you no longer trust their opinion. She was caught off-guard. Again, when you look at the dimensions of People Judgment,

Relationship Building comes to mind. Unfortunately, Jamie did not effectively demonstrate this capability. She was so focused on the need for the data, she forgot about people. Even worse, her first reaction to the concern of a long-time associate was to think about quickly firing him unless she could get him to see things her way.

Jamie's hours-long dinner discussion with Carl was reactive. This was low Decisiveness. She demonstrated enough Data Savvy to convince him of the plan benefits. She could count on the many years of goodwill the two had built working together to overcome the uneasiness of the day. Jamie was empathetic, and she did what she should have done earlier in the year— strategized with Carl on ways he could lead the charge to ensure the entire sales team recognized the value of data to the company and their checkbooks. From her account of the evening, the dinner was effective. However, we wonder if she has built a degree of mistrust between the two and will need to closely monitor Carl to ensure he truly agrees with the plan. She might also find she quietly ignited a revolt among her sales representatives that Carl will passively fuel. We have made a note to check in with Jamie on salesforce morale and the results of the data initiative on sales.

Jamie's impact on e-Dine's results is mixed. As the data is not yet collected or implemented in planning and forecasting, the market and financial results are unknown. The immediate people results are not optimal. Not only is Carl's motivation questionable, but the morale of Jamie's other executives is also affected by what they saw at the kick-off meeting. We know Jamie is hoping she has diminished any issues from the salesforce, but that is yet to be seen. Operationally, there is no doubt that expanding the already proven methods for using data to make better decisions within e-Dine is a positive result.

Scorecard

Business Judgment			People Judgment		
① —— ② ▼ ③			▼ ① —— ② —— ③		
Data Savvy		3	Engagement		1
Strategic Mindset		3	Relationship Building		1
Customer Focus		NO	Team Development		NO
Financial Awareness		NO	Individual Development		NO
Balanced Decision-Making		2	Decisiveness		1
Results					
↔	↓		↔	↑	
Market	People		Financial	Operations	

How did you assess Jamie's leadership in this situation? Where do we agree? How do we differ? Why?

Think of a situation where you and a member of your leadership team did not align. What did you do?

What happened?

What would you do differently?

Chapter 15

The Ultimatum

A key salesperson is considering leaving the organization for a similar position. The new job comes with a considerable salary increase. After discussing her opportunity with Carl, the VP of sales, he petitions Jamie to match the offer to keep the associate. Once again, Jamie is at odds with her sales team.

Tell me about a specific people challenge you experienced this past quarter.

You might remember Roxana from one of our earlier interviews. She is a senior sales representative and was one of our VP of sales, Carl's, first hires. Because Roxana was here early and we were trying to grab as much business as possible, she built a large territory—almost two and a half times the size of any other reps. She's written a good piece of our POS business. I thought Roxana was happy here at e-Dine. The other reps seek out her advice. Carl regularly spotlights her when his team does any type of professional development. Every new salesperson meets her during their training. Everyone wants to be the next Roxana. But last quarter, about a month after we lost the Che Jacques account, I got a late-night email from Carl telling me she was planning to leave us. He was anxious for us to speak the next morning.

What did you do?

Well, of course, I told him we should get together first thing, and we did. Carl explained that Roxana had come to him and said she was planning to resign. She had been offered a job selling CRM software at a large, established firm. Although the commission plan was like e-Dine, the base salary was higher. Roxana also expressed frustration with how e-Dine was changing. For example, she did not like having her field data collected and felt we were scrutinizing salespeople's work. I thought this was odd because her data was the most telling about what salespeople should be doing to succeed in the field. Carl said it was clear the loss of Jocko's business weighed heavily on her mind.

Carl and Roxana have a good relationship. Carl has been a mentor, and she has been a superstar on whom he can count to motivate his team and ensure his numbers. He did not want to see her leave. He told me about their conversation. After a lot of soul-searching, he helped her recognize much of her unhappiness with the organizational change, which was natural. He told her that successful early team members must adapt. When a company grows quickly, it means good things for everyone involved. He then got her to the point where he asked, "If you had the same salary here as they were offering, would there be any reason for you to even think of leaving?" When Roxana said no, Carl told her he would talk with me about how we might be able to make that happen.

Your reaction to Carl?

I was not particularly pleased he put us in the position where an employee was dictating their salary. Carl's reasoning was it was a 15 percent jump in her base. Had it been more, he would not have been able to convince her to consider staying. He felt matching the salary offer was more than reasonable for a rep who had been with us for so long and brought us so much value.

I understand why Carl was concerned. Roxana is great. She is responsible for a lot of business in a territory that's disproportionally large yet she churns out new customers every month. Plus, the way she sells has been a model for our people.

Roxana's success motivates other salespeople. But I was worried about the precedent this would set. We pay well. Our salaries are more than competitive, and our commission plans are built to make salespeople win when we win. If you start letting people negotiate salaries throughout the organization, you are setting yourself up for a constant barrage of salary matching. I have seen it a thousand times. Even if you make an exception for one person, what does that say about how you value all your salespeople and the opportunities each has to succeed? I told Carl I understood her value to the company, and I knew how close they were, but if her continued tenure at e-Dine was going to be based on a 15 percent increase in salary, it's not going to happen.

Carl's response?

He told me he thought this was the wrong decision, and we were going to take on a lot of damage to our numbers and team morale. Carl wanted to make a one-time exception. I told him that it was just not an option. I knew the implications of her leaving. I tried to think of some things he might do to incent her. I asked if he thought giving her some significant intangibles, like promising a considerable number of the prequalified leads, might work. We could carve out some of her time later in the year and ask her to be more involved in the new central region launch in a training capacity. We could pay her for that time. Carl said he would try, but he knew this was not going to move her—we should be prepared to see Roxana depart in two weeks. I knew he was right. I knew we were going to take a hit for it. But if we gave Roxana a raise just because she went out and got a competitive offer, do you know how quickly we would be fielding salary increase demands from people across every department? I was not going to open us up to that.

I asked Carl to let me know what happened, and if she chose to leave, he and I should quickly sit down and plan to address her departure. We needed to quickly find a good fit for the role. We were also going to have to adjust our short-term projections for the next few quarters and figure out how much of an impact her departure would have.

Were there other options you might have considered to keep Roxana?

No, and it was not worth the effort. Yes, it was a big deal, but Carl needed to accept that no company lives and dies by one person.

What happened?

As expected, Roxana did not find any offer worth staying for. She left us two weeks later. There is a part of me that thinks this might have been a blessing in disguise. For a long time, I have been bothered by the size of that territory. It was way too big for a single rep. We could never have scaled it back while Roxana was here; she would have quit over something like that. We broke it into two separate territories that align with our standards for profitable and manageable territories. We also took some of the outlying portions and appended them to existing reps' territories. This helped us to limit some of the short-term losses.

We hired two new representatives who started about thirty days after Roxana's departure. No one had been selling in most of Roxana's territory for that time. Our sales targets are down 6 percent this quarter. The two new reps show early potential, but it will take a good three months for each to hit a pace. We are hoping to limit our losses to 4 percent next quarter.

Any other implications of her departure?

Carl and Matt, our HR manager, are concerned about the hole Roxana has left. They both think many long-time employees feel we are not loyal to the people who helped build the company. Carl is anxious about our plans to expand into the central region at the end of the year, coinciding with our software's next version. I keep telling him that everyone is replaceable. We have several exceptional salespeople. Perhaps some were in Roxana's shadow. I suggested he start trying to encourage those with the drive and potential to take on training opportunities within the team. I think we will be fine in that area. I plan to spend more time in the field with the team, encouraging them and identifying talent.

Authors' Insights

Earlier in the year, Jamie took a hard line on discounting and lost a major customer. Once again, she is in a situation where her firmly held belief appears to mean more to her than any fiscal or people losses.

Jamie continued to demonstrate a Strategic Mindset by recognizing the long-term value in realigning Roxana's territory. She knew the most effective size and demographics for a rep to manage successfully. That territory was bothering her because it could become inefficient. Similarly, she recognized that a top-performing salesperson's departure would represent more than just a short-term loss. She wanted to understand the impact of her decision on the fiscal health of e-Dine's sales for successive quarters. This was the type of Financial Awareness one would expect from a PRG leader. Her decision to let a top salesperson leave was an example of Balanced Decision-Making—it was timely, she evaluated the risks. She accepted the short-term loss of Roxana's departure balanced against the likelihood of quickly hiring new reps and improved territory efficiency in the future. In our view, this was an example of solid Business Judgment. Was it the right decision? No one knows. But the

Business Judgment capabilities Jamie demonstrated in making the decision were thought effective.

Jamie's People Judgment was repeatedly less than effective because of the rigidity she continued to show when it came to core beliefs—*how things must be done*. Her conviction tends to blind her to the things her key people say. More importantly, this blindness weakens these relationships so critical to her success as a leader. Carl came to Jamie with genuine concerns over Roxana's departure. As the head of the sales organization, he, more than any other, should have insight into the effect Roxana's departure would have on sales and his team. Carl made it clear this was not the right time; they needed her. He pleaded that she make the deal. Jamie's dismissal of her VP of sales' concerns was an example of less-than-effective Relationship Building capabilities. Jamie's lack of Engagement also stood out to us. This was a long-time associate and her top salesperson. Never once did Jamie directly have a conversation with Roxana. She did not consider her associate's needs and concerns. What might the outcome have been if Jamie had agreed to the salary? Was this the stage in the company's growth where that action set the standard forevermore? Could she have considered promoting Roxana? E-Dine is planning a major regional expansion. Carl and her work well together. The organization is likely to need another layer of managerial support.

Although Jamie was quick to think about the financial implications of Roxana's departure, she never bothered to consider how the sales team would see this move. For that matter, what might the many early members of the e-Dine team think her leaving said about their value and contributions? She demonstrated less-than-effective behavior in Team Development.

We can see the impact of Jamie's leadership across our four result categories. First, e-Dine's market is down because the territory lacks coverage. The company is losing market share and visibility each day a rep is not in the territory. Second, current customers will inevitably be shuffled around internally, and there are always opportunities for customer service issues. Her impact on people was immediately negative. Roxana's departure shakes many long-time associates. Also, one begins to see a trend with Carl—he always appears to go to Jamie with a plan and never gets to execute his way. Where do you think his motivation is at this point? The financial impact was significant. Not only are sales down for this quarter, but they are also expected to be in Q3. There is one upside to Jamie's decision. Operationally, e-Dine saw some short-term improvement. A legacy territory could be "right-sized" into two that are more representative of the rest of e-Dine's territories.

Scorecard

Business Judgment			People Judgment		
①——————②▼——————③			①▼——————②——————③		
Data Savvy		NO	Engagement		1
Strategic Mindset		2	Relationship Building		1
Customer Focus		NO	Team Development		NO
Financial Awareness		2	Individual Development		NO
Balanced Decision-Making		3	Decisiveness		2
Results					
↓ Market	↓ People		↓ Financial	↑ Operations	

How did you assess Jamie's leadership in this situation? Where do we agree? How do we differ? Why?

What is your philosophy for negotiating salaries? Are you as resolute as Jamie?

Have you experienced a situation like Jamie's?

What happened?

What would you do differently?

Chapter 16

Remote Work

Since its first year of business, e-Dine's offices have been the home to all employees. Outside of a handful of salespeople and on-site support technicians local to each region, Jamie's people have worked and collaborated in this unique space. She has always thought of the home office as the heart of the company's creativity and innovation. Now associates are suggesting e-Dine would benefit from remote work.

Tell us about your decision to adopt remote work options.

Recently, I announced we would be offering all associates hybrid work schedules in which they could take advantage of remote working technologies. Each month, any of our people can choose three days to work from home, a favorite destination, even an inspiring location. I am still not convinced this practice is good for our productivity and creativity, but it at least keeps us competitive with other employers for attracting talent.

How did you recognize the need for this program?

My HR manager, Matt, came to me with a plan earlier this quarter. I had to be convinced.

During the pandemic, we, like the entire industry, were forced to adopt remote technologies to maintain some semblance of daily operations. Now that we have moved back to a new normal, some employers think remote working allows for lowered costs while achieving the same, if not better, productivity. I am not one of those people. I think we were less productive, and associate accountability was not reliable during the pandemic. I was thrilled when we could get everyone back into the building.

When we were first starting, I was looking for office space. Here was this old public tuberculosis sanitorium owned by the city. The city council was willing to practically give it away to a company that would bring new business to the town. The building is unique. All four floors are centered on a five-story, glass-ceiling atrium—daylight emanates from the center of the building. There are large rooms, little gathering spaces, and an old-time elevator. When we are here in our departments, and as people talk in the breakroom or share stories over a game of ping-pong, big ideas come to life. That's the company culture we've built—collaborative and creative, one where people from every group are comfortable walking over to another area and sharing an idea or problem. You lose that when everyone is sitting at home and logging into a bunch of video calls.

Matt told me he knew how I felt about remote work. Still, he received a steady stream of inquiries from associates across the company asking about opportunities to work from home. Matt had collected several articles and blogs about millennials working better in their own spaces. He showed me workforce studies indicating traditional workers who had been forced to work remotely now began to value the flexibility. Matt told me plenty of studies say the exact opposite, but remote working is on-trend right now. He saw this as an important way to keep us competitive in the talent market. He had collected job descriptions for all kinds of jobs at several competitors. All offered some degree of on-site and remote work. Matt proposed introducing a flex plan where all associates could remotely work at least two days a week. He developed a program he believed would make our people happy, keep the company competitive in the jobs market, and honor our collaboration culture here in the home office.

What did you do after hearing Matt's recommendation?

As I said, I had to be convinced. I told Matt I appreciated his effort, and he had given me some things to think about. My husband, Dave, is a professor of human resources and organizational development at the local university. I said I would ask Dave his thoughts on the initiative and get back to Matt later in the week with my decision.

I shared the idea with Dave, who knew I just hated the thought of our company becoming a virtual workplace. He told me Matt's information was accurate, but Dave's research suggested a good portion of HR executives and leaders believed remote workforces were significantly less collaborative and failed to innovate. Knowing how much I value collaboration, he suggested we adopt a policy of three flex days each month. This would allow us to talk about our recognition of remote work but keep the culture focused on-site. I thought he made some excellent points.

What did you decide to do?

Later that week, I met with Matt. I thanked him for recognizing ways to make our people happier and identifying a potential competitive weakness that could impact our hiring practices. I let him know that I talked with Dave and shared some of our concerns with the twice-a-week remote option. We thought it would be too disruptive because our primary workplace should be here at the home office. I gave him some notes on how I wanted to adjust the program and asked him to get to work, making this a priority. I wanted to announce it as soon as possible.

What happened after you green-lit the revised plan?

I was excited to announce the new program because it looked good internally, and this approach kept us competitive in the jobs market. Matt seemed less enthusiastic about the program.

I was a bit surprised because he knew I was not readily a proponent of any remote work programs. I guess he disagreed with the structure of the program. But Matt put together a great rollout in just under three weeks. I sent out a company-wide announcement that was well received. Our people wanted some flexibility. So far, so good — I guess.

Authors' Insights

E-Dine is not the only organization trying to navigate post-pandemic work arrangements. Jamie, like many executives, was anxious for associates to be back in the office. Although most companies' operations were efficient when employees were forced to shift to virtual work, numerous leaders believe the creativity and ingenuity resulting from daily engagement were lost. But employees have become comfortable with the flexibility they discovered working from home (or wherever) during the height of the pandemic. In the summer of 2021, Apple announced its plans for employees to return to the sprawling Apple campus. Many associates complained, sending an open letter to CEO Tim Cook. On the company Slack channel, over 2,800 remote work advocates suggested looking for new jobs if the company did not embrace offsite, remote, and hybrid work options. Morgan Stanley's CEO made news by saying, "If you can go to a restaurant in New York City, you can come into the office." Business leaders across the world are still reacting to the effects of the pandemic. Remote work will have a place in offices across the globe, but we are all trying to understand just what the new model looks like.

Jamie's HR manager came to her with a genuine problem, representing internal and external weakness in the near term. There was no doubt that employee demand for flexible working options was on the rise at e-Dine as it is in most industries. Matt was frequently fielding requests for remote work. He also observed e-Dine competitors were embracing more virtual positions. Having worked with Jamie through the pandemic and seeing her frustration with the virtual workforce, and watching her anxiously awaiting a return to on-site work, one can imagine Matt must have believed this a critical program. He came to her and laid out the problem, the data, and a solution.

What did Jamie do? She chose to say she would consult her husband, the HR professor. In effect, she told her HR expert that his opinion was not enough. We thought this was the extreme of a less-than-effective Relationship Building. Her deferral of a decision was also low Decisiveness. She could have said she would consider his proposal and quickly get back to him with her decision. She might have spent more time with Matt, digging deeper into her concerns and allowing him to convince her this was the right program for the company. This is what an engaged leader would do. Also, by hijacking Matt's initiative and dictating the program's terms, Jamie threw a roadblock in his professional growth (Individual Development).

Let's talk about a Derailer that was the elephant in the room. Informal Influencers are people outside the organization, often with no vested interest in your company and sometimes without credible background or knowledge. Sometimes, a leader allows these individuals to have considerable influence on their decisions. When you look beyond the advice of your key people, you are conveying one message: "I lack confidence in your abilities and insights." Often, Informal Influencers are obscured, but your people have a pretty good idea who might be whispering in your ear. In this case, Jamie made it clear— her husband was the one who convinced her of the need for a remote work initiative, not Matt. Is it surprising to you that Matt appeared "less enthusiastic" about his initiative after Jamie told him how Dave had suggested she adopt the program?

The results Jamie achieved through her leadership were negative and primarily in the people category. Although e-Dine associates now have a slightly more flexible and people-centric work environment, a key member of Jamie's team has been disenfranchised. As a result, the success of that relationship has been compromised. Also, by all indications, the new remote work plan appears to be less than in line with the associates' expectations that Matt was hearing. We suspect e-Dine employees are not as enthusiastic as Jamie may have convinced herself that they are.

Scorecard

Business Judgment			People Judgment		
(1) —— (2) —— (3)			(1) ——▼—— (2) —— (3)		
Data Savvy		NO	Engagement		2
Strategic Mindset		NO	Relationship Building		1
Customer Focus		NO	Team Development		NO
Financial Awareness		NO	Individual Development		1
Balanced Decision-Making		NO	Decisiveness		1
Results					
↔ Market	↓ People		↔ Financial		↔ Operations

How did you assess Jamie's leadership in this situation? Where do we agree? How do we differ? Why?

How have you addressed changing norms and expectations for flexible work environments?

How have your choices impacted your employees and your business?

What would you do differently?

Q2: Terry

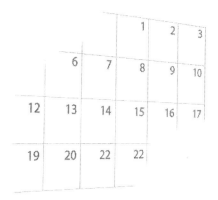

Chapter 17

Watering Rocks

Terry has begun to recognize that much of his time is spent on store-level tasks that preclude him from executing his strategic plans. For years, he has served as the manager of each of his three stores, collaborating with the assistant manager at each location. Terry's approach to the hiring process leans heavily on promoting from within, and he finds the next in line is not always the best in line.

Tell me about a people challenge you faced this quarter.

Lately, I've realized I didn't have the bandwidth to continue as head of the company and as the manager of each store. Earlier this year, I decided to let go of being the store manager. Quickly, I became aware that this was a notable event for associates across the organization—who would take that role in each store? Even if we had assistant store managers, they only executed what was decided versus leading. Everyone knew I was controlling what happened in the stores. Now, someone else would lead, and that someone was their peer. The hiring of store managers was a big deal—it meant a lot to the potential candidates. This was an opportunity to oversee the store, which was a big responsibility.

To be perfectly frank, I had always assumed the current assistant managers would move into the store manager roles. In two of the stores, I thought the assistant store managers were a given. They had been with me for a long time; their values closely aligned with mine, and I felt they could do the job. In the last store, the assistant manager, Allen, was a great person who always did everything asked of him with a smile. However, he had not been with us that long. We brought him in from another grocery store after Lars, a man who held the job since my parents ran the company, had retired. I was less sure Allen had the drive and initiative I needed in a store manager.

How did you make that assessment?

I assume it was partially my gut, but it was also based on our interactions during this last year. As I said, he always did the things I asked of him but didn't go beyond that. He would see things that needed to get done, but if it weren't something we had agreed on, he would not do it without asking.

Was he coachable?

I am not sure if you can teach someone to think outside of the box and take the initiative. I've often found myself saying to him, "It's great that you saw this needed to be done, but you don't have to ask me for permission. You know what we are trying to accomplish, so you are welcome to go ahead and do it."

How did you approach the hiring process?

Since the store manager position was so important, and a very visible sign that Eat Fresh was growing, I made it clear we would consider all qualified applicants from any of the stores. I let everyone know that no one had a lock on a position, and we would evaluate all applications and conduct interviews based on a clearly-defined job description. Even if I was reasonably sure of the two assistant managers, I wanted my decisions to be unquestionable. Also, I wanted to know I hired the three associates who would be great store managers.

What did you do to achieve those outcomes?

I sat down with Helen, our head of human resources, to create a job description that included job requirements, qualifications, and expectations. We also created a list of the characteristics we thought defined a great store manager. We would use this list to evaluate different candidates.

We posted the job and all three assistant store managers applied, as expected. Several department managers did as well. We evaluated each—first against the job description. Those candidates who passed the initial screening were reviewed again, this time considering our list of great store manager characteristics. It was exciting. I gained a better perspective of people's strengths and weaknesses. Helen has a lot of experience in recruiting. She helped me to get the most insight into the candidates.

The next step was the interviews. I shared the list of characteristics with each candidate and asked them to talk about characteristics they strongly identified with. We discussed examples of each. I was surprised by some of the things the candidates chose to talk about—several were more about good management than leadership.

What was the outcome of the selection process?

We promoted the two assistant managers who I thought, from the beginning, would be good store managers. The process allowed us to identify what type of training each needed to ensure they would succeed in the new role. Had we not been so thorough in developing the success factors for store managers, I doubt we would have had such great insight into how to support these new leaders.

As for the last store manager, I had three choices regarding what to do with Allen. He clearly was not as confident or capable, but I could promote him and commit to spending time coaching him. I could also simply promote him and hope he grew into the role. My final option was to not promote him. I could explain why he was great as an assistant store manager but, at this time, did not demonstrate the potential to succeed as a store manager.

Your decision?

I chose to go ahead and promote Allen. He was liked by the people, had a great attitude, and during the interview, he acknowledged his shortcomings and indicated what I thought was a real desire to improve. I think it necessary we give people a chance. Had we not promoted him, he would probably have left. Then I would have had a store that was down both a manager and an assistant. Even though some of the other candidates were disappointed they were not promoted, they knew from the beginning the assistant store managers were the most likely to get the jobs. But they all knew they had the opportunity to be fairly considered.

How successful have your selections been?

Two have been solid performers. Allen had a difficult transition. I found myself working closely with him for the first two months, coaching him daily. He was not adapting to the role. He appeared to become less engaged each week no matter how I tried to support him.

He just resigned. He said he wasn't enjoying the job. Allen thought the decisions were difficult and felt he couldn't make them well—he didn't think he was doing a good job. When we asked the associates in his store, they all said they felt Allen was trying but had difficulty making decisions.

How will you address his departure?

We are looking to take one of the other candidates, Maggie, who we thought could also be a great store manager, and promote her to the role. Unfortunately, this will mean more time to help get her up to speed, even though she had recently become the assistant store manager.

Authors' Insights

Hopefully, Terry's experience with Allen teaches him an important lesson from which all of us can learn. Good leaders recognize the needs, aspirations, and feelings of their people. They recognize the importance of associate engagement and morale and they work hard to maintain high levels of both. On occasion, however, concern for the well-being of one individual outweighs the impact it might have on the organization as a whole. That is what happened to Terry in dealing with Allen's promotion.

Before the process began, Terry had considerable reservations regarding Allen's ability to assume the broader responsibilities of a store manager. Helen's evaluation process confirmed Terry's initial observations of Allen; nevertheless, he promoted him—recognizing his potential for failure. *Why?* We think you know why—a leader's propensity to avoid injuring the morale and self-confidence of their associates. Most leaders tend to see the positive in their people and do not want to hurt their feelings. They also want to avoid making those difficult people decisions requiring them to put an individual's shortcomings into perspective. The result of this mindset is that leaders avoid difficult conversations and make poor people decisions.

An associate once told us, "You need to stop watering rocks." He meant good leaders know when they need to stop trying to develop, stop giving more time for improvement, and stop procrastinating on a decision to fire, demote, or move someone to another role. Many leaders we have spoken to over the years have told us they knew as much as a year in advance that a struggling associate was not going to make it. But they let it go until the damage to the organization and individual was out of hand.

So, let's return to Terry and Allen. Although he knew Allen would not cut it based on low initiative and slow, poor quality decision-making, Terry promoted him anyway. What were the implications of that decision? First, Terry would have to spend more time coaching and looking over Allen's shoulder; thus, negating the need to create store managers to free up Terry's time for more strategic activities. Second, Allen's lack of initiative and poor judgment were critical factors to his success as a leader and would affect the day-to-day morale of his associates. Although the store employees may have liked him as a person, his role as their leader would be a problem. Third, it would be obvious to those who applied for the role and other associates that Terry did not use the process appropriately but went with who he had in place. Finally, we don't know the financial implications of his decision, but we can assume that Allen has missed opportunities for efficiency, productivity, and profitability. Fortunately, he lasted only two months, which minimized his negative impact on engagement and productivity.

What does all this mean in terms of our leadership model and what Terry demonstrated? In this case, it is simple. This was primarily about People Judgment and Terry's Decisiveness. Remember, part of the definition of Decisiveness is making timely, considerate, but resolute decisions resulting in the best outcome for the individual and the organization. Terry's decision on Allen did not turn out well for either Allen or the company. Terry tended to assess his options in terms of Allen's feelings and Terry's need to spend time supporting Allen. Impacts on Allen's fellow associates, those who had applied for the role, and the efficiency and productivity of the store were not weighed in his decision. Let's give Terry credit, however, for a degree of Engagement and Individual Development. He created a transparent promotion process. Terry invested in coaching and training both Allen and those who applied for the role.

Again, the big takeaway here may sound harsh, but beware of watering rocks, and do not be afraid to have difficult conversations with associates. You may be surprised that the associate is relieved to have had their issue addressed. Just do it with consideration and sensitivity but resolutely.

Terry's less-than-effective People Judgment affected his results in many ways. During this quarter and for the foreseeable future, his people will question his methods for hiring and promoting associates. Throughout Allen's tenure, he and his store staff were less productive, and morale was low. Allen's leadership led to inefficiencies in the store, and this disorganization had some effect on fiscal performance. We are not sure Allen's time in the store was long enough to make a lasting negative impression on customers—there was no discernable impact on market variables. Terry is lucky this location did not become a drag on the Eat Fresh brand.

Scorecard

Business Judgment			People Judgment		
(1)————(2)————(3)			(1)————▼————(2)————(3)		
Data Savvy		NO	Engagement		2
Strategic Mindset		NO	Relationship Building		NO
Customer Focus		NO	Team Development		NO
Financial Awareness		NO	Individual Development		2
Balanced Decision-Making		NO	Decisiveness		1
Results					
←→	↓		↓	↓	
Market	People		Financial	Operations	

How did you assess Terry's leadership in this situation? Where do we agree? How do we differ? Why?

Have you fallen into the trap of watering rocks?

How long did you wait before you talked with your associate? What would you do differently?

Chapter 18

Diversity Challenge

When an outspoken minister and influential leader in the local community visited his neighborhood Eat Fresh store, the reverend's first impressions were not favorable. He reached out to Terry, questioning the lack of African American employees in all but a few stock clerk positions. Terry must not only promptly address the minister's concern but also needs to quickly understand how his current hiring practices support his commitment to diversity and inclusion.

Terry, tell us about the incident concerning diversity at Eat Fresh.

It started when Reverend Pinkney, the minister of the First Church of the Savior, visited our Blakely store and felt the proportionality of people of color did not reflect the community's population. The minister sent me a rather strongly worded note in which he told me about our failings. He said if we wanted to be part of the community, the store should look like the community. What he was implying was that our stores did not represent the black community. He felt we lacked at every level of the store. He said he felt outraged the only black employees appeared to be in entry-level positions.

What did you do?

I immediately gave Reverend Pinkney a call to thank him for the note and set up a face-to-face meeting. I wanted him to know I took his complaint seriously. We met the following day and spent a lot of time talking about what representation of the community meant to him. We also discussed the potential challenges to accomplishing this. All in all, we had an excellent talk, and we ended with me letting him know I would personally be involved in addressing this and keep him updated.

How did you evaluate the potential issue the minister shared with you?

After that, I sat down with Helen, our head of human resources, to analyze the organization and understand why so few people of color had been promoted. Helen agreed that we need to create an organization that represents the community through a diverse workforce. However, she was rather upset with me because I didn't bring up with the minister the diversity initiatives we have going on that are much broader than just color. Diversity is supposed to represent the broad spectrum of people, genders, religions, ethnicities, ages, and the like. It would have been appropriate for Reverend Pinkney to understand the scope of our commitment to diversity.

I agree that it would have been good for me to bring this up at my first meeting. I believe I was so caught up in listening to the minister's concern about color and our lack of having anyone at the managerial level that I missed the bigger picture.

Helen and I agreed that we needed to analyze what our racial and other diversity factors were at every level.

What did you learn from that analysis?

This turned out to be a more pervasive issue than just promotion. Our racial diversity at the lower levels was poor and then reflected in the lack of diversity at the supervisory and management levels. We also discovered that we had a recruiting issue. It boiled down to where we were looking for people. Previously, it was done by word of mouth and some advertising in the local papers. However, these channels did not reach all groups of people in the community.

We know we hire good people, and we hire them because they show the potential to be successful here—now and in the future. We also promote based on who would be the best person for any new position. But if the pool of people we promote from is not very diverse, then it becomes impossible to get diversity in our senior ranks. Although our selection and promotion processes are merit-based, we were systemically discriminating because our base lacked diversity.

We did find that our employees thought we cared about diversity. We had implemented great initiatives to make sure people felt like we treat everyone with respect. For example, we have created personal space for people to nurse their babies. We recognize times when more devout members of religious groups might need time for daily prayers and religious holidays.

Based on your findings, what did you do?

Our first step was to analyze how to reach people of color and other minorities in the job application process. Once we saw how and where these different groups looked for work, we made sure that all of our job openings were highly visible in these channels.

I also worked closely with Helen and our human resources team to change our application, screening, and interviewing processes. We needed to adjust these as well, so we didn't exclude people using an old method. We didn't change our hiring criteria, as we still want the best people who will be good performers, but expanding the search gave us a more diverse candidate pool from which to screen and interview.

When it came to promotions, we saw that there wasn't any immediate fix, as we didn't have a big enough pool of people to pick from due to our hiring process. However, we are trying to ensure, if possible, we promote people of color and other minorities while still making sure we selected based on competence. Hence, we will be confident the person would succeed. We made a special effort to communicate our new recruiting strategy and promotional process to all our associates.

How have the changes you introduced affected your company?

Over time, we believe this will be great. Our outreach and programs will create a workforce that reflects the people living in the community. Even though the work was more than I initially thought, I believe it was essential to get it right, so I am happy I was involved.

What feedback have you received from the minister?

Well, he is less skeptical than before, but we still have a way to go. I kept him informed of our findings and our actions, but he felt we should have done some of it from the beginning. He is also not convinced we will hire and promote people of color because we have more candidates of color. Suffice it to say that he won't be satisfied until he sees black people in key roles.

Authors' Insights

Establishing relationships with key stakeholders in the community and society is a critical role for leaders. Equally important is the need to ensure your organizational make-up reflects the population you serve. Having the processes and discipline in place to ensure you achieve your diversity goals is also a key responsibility of the PRG leader. Terry took Eat Fresh a long way toward achieving those goals. Let's talk about how he did that.

First, Terry took the initiative to reach out to Reverend Pinkney immediately after receiving the note describing the minister's perception of a lack of diversity in his store. Although Helen chided him for not including her and not being aware of the diversity initiatives already in place, we could make the case Terry was better off going to see the minister without a lot of data and descriptions of initiatives. Showing up at the church door armed with data and his HR manager could have changed the tone of the meeting from one in which a business owner was eager to hear from a valued community leader and establish a relationship based on mutually beneficial goals to one in which he would appear defensive. Terry illustrated Decisiveness in his timely decision to solicit the minister's perspective in more depth. He also demonstrated the ability to communicate and engage the reverend as a key stakeholder. As a result, his Relationship Building capability came into clear view.

One could make the case Terry should have known about the diversity initiatives Helen described. Still, we will give him a pass based on the degree to which he became engaged with the HR team to collect and analyze the demographic data on Eat Fresh's recruitment and promotional activities. They did a thorough analysis (Data Savvy), and he and Helen took action that dramatically changed their recruitment and promotional processes. Those quick and resolute actions illustrated another example of Terry's Decisiveness.

In addition to the positive significance of his actions, Terry and his head of HR were highly transparent in communicating the nature of the changes and the processes' goals to their employees, the community at large, and Reverend Pinkney. These are solid examples of Engagement. Their actions, in terms of recognizing individual differences and needs (for example, time for daily prayers and recognition of different religious holidays), were significant for creating a culture in which individuals feel respected and added to the team's strength.

We don't want to give Terry all this positive feedback then slip in a negative nugget to tarnish his good work. We will mention, for future observation, the depth of commitment and involvement Terry illustrates when he has a problem to solve. As he gets In the Weeds on some issues, he may tend to infringe on his team members' responsibilities. He may have overreached with Helen in this scenario, but we do not have enough information to be sure. Suffice it to say, Terry's tendency to get In the Weeds is a reflection of a potential Derailer. Let us see if this observation generalizes to multiple situations.

How did Terry's leadership affect results across Eat Fresh? The Eat Fresh commitment to diversity should affect customers who, in the future, may reward the diversity they see with their patronage. For now, market results are not changed. Although Terry believes the long-reaching effect on people will be positive, the immediate impact of his leadership on people results is neutral. Even the Reverend Pinkney is waiting to see if Terry's emphasis on reducing the heterogeneity in the entry-level ranks correlates to upper-level diversity. We can see the immediate impact of improved recruiting and hiring practices on operations—more applicants from which to find the very best associates. There were no significant financial impacts. We suspect Terry thinks his efforts are a wise investment that will yield returns across all the results categories in the mid-to-long term. We agree.

Scorecard

Business Judgment		People Judgment	
Data Savvy	2	Engagement	2
Strategic Mindset	NO	Relationship Building	3
Customer Focus	2	Team Development	NO
Financial Awareness	NO	Individual Development	NO
Balanced Decision-Making	NO	Decisiveness	3

Results			
↔	↔	↔	↑
Market	People	Financial	Operations

How did you assess Terry's leadership in this situation? Where do we agree? How do we differ? Why?

When you look around your company, how diverse is your workforce?

How do you ensure diversity and inclusivity?

Chapter 19

Safe or Sorry

During the summer, Terry had a situation in which an extra-large shipment of baby food might have gone bad. It may seem like a *no-brainer* to discard the batch of product, but Terry believes the decision may not be so cut and dry. He wants to check his facts before discarding the product and losing valuable customers eager to purchase this particular baby food.

Terry, let's talk about an operational challenge you faced this past quarter.

Sure. One of my receiving employees called me from the loading docks. He had identified a large shipment of baby food sitting out for longer than what is safe for the product. He was also worried because the weather was particularly hot that week. To make matters worse, we had just begun a major sales promotion for this popular organic baby food, so this shipment was three times the typical order size. Discarding it would have a significant financial impact; plus, if I were to re-order the product, it would take three weeks to receive it. On top of that, anything that involves children is more sensitive than most other customer groups, making it even harder for us to consider still selling the baby food.

What did you do?

I wanted to determine if the baby food was spoiled. I started by contacting the manufacturer. They said even though it wasn't ideal, there should be no problem with the food. I also contacted a government agency. It was hard for them to give any indication of what to do other than recommending that if I discarded the potentially spoiled baby food, I'd be safe rather than sorry.

Since the answers I received didn't convince me in one way or the other, I decided to get a team's input. I gathered Vince — the associate who called me about the situation — and Peter, my head of customer service, and head of operations, Kathy.

Why did you choose this particular group?

I wanted to make sure I got input from multiple sides of the business. Kathy would look more from a business perspective, whereas Peter would see it from the customer's point of view. I also wanted Vince to tell me the facts and details of how the shipment had been handled, as he raised the red flag, and I wanted him to feel ownership in what we were going to do.

How did the team address the issue?

We needed to quickly decide to sell it or dump it. I asked everyone to consider both sides: discarding the shipment or selling the products as planned. I wanted everyone to think of the alternatives rather than digging in and taking a single position.

Each person spent ten minutes writing a note for themselves as to why we should discard the baby food. Then they spent an equal amount of time considering why we should keep and sell the baby food. In two different columns on a whiteboard, we wrote down everything the team had come up with. Then we discussed the various arguments.

I thought Peter would just insist that we should discard the baby food because it was the safest thing to do, but that wasn't the case. He said many customers rely on that brand of baby food, and no nearby stores carried it. We carry limited brands, which meant the clients had to go to someone else, and it also suggested they either had to drive far to find it, try another brand, or possibly order it online. Whatever they ended up doing, we would probably lose customers as they would find a new place.

Did you discuss the long- and short-term implications of the choices?

Absolutely. I think we all understood the short-term financial impact of discarding the food. However, we struggled most with the long-term effects of our brand and reputation. If we kept the baby food, sold it, and children got ill, that could hurt our brand.

On the other hand, not having the baby food when people are coming in to buy it would frustrate our customers. We would have to tell them what happened, which might be good because we'd be seen as upfront and honest. But on the other hand, they would wonder what else is not working in our stores. We could build trust or erode it.

What did you decide?

After all the discussions and weighing each of the pros and cons, I know the team saw merit in whichever decision we made. In a case like this, someone had to decide, and I felt it is my role to do so. I had listened to everything that was said and taken it all into consideration. It was not an easy decision, but I decided that the probability was low that the baby food had spoiled and that we should sell it.

How did you arrive at that decision?

A few things played a role in my decision. First, the manufacturer of the baby food was not overly concerned; and when we dug into the details of how long the food had been out in the heat and the temperature of where the food had been, I wasn't so sure it was as bad as I initially thought. The financial impact of discarding the food wasn't going to make or break us, but we are often faced with decisions like this. If we always go the safe route, it would hurt us eventually. So this is one I felt willing to risk despite it potentially affecting children. I also thought the weather would be hot for a while, so there is an almost equal risk that the customers could leave the food in the heat too long, and that's something we couldn't control. Regardless of the decision, we needed to work hard to keep our reputation and brand with our customers. I was willing to do that, no matter what. So I decided to put it on the shelves.

What was the team's reaction?

Since we had worked through it all together, and I told them how I came to my decision, they were behind it. Of course, we were worried that we could be wrong, but it felt like we were all in it together.

What happened?

It turned out the baby food was okay. We heard no unusual or negative feedback from the customers, so I guess it was the best decision. I faced difficult trade-offs. The "easy" decision is not always the best, and if leaders were always to take it, they would have a hard time making enough profits to grow.

I learned afterward that several employees have expressed concerns that we risked our customers' well-being for the sake of profit. They just don't know the whole story.

Authors' Insights
Given the potential negative health, brand, and financial implications of the scenario, we considered retitling this chapter:

Better to be Lucky than Judicious.

Let's talk about why we disagree with Terry using the dimensions of Business Judgment as our guide.

If we start with Data Savvy, we see Terry pulled key staff to get their opinions on the pros and cons of discarding or putting the baby food on the shelves. That was a positive approach, but Terry was gathering their opinions based on insufficient information. He did not obtain additional sources of information beyond the manufacturer's thoughts and the government agency. Both responded as you would expect given each one's mission and role. What information could he have solicited? At the store level, he could have been more precise in determining the actual time on the loading dock and the temperature. He could have sent a sample of the food for testing. He could have spoken with his attorney to understand the implications of a child becoming ill, or worse, dying. The reputation implications are obvious. From a sourcing perspective, he could have pursued purchasing some of the same brand from a competitor at retail price. Although he would have lost his margin, he could have delivered on the promotion. We are sure you can think of other information he may have been able to acquire. Regardless, had he and his staff had the above information, he would have received a much more informed opinion and potentially, a different point of view.

How about Strategic Mindset? Terry's business model is predicated on promoting healthy eating. Does ingesting potentially spoiled food align with Terry's mission? The same could be said about Customer Focus. Terry's decision gave lip service to the customer by being concerned they would have to travel to get this brand of baby food. We feel Terry weighed the immediate negative financial implications of discarding the baby food more heavily than customer welfare. This leads us to Financial Awareness, an area in which Terry has demonstrated strength. This scenario is no exception. Terry knew exactly what the short-term financial implications were for keeping or discarding the baby food. He chose to put the baby food on his shelves, which leads us to Balanced Decision-Making. He neither developed any significant alternative solutions nor did he adequately consider the long-term legal and financial implications of his decision.

The analysis of Terry's behavior relative to Business Judgment illustrates a low level of effectiveness in four of the five dimensions. As a result, we reject his premise substantiating the decision—"the easy decision is not always the best, and if leaders were to always take it, they would have a hard time making enough profits to grow." The fact is *this was not a tough decision.* Considering Eat Fresh's mission and the potential negative reputation and long-term financial implication of even one child becoming ill, this was an easy decision to be made definitively and by Terry alone—discard the order and look for alternatives!

Before we complete our insights, let's take a quick look at how Terry fared on the People Judgment side of the ledger. Terry illustrated positive behavior by consulting with associates and seeking their perspective. He was extremely transparent and honest with this team about the situation and how he arrived at his decision to keep the baby food on the shelves. He gets points for Team Development.

The impact of Terry's leadership decisions relating to the potential baby food spoilage? Be it the result of a quality decision or plain old luck, the immediate market and financial impacts were favorable. Eat Fresh was able to deliver a high-demand product that few competitors could offer. Terry was able to attract existing and prospective customers and generated sales on the baby food. When considering the impact on people, we are sure some are relieved to have a stock of the popular product. But you must wonder how many associates question or are downright uncomfortable with Terry's decision to place a short-term gain over the health and well-being of customers, especially children. Terry avoided a critical inventory issue that would have been problematic from an operations perspective. Did he take steps to ensure similar challenges would not impinge on company operations?

Scorecard

Business Judgment		People Judgment	
①———▼———②———③		①———②———▼③	
Data Savvy	1	Engagement	NO
Strategic Mindset	1	Relationship Building	NO
Customer Focus	1	Team Development	3
Financial Awareness	3	Individual Development	NO
Balanced Decision-Making	1	Decisiveness	NO
Results			
↑ Market	↓ People	↑ Financial	↔ Operations

How did you assess Terry's leadership in this situation? Where do we agree? How do we differ?

Have you been faced with a business decision in which the outcomes were equally vague?

What did you do?

What would you do differently?

Chapter 20

Is Now Really the Time?

The story of the Organic Dangle acquisition continues. Six stores now bear the Eat Fresh name. Terry and his team have been working to integrate two organizations, but new challenges continue to arise. Should a people-management system used in the previous Organic Dangle stores be adopted across the company? Terry worries this formal HR tool will make the organization feel bureaucratic and cause his company to lose its entrepreneurial edge.

Talk to us about a challenge you faced relating to the recent acquisition.

One comes to mind right away. After we bought Organic Dangle, Helen, my head of human resources, wanted to leverage the people-management system they had been using to support employee training, time tracking, and benefits enrollment. She had talked about us investing in such a system before; however, we have managed to do well without it. I never saw this type of system as an urgent need. Now, having almost doubled in size, she said it was a must-have.

How did you evaluate Helen's request?

I thought she made some valid points relating to the productivity and efficiency gains the system would provide. We would benefit from a program that manages everything — recruitment, payroll, training, and other HR functions. The more employees we bring on, we risk making errors that could be costly. Also, we will soon hit a point where Helen and her team would simply become overloaded.

She convinced you to adopt the system?

No. Ever since I decided to grow the business, I have thought about how to keep our entrepreneurial spirit. With the growing number of employees from the acquisition—lately, I've been mindful of losing that aspect of our culture. I feel stuff like this is just needless bureaucracy, which, in turn, kills the entrepreneurial spirit. Sure, I understand that at some point, we might need a people-management system, but not yet. If I do this, what's next? I just thought we were inviting a degree of formalness that would slow us down and make us a less nimble company.

I was less than comfortable with the idea but I did not share those feelings with Helen. Instead, I thought it best to bring the entire management team in on the decision. If they all agreed, I would likely go with it. I asked Helen to present it at our next management meeting.

What happened at that meeting?

Helen presented her thoughts on the need for the people-management system. She explained how it would streamline our recruiting process, ensure we were well-positioned to hire quality employees, manage associate hours, salaries, and benefits, and provide a training platform that aligned us to government requirements for companies of our size. She said that if we didn't do it now, we needed at least two additional HR staff to manage our current associate load using the existing processes.

George, our head of finance, had collaborated with Helen on the proposal. He walked us through a breakdown of costs and the financial implications of implementing the system. It was not cheap. We needed to buy software and hardware for our original stores and pay a transaction fee for every associate managed by the system. We were already paying these fees for the three Organic Dangle stores even though we had not been using most of the system's components. Despite the costs, George thought adopting the people-management system would make both human resources and operations more efficient. Also, it would limit the need for additional HR staffing. He believed the benefits outweighed the time and investment.

Kathy, our head of operations, talked about the implications of a changeover to the system. Several of our home-grown solutions would become obsolete — she was concerned important data might be lost in the transition or become inaccessible in the future. The people-management system required considerable training and coaching for everyone across the organization. She felt some long-time associates and managers might be opposed to this new and formal system. However, she believed all would eventually see the benefits of the people-management system. If her concerns could be addressed, she too was an advocate.

Was the entire leadership team in agreement?

No. Paul, our head of sales, and Susan, our head of purchasing, were both against it. Like me, they thought the system was overkill for a company of our size, and it would slow us down. They argued it would change the company culture, which is such an integral part of our success. Rinjat, head of IT, felt our data ubiquity would be challenged by pushing so much critical internal data to a system that was not specifically designed in-house.

George was on the fence. He saw the advantages — better oversight, control, and analysis. He believed it would make us more efficient and profitable. George also worried the implementation would be more difficult than anticipated. Others did not voice a strong opinion for or against it.

What did you decide to do?

If I had to decide, it would have been no. But I could read the room and thought it would be better if the majority of the team shared the view on something this close. So I asked the team to vote.

The result?

We decided not to adopt. We agreed we could just add two more people to Helen's team and save the investments of time and money. We also decided to pause using the software at the former Organic Dangle stores. This would save us the transaction fees for associates in those three locations. The move away from the formal system will help us foster that entrepreneurial spirit we felt was lacking in the newly acquired stores. Besides, we have so much going on right now.

Helen's reaction?

She was understandably disappointed. She feels we are not addressing the needs of her department by taking the appropriate steps to manage people in an organization of this size. The growth we have experienced is making HR's job more difficult. She thinks we are short-sighted. She said, "I truly hope this decision doesn't come back to bite us all in the behind."

Authors' Insights

An important lesson illustrated in this scenario is: *no behavior is behavior.* Terry's lack of initiative in this situation tells us more about his leadership effectiveness than his overt actions. Let's see if we can explain how a lack of action can negatively impact your leadership effectiveness.

Instead of expressing his opinion and responding negatively

to Helen's recommendation to implement the people-management system, Terry chose to delegate the decision to his management team. Helen presented the concept and allowed team members to voice their opinions on the system's benefits and value, as well as the negative implications. Helen made a robust, fact-based case for adopting the system. She pointed out how it would help streamline recruiting, increase the quality of hires, enable more timely and accurate compensation decisions, and other benefits. The head of finance provided his analysis of the financial and resource implications. His summary conclusion? George believed the benefits the system created outweighed the costs and time investment. Similarly, the head of operations expressed concerns relating to training and possible loss of data that she felt should be addressed, but ultimately, she was on board.

The head of IT suggested the system required disengaging from several home-grown solutions and wanted no part of it (this sounded like he was guarding his territory more than thinking about the company's best interests). The head of sales and purchasing shared in opposition to the system. Both felt it unnecessary—it would slow down daily operations and negatively change the culture. Unlike Helen, George, and Kathy, Paul's and Susan's objections were less fact-based and highly opinion-based. What about Terry's impact on the decision? He did not take a strong position during the discussion and then voted with those who opposed the system.

Where does "no behavior is behavior" reside in this situation? When Helen first recommended the people-management system, Terry had the opportunity to solicit information from providers and comparable users on the impact and long-term implications of such a system. He failed to do this. Not only did Terry fail to solicit additional external data, but he also did not endeavor to understand the value of the existing people-management system currently in use throughout the former Organic Dangle stores. Collecting this additional information may have allowed Terry to weigh the long-term implications for his newly doubled-in-size organization versus his concern for "killing the entrepreneurial spirit." Terry's inaction relative to soliciting information (poor Data Savvy) negatively impacted his Business Judgment—failing to weigh the long-term implications on his strategic vision for the organization.

We will give Terry credit for providing his management team the opportunity to weigh in on implementing the people-management system. We are certain his team appreciated his confidence in them to provide insights and debate the merits. His approach illustrated positive Team Development behavior. Did his leadership team expect the situation to turn into a pure democracy where Terry did not express his opinion and allowed his vote to count the same as his team members? Given Terry's previous behavior, we doubt it. Typically, effective leaders solicit their staff's input to get various perspectives and data points to help them make a higher quality decision. A vote may show where the preponderance of support resides for a given issue, but effective leaders seldom are bound by a vote. That is why they are the leader. In Terry's people-management situation, he abdicated his leadership—intentionally choosing to let the team decide after reading the room and realizing he could let the majority make the decision he secretly wanted to make. *No behavior.*

From previous scenarios, we know the strength of Terry's financial acumen and the degree to which it has impacted his behavior and decisions. Although George provided a positive fiscal picture regarding the system's implementation, Terry took no action to reinforce the financial benefits. Nor did he react to the implications of adding two HR staff to keep HR afloat. Finally, he decided to suspend using the former Organic Dangle stores' system without identifying the operational and financial implications of doing so. "No behavior is behavior" in each of these examples. His staff's empowered feelings might mask Terry's lack of action due to their majority decision to scuttle the people-management system. Our bet is it will come back to bite him — later implementation will be equally if not more difficult. The long-term benefits of adopting the system earlier will be lost, and the short-term financial liabilities will be realized.

The importance of maintaining the entrepreneurial spirit for Terry is not unusual in highly motivated PRG leaders who want to see themselves in the culture they are building. They see their unbridled enthusiasm, initiative, and focus on the customer as the key to success. However, they must weigh those behaviors with the reality of running a business growing in size and complexity. In Terry's case, his strident position on maintaining the entrepreneurial spirit and his lack of initiative to dig deeper into the system's value may be evidence of one of our Derailers — Formality-Structure Disconnect. A key illustrative behavior for this Derailer is minimizing the importance of structure and process. That is exactly what Terry did. He underestimated the value of the people-planning strategy without appropriate scrutiny. Terry may have been right about not being ready for the new system given the acquisition's recency. However, he did not know if he was making an effective decision for the people or the business because he did not do the necessary diligence.

For the present, Terry's decision not to implement will be received positively by some of his staff. The leadership team were all part of a critical decision and they feel trusted and engaged. Many associates and managers will be pleased to have avoided a system they see as time-consuming and bureaucratic. But mid to long term, the impact on people results is likely negative on both HR effectiveness and all associates. Terry eliminated a costly system representing a high fixed cost. Adding two additional HR associates was, comparatively, a minor cost. Thus, the immediate financial results were positive. However, the operational implications are problematic. Abandoning a state-of-the-art Human Resources management system to adopt the current and clearly less effective HR processes is immediately inefficient.

Scorecard

Business Judgment		People Judgment	
Data Savvy	1	Engagement	2
Strategic Mindset	1	Relationship Building	NO
Customer Focus	NO	Team Development	3
Financial Awareness	NO	Individual Development	NO
Balanced Decision-Making	1	Decisiveness	1

Results

Market	People	Financial	Operations
↔	↔	↑	↓

How did you assess Terry's leadership in this situation? Where do we agree? How do we differ? Why?

What's your reaction to the "no behavior is behavior" concept?

What situations have you confronted in which you took no action (i.e., tended to abdicate your leadership responsibilities)? Why?

What were the results?

What would you do differently?

Q3: Jamie

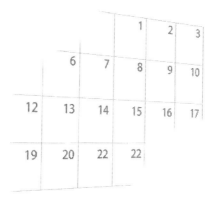

Chapter 21

Pricing Model Change

Jamie and her team are debating the merits of selling software using the traditional perpetual license versus a subscription. Some believe *now is the time*, as many companies across the industry have successfully made the shift. Others are concerned the company will lose customers. Is this the time for e-Dine to make a fundamental change to its pricing model?

Tell me about a business challenge you dealt with this quarter.

There is a trend occurring across the industry that I believe will change how everyone sells software. I've been monitoring this movement for the past few years. The implications for producing our product, maintaining it, charging for it, and recognizing revenue over time are dramatic.

I don't want to bore you with all the technical stuff, but the long and short of it is this. We sell our product for a one-time price—buy the software, and you have the right to use it forever. It's a perpetual license. Our POS is $3,800. Every eighteen to twenty-four months, we release a new version. We try to build compelling new features into the new versions that entice current users to upgrade. A substantial group does. Upgrades are discounted—typically $1,495. Software companies need to release new versions regularly. Without those upgrades, our model would be a one-time sale. Our only revenue would come from new customers.

Over the past five years, the industry began moving away from perpetual licenses. Companies started selling access to software as a subscription. The move was positioned as a benefit for customers. Their acquisition costs would drop dramatically.

You always have the latest and greatest version. When you are no longer using the product, just cancel the subscription. Adobe was one of the first. They combined their entire line of creative products into the Creative Cloud and charged a monthly fee. They now regularly introduce new features across the suite every fall and spring. Then Microsoft made Office a subscription. Many online services are based on this model.

I felt we should consider changing our pricing model from a perpetual license to a subscription, with the next release scheduled for the end of the year.

What did you do to further evaluate this change?

I scheduled part of our weekly leadership meeting to discuss the merits and asked all to come prepared with any data to supplement what I had provided.

Tell me about the meeting.

I began by explaining my read of the landscape—subscription pricing will be the industry standard in less than ten years. So, this discussion was about when we go there, not if e-Dine will move to subscriptions. People had differing opinions on the issue.

Our CTO, Mike, agreed and wanted to move as soon as possible. The short-term cost of switching was not an issue. But he suggested customers would need time. If this was going to work, we needed to promote the value of subscription pricing now so that our current customers' switchover to version two was automatic without having to budget for the cost of a major software upgrade. Denise, our VP of marketing, also agreed. She also shared a customer survey in which she had tested monthly pricing. Close to 80 percent of existing customers said they would pay a monthly fee for a product that received frequent updates and feature enhancements without additional upgrade fees.

Carl, our VP of sales, was eager to have a monthly option. He noted the most frequent objection the salespeople encountered was the cost of our POS. Carl thought we should sell the perpetual license and the subscription version because some customers would object to being forced into paying a monthly fee for something they already bought. He argued up to 40 percent of users typically do not upgrade to each new version.

Perrin, our VP of finance, did not have a strong opinion but wanted us to see the effect of a switch on the timing of our cash flow. There were tradeoffs. Our sales projections for the year were based on perpetual licenses—a mix of new sales at $3,800 and upgrades at $1,495 per license. As a $349 monthly subscription, that same income would take eleven months to recognize. She suggested the average revenue per customer would increase by at least $1,745 because we would be paid the subscription every month—under our current model, a customer paid $3,800, and we looked to upgrade them in two years.

Perrin and Mike both thought a subscription system would improve our receivables. Customers would be charged every thirty days through the software using credit card payments and bank withdrawals. We could also move the premium support subscription fees from our invoice approach to the automatic billing system.

What choices did you have, and what were the implications of each?

There was never a question about switching to a subscription model. I was focused on the timing. I have been watching the industry and keeping close track of analysts' opinions. This is what most consumers want. It is also a better way to do business. You can better project monthly revenue, the product becomes more accessible, and your product cycles can be more focused—you don't always have to try and fill up the kitchen sink with cool stuff, trying to get people to upgrade.

I could have waited for the product to release, get six months into the upgrade cycle, and then make the switch. But that's almost a year in which our competitors could make the switch, undercut me on price, and beat us with new features. In the meantime, we would lose an opportunity to overcome our single biggest objection to a sale—price.

There was no reason to offer a standard license and a subscription in the long term. First, the operational complexity in marketing and supporting virtually two versions of the same product would be inefficient and costly. I also knew from reading about some of the earliest adopters of subscription models there were always a few customers who made a lot of noise. They were always the minority, and their complaints were never more than a blip in certain corners of the internet.

What did you do?

There were far too many upsides to moving now. We began planning the changeover the following week. Later that month we moved the current version to a subscription. New customers are using the same software as clients who have perpetual licenses, but their subscription is billed every month. When we release version two, our existing customers can keep using the old version at no cost, or they can sign up for the new version as a subscription. It allows us to take advantage of the next six months to educate customers and promote the change as a significant benefit. More importantly, we are selling our current product as a subscription, which allows us to reach a huge group of previous prospects who said they loved our product but simply could not afford the upfront costs.

I expected we would see a surge in new customers because of the pricing. We would have to watch our cash flow—monthly revenue would fluctuate, but long term, that license revenue would increase and be more reliable. The support team would be more efficient when they no longer had to support multiple versions. Plus, bugs could be addressed quickly and uniformly when the software is checked each month. I also thought that moving to incremental updates made us better able to respond to customer requests and competitors' features.

What happened since converting to the subscription?

We won't see the full impact until the launch of our next version and the transition of our existing users to the subscription model. But, I can tell you, I have received a lot of pushback from customers whose immediate reaction has been that we are about to gouge them for $349 a month and force them into an endless upgrade cycle. We need to work quickly to educate our customers and promote the value of subscriptions.

Short term, we saw a big spike in sales. Carl was right—a lot of people would buy our software if the entry price were lower. In this first month, we exceeded our goal for new customers by nearly 300 percent. Let's see how many of those users are still subscribed a year from now.

As expected, we took a hit in cash flow. Despite all those new customers, the revenue they generated this month was about half of what we would have earned if we had met our target and sold perpetual licenses. An early issue—only 20 percent of the new customers purchased premium support, which is a significant profit center for us. I didn't expect such a disparity. We need to address this in our selling approach. We are going to have to start managing our customers with an eye on the churn rate.

Authors' Insights

Jamie was monitoring a trend within the industry, gauging the adoption of subscription software. She considered industry information, monitored business events, and evaluated data from within the company to create scenarios of what a subscription model might look like—for her customers, in the market, on the balance sheet, and throughout the company. These are good examples of her applying her Data Savvy and Strategic Mindset.

Much of Jamie's decision was about the most appropriate time to shift to what she had concluded would become the industry standard. She balanced the risk and rewards of moving now versus waiting. There was an opportunity to expand the product's market reach by lowering the acquisition cost. A customer would be worth more, representing a continual line of revenue. She was also keenly aware of how the change would impact her cash flow for the rest of the year. She also identified potential for higher user turnover from price-conscious new customers. Jamie thought about the fiscal implications her decision would have on the health and well-being of the organization. She showed Balanced Decision-Making demonstrated as a function of her market analysis and Financial Awareness. Jamie did not demonstrate effective Customer Focus. She was quick to report how other companies' customers reacted to shifting their pricing models. Yet, never took the time to reach out to even long-time clients to gauge their reaction to what was, by all accounts, a dramatic change in how e-Dine did business.

Turning to People Judgment, Jamie was upfront and honest with her leadership team—she had determined the industry was moving toward subscriptions. This frankness about her motivation and the positive effect the move would have on the company demonstrated a degree of Engagement. The question for her team was—when and how do we get there? We thought Jamie's involving the leadership team to debate approaches to a new pricing model was an excellent example of Team Development. Her key people brought expertise and diverse insights to the debate. Their collaboration led to an agreement that e-Dine needed to adopt a subscription model.

The CFO of Turbine Entertainment Software once told us you must look at industry trends and recognize that some are not negotiable—they will become industry standards. Rather than fight, start thinking about how and when you can make the change work to better your products and services. This type of thinking helped Turbine to early-adopt 3D gaming technologies that are now the foundation of every computer and gaming system. Companies in the PRG are often better equipped to be early adopters of changing standards. Like Jamie did in this scenario, a high-impact leader needs to continually monitor the marketplace, looking for patterns and indicators that suggest a change is not a trend but an industry disruption.

Jamie's leadership decisions' impact across the results categories is difficult to quantify. New sales are up, but will these customers become reliable, long-term users? The shift to a new subscription model means churn rate will become a significant factor in how the organization grows its market and expands the customer base. She has buy-in from her leadership team that will undoubtedly help to build acceptance throughout the company. Financially, monthly revenue is down, but it appears year-end income will meet or exceed company targets. The company must adapt to the timing of incoming cash, which Jamie and her team planned. We have seen the short-term impact of this transition on operations— the e-Dine staff has an influx of customers whom they were not fully prepared to support. This is assuredly a short-term hurdle.

Scorecard

Business Judgment		People Judgment	
①————②——▼——③		①————▼②————③	
Data Savvy	3	Engagement	2
Strategic Mindset	3	Relationship Building	NO
Customer Focus	1	Team Development	2
Financial Awareness	2	Individual Development	NO
Balanced Decision-Making	3	Decisiveness	NO

Results			
↑	↔	↓	↓
Market	People	Financial	Operations

How did you assess Jamie's leadership in this situation? Where do we agree? How do we differ? Why?

How effectively do you monitor and assess changing industry standards?

What could you do differently?

Chapter 22

The Departure

As the third quarter closes and e-Dine readies to launch in a new region, a key member of Jamie's leadership team comes to her to tender a resignation. Jamie is surprised—she never saw it coming, yet everyone else did.

We had to reschedule last week's interview because you were dealing with a critical people event. Let's talk about that.

That's probably a good idea because I was genuinely shocked. I am concerned at how blinded I was to this situation, and I'm starting to wonder if I need to do some things differently if I want to continue to succeed here at e-Dine.

What happened?

Last week, my team and I were all getting ready for our strategic planning meeting, so things were hectic. We have big plans for the fourth quarter, including the latest version of the software and our new launch into the central region. I went to my office and found my VP of sales, Carl, waiting. He was pale and kept looking down. I asked him what was wrong, and he handed me an envelope and said, "I'm so sorry, but as much as I did love my early experience here, it's just not working anymore. I have to leave."

What did you do?

I sat down and asked him what was going on. He said something about this having been a great run and a unique experience that a guy like him, from a corporate background, never thought he would be a part of. "Then why would you want to leave?" I asked him.

I guess those were the magic words. Carl opened with a litany of grievances. Most were about our working relationship—how it had deteriorated to the point where he did not know why he needed to be in the office at all. He told me I have been alienating him for over a year now. As we started growing, I began focusing on the outcomes and less on the people who could help me achieve the things I want for this company. In Carl's case, he thought I have been dictating what I want to be done instead of letting him tell me how he and the sales team can best achieve what e-Dine needs. I don't know. Maybe I should have heard what he said about the impact of Che Jacques on the sales group and our market perception. Maybe he could have found a way to keep Jocko on board. It was the same thing with Roxana. He told me he wanted her in this organization, and I didn't care.

Carl also told me that I have every right to think big and plan for the company. He said that we'd done well. But just because I know I want to do something doesn't mean my closest people understand why. He brought up the whole data issue. How could he help convince the organization of the value of tracking all that field sales data if he had barely come to grips with the implications?

I guess I wasn't always like this. Carl even said, the first four years together, we were productive, had a lot of fun, and he felt like a trusted part of my team. Until this year, he never thought I would make a major decision relating to sales without his buy-in. But he was right. That is not how my approach has been this year. I could see why he felt I don't trust him or need him.

What was your reaction to Carl's perception of your leadership?

At first, I was shocked. Right then and there, I realized he just told me I was not listening. Maybe I had not been for a long time. I got a pit in my stomach. I looked at Carl and said, "I think somewhere and somehow along this journey, I have failed you, and I am sorry." I must tell you, that was an eye-opening event.

What did you consider doing at that point?

Part of me thought of asking him if we could start again—throw out the resignation and clean the slate. I would give him my word things would be better. I do value Carl. He knows the team, has excellent sales insight, and knows how to structure compensation plans. He is the one who is going to make the central region expansion work. Plus, we have the new software launch.

I realized, though, this was the end of the line. You can't go this low and expect things to go back to how they were. Even if Carl were willing to let me turn this around, I would be forever stepping on eggshells in my interactions. I probably should leave this as a sincere apology and thank you, go home, regroup, and plan for how to move ahead. His departure likely meant I would need to put our expansion on hold. We could not launch a new version and simultaneously sell in a new region.

I thought maybe I could find a way to incent Carl to stick around for more than two weeks and help me firm up the plans for the software launch and new region, as well as help onboard his successor.

What did you do?

I wanted to minimize the impact of his exit, both organizationally and financially. I suggested he stick around for forty-five to sixty days to keep the organization steady. I wanted him to spend most of his time focused on the two rollout plans. In exchange, I would give him a cut of the launch. Once I located his successor, I asked that he work with that person for a week to help onboard them and familiarize them with the team and Carl's sales and organization approaches.

What happened?

I don't think Carl was expecting any of this. He told me he was pleased but somewhat surprised that I listened to him and came to see what I had been doing. It is not quite the fairy tale ending I would have hoped for, but it was an effective outcome. Carl agreed to stay on board as I asked.

What did you do next?

We started a search right away. The first few weeks were challenging. Several people internally were jockeying to be promoted. I decided we needed to go outside. We have an exceptional sales team, but the gap in experience between even the most tenured and what we need in a VP of sales was significant. I sat down with the sales group and explained the rationale. We talked a lot about the benefits we would gain by bringing in someone with substantial sales management experience. I also asked for volunteers to join an interview panel to share their feedback on the final candidates. The team was much more amenable to the search after that meeting.

Matt, my HR manager, and I had talked about our goals and a timeline. This was our first executive search, and he knew exactly how to put the process together. I am happy with our hire. Brandon was the national VP of sales from a global restaurant supply company. He had retired early and wanted to focus his energy on something new in the restaurant business. He has the industry knowledge and a network that can grow our sales nationally. So far, he is a good fit with the team. People are excited about the possibilities he represents. Carl spent a week with Brandon before his arrival and then made his exit in just about a month and a half. We are going to delay the central region launch, but only for forty-five days. Brandon is confident he can use Carl's plans and adjust as he gets to know our current sales operations. I have had to spend some time in the field helping, which is more than I would like at this point in our cycle, but our new VP needs to know I support him.

Authors' Insights

Faced with the decision of accepting Carl's resignation, Jamie quickly determined she had few practical options. She was focused enough to think about how she could minimize the damage of his loss on her expansion plans and new software launch—always thinking about her business strategy and how to overcome obstacles that could impact her plans. Jamie's immediate focus on the effect her next steps would have on the fiscal well-being showed her Financial Awareness. We are not surprised by Jamie's consistent Business Judgment.

From the People Judgment lens, Jamie demonstrated a genuine willingness to listen to Carl. In the end, she was honest, acknowledging her role in fracturing the relationship with her VP of sales. Her openness and sincerity likely helped her convince Carl to stay on beyond his intended two weeks. Jamie was equally forthright and open with the sales team regarding choosing to seek a candidate from the outside. Although there may be a bruised ego among the group, we agreed with her read of the room: the salespeople recognize that e-Dine needs an experienced sales executive with industry connections to support continued growth.

We disagreed on Jamie's Decisiveness. Jonas and Jonathan judged her behavior as effective. Jamie considered Carl, the future work environment, and the likelihood the relationship could be repaired. When she decided Carl could not stay, she thought about the short term and persuaded Carl to stay for sixty days. Jamie created a win-win outcome for e-Dine and Carl. Richard disagreed. In his assessment, Jamie did not attempt to reengage Carl, convince him to take back his resignation, and move on. Her rationale that "she would be walking on eggshells" was not a reasonable excuse for a PRG leader.

A long-term effect of Carl's departure may be that Jamie reacts to and communicates with people more effectively in the months and years ahead. She appears to recognize the impact her leadership can have in building and maintaining an organization of driven, thoughtful, committed, and company-centric associates. This is a critical moment in her professional development—an opportunity. Jamie will not become highly effective overnight. If she builds her recognition of and regularly thinks about the behaviors illustrating the various capabilities of People Judgment, her leadership impact will improve.

Jamie's immediate leadership impact throughout e-Dine was primarily negative but could have been significantly worse. Yes, the salesforce lacks a leader in the short term, and the central region's delayed expansion will affect sales. Some long-time associates may be bothered by Carl's departure, but the core constituency, the sales team, appears to have accepted the change. The delays will slow projected revenue growth too; thus, financial results are down. Finally, operations are down for many of the same reasons: a lack of new staff, a transition in leadership, delayed coverage areas, etc.

Scorecard

Business Judgment		People Judgment	
(1)————(2)——▼——(3)		(1)————(2)——▼——(3)	
Data Savvy	NO	Engagement	NO
Strategic Mindset	2	Relationship Building	2
Customer Focus	NO	Team Development	2
Financial Awareness	2	Individual Development	2
Balanced Decision-Making	3	Decisiveness	3
Results			
↓ Market	↔ People	↓ Financial	↓ Operations

How did you assess Jamie's leadership in this situation? Where do we agree? How do we differ? Why?

How have you dealt with the departure of members of your leadership team?

What happened?

What would you do differently?

Chapter 23

High Performer—Low Values

One of e-Dine's senior developers is a superstar. He can code in just about every language, develops algorithms over his morning coffee, and scripts as fast as a sports car on the Autobahn. So why is Jamie talking with her CTO about firing the guy?

Let's talk about a people or staffing issue you had to deal with this quarter.

How about the fact I just fired our top developer?

Tell me more.

As you can imagine, our developers need to be great coders and exceptional team players. Our company culture is extremely collaborative. The technology group doesn't just build our product. They troubleshoot with quality assurance and customer service, help the salespeople, and work closely with marketing to showcase our software. Everyone here follows an unwritten rule: we help each other out because it's good for the company. This brings me to our developer Eric. He had been with us for about a year—came to us from Silicon Valley and started as a senior developer. Our people are good but this guy was a notch above the rest. He was faster, a better problem-solver, and the most efficient coder in the room.

What was the problem with Eric?

Just about everything except his ability to code. He was just a bad fit. Within the development team, he let the junior developers do his grunt work and talked about finished projects as if he were the only contributor. We expect our less-experienced programmers will learn from the senior folks. Eric never helped others troubleshoot their projects or gave them tips to write better code. He wasn't a team player. If a call came in from our QA or tech support group, he would let it roll over to the room where the developers tended to hang out and work. Eric did the bare minimum outside of his official duties, but he quickly told everyone how great his work was. I sat in a few developer meetings with the team and our CTO, Mike. I was rather taken aback by the pompous way Eric talked to Mike and the other developers. I asked Mike about this. He brushed it off as typical prima donna developer behavior.

Over the past six months, I started to understand Eric's impact on the company better. You know, I am all over this place. I see things, hear things, and talk to people. I began asking some of my people, like the head of QA and customer service, about their experiences with Eric. They all had similar stories—not the most likable guy, not a team player, tough to work with. I quickly realized he was not a good fit. Something had to be done.

What did you do?

I went to Mike and told him what I had heard and some of the things I saw. I asked him if he saw the same.

Did he?

He said he did, but he figured that's the price you pay for someone who codes so well. I told him I disagreed. First off, no one is indispensable. Is anyone so valuable that they get a pass on acting like a decent person to others? You can't tell me there is not another developer out there who can do what Eric does. More importantly, although Mike may tolerate it, Eric's professional behavior dragged down his team and the entire organization. I suggested he sit Eric down and try explaining what we expect from everyone at e-Dine. He should spend the next few weeks working closely with Eric and coaching him. Mike said he would give it a try.

What happened?

Nothing. Over the next few weeks, I would ask Mike how things were going. He would tell me he thought they were making some progress. But I did not see any changes. After three weeks, I went to Mike's office and expressed my frustration. I let him know I thought it was time to formally address our expectations and put a timeline on it. He told me he had never fired anyone from his team. I said, "This kind of stuff comes with the territory." If he needed help putting together an improvement plan, he should sit down with Matt from HR who could walk him through the process. I assumed this would be the beginning of the end for Eric, and we would move on. I wasn't so lucky, though.

What do you mean?

Well, a week later, I was coming back from a meeting and walked past the developers' war room. I got there just as Shikha, our QA manager, was looking for a developer to help with an urgent tech issue her team was encountering. The only person in the room was Eric. Shikha told him they had a major problem in the field and needed a developer to come down and remote access the customer's site to work with her field team. This is our practice—when QA escalates something to a level three, one of our developers takes care of it.

I sat there listening as Eric looked at her and said, "You'll have to find someone else—I don't do bugs." Shikha told him this wasn't up for debate; this was a level-three support issue. They needed to address the bug immediately. He again looked at her and replied, "Hey, everybody gets a bug occasionally. They can wait for a while until one of the juniors gets here." At this point, I was about to walk in and take over. Shikha had seen me from the corner of her eye and given me a hand signal as if to say, "I am going to handle this." She asked Eric if he recognized she was not asking him but telling him to go work on the case. He ignored her. Shikha told him she would follow up with Mike later that day and walked out.

I met her in the hall and followed her back to her office. I asked her why she didn't just tell him to get down there or let me tell him. She said his presence would do nothing to help the customer and would make a poor impression. She was planning to text one of our other developers.

This was near the end of the day. I told her to meet me in my office before heading home. I sent an email to Mike and Matt and let them know to be there too. At that point, I was more than annoyed—I was angry. All I knew is that this guy was going to be gone.

What happened next?

I had Shikha tell Mike and Matt about the incident. I told Mike this was it. I wasn't going to have this kind of associate poisoning the company. I asked Matt to fire him for gross insubordination and make sure Eric was out of the building the next day.

What reactions did you get from your people?

Mike was shocked, admitting he never thought Eric was that much trouble, but he agreed.

Matt pushed back. He told me that he and Mike had just

started the performance improvement plan two days earlier. This incident should be documented, but we needed to wait for the forty-five-day period. Matt said he didn't think the incident qualified as grounds for immediate termination. I asked about associates being employed at will. He said this was the case, but that didn't mean you can fire an employee without being prepared. We could face a lawsuit, even if it were a nuisance case. I didn't care. I could not imagine forty-five more days of this guy and the effect he would have on morale and the company culture. I told Matt to get it done tomorrow by the end of the day.

Matt walked Eric out the door the next afternoon.

What happened as a result of your decision to fire Eric?

Surprise—he's suing us for wrongful termination. Our attorney assures us he has no case. I could do without the wasted time, lawyer fees, and all the extra paperwork, but it is what it is.

Fortunately, we were able to find a replacement—a referral from Shikha. So far, she has impressed us all. Here's a sad fact— female developers are a minority in tech and often underrated in large firms. I absolutely believe this woman was a superstar ignored in a Silicon Valley startup, mostly because she was an Indian woman. She is not going to have that problem here. We were lucky with the timing and circumstances. If this had happened a few months later, we would have been right in the crunch of the final development push for our new release and likely behind.

Any other repercussions?

Yes, I'm questioning Mike's ability to lead and manage the developer group in a manner that will support us long term.

227

What are you doing to address your concern?

I'm having bi-weekly meetings with him to review what he's doing to coach and develop his team. I need to help him understand how to lead that group and not just manage them.

Authors' Insights

One of the characteristics of being Success Driven is that PRG leaders often build unique cultures they believe communicate their personal values and help their company succeed. Tom Peters and Robert Waterman's book *In Search of Excellence* confirmed that leaders who emphasized shared values created companies with incredibly powerful cultures focused on achieving remarkable things. Jamie is working to build such a culture at e-Dine. The behavior of one employee, regardless of his considerable abilities, was unacceptable to her.

Everything we observed in this interview related to People Judgment.

Jamie quickly identified Eric's poor fit within her organization because she spends time in the building talking with associates, listening, and observing what is going on. She is aware of the day-to-day operations. We saw that people felt comfortable giving her feedback on an uncomfortable subject—how an associate appeared to get along in the organization. These are examples of Engagement.

Matt outlined genuine concerns about immediately firing Eric. When she told him she did not care about the implications, she was summarily dismissing his counsel. We have seen her do this with Matt and others several times throughout the year. Which leads us to ask: What kind of relationship do you think Jamie is building with Matt and the members of her leadership team? She continues to demonstrate behavior that is less-than-effective Relationship Building.

The decision to fire Eric was made quickly but honestly

communicated. Jamie's rationale was simple—Eric was more than a poor fit. He was toxic to a culture where teamwork and service to the customer were valued. She weighed what she characterized as insubordination heavily in her decision. At this moment, we would say she showed Decisiveness. We will have to see if her decision indeed served the long-term needs of the organization.

On the other hand, she seemed slow to recognize Mike's reluctance to address difficult performance issues but took action because of this situation—also decisive. We need to see how effectively she demonstrates Individual Development in addressing Mike's shortfalls as a leader in the months ahead.

What was Jamie's immediate impact throughout the organization? We saw that Eric's departure made a difference in workplace morale. Associates are less worried about having to deal with the rebel in the technology group. For now, there is no financial impact, but in the future, there could be damages from the lawsuit if Eric's claims hold any merit in court. The team appears to have moved quickly, replacing Eric with what may be a surprisingly great new hire; thus, operations were not affected.

Scorecard

Business Judgment			People Judgment		
①——————②——————③			①——————②——————③		
Data Savvy	NO		Engagement	2	
Strategic Mindset	NO		Relationship Building	1	
Customer Focus	NO		Team Development	NO	
Financial Awareness	NO		Individual Development	1	
Balanced Decision-Making	NO		Decisiveness	3	
Results					
↔	↑		↔	↔	
Market	People		Financial	Operations	

How did you assess Jamie's leadership in this situation? Where do we agree? How do we differ? Why?

How do you evaluate associates' "fit" within your organization?

What have you done when an employee did not align well with your culture?

What would you do differently?

Chapter 24

Feature Creep

With less than four months to launch, Jamie's heads of technology, marketing, quality assurance, and sales are vying to add *one more little thing* into the next version of the e-Dine POS. Among the many last-minute additions are several innovative and competitive features. What, if anything, will Jamie and her team add to the feature set? Could these changes impact the launch?

Tell me about an operational challenge you dealt with this quarter.

I'm not sure how familiar you are with the software industry, but right at the point where your team should be wrapping up a new release's features and focusing solely on testing, it's inevitable that people throughout the organization come up with features they believe must go into the release. We always build a bit of a cushion into the development schedule to allow for features or user experience improvements that add value or bring competitive parity. But the list of late-in-the-game requests is always much bigger than any development team can handle. If you aren't careful, the last-minute stuff can kill a product launch. We call it feature creep. Earlier in the quarter, our CTO, Mike, looked at a list of requests way too big to be accomplished. He had broken the suggestions into categories: not technically achievable, too time-intensive to be realistic, and reasonable to consider. Mike had allocated the time and resources each practical feature would require.

That was when I had to step in.

What did you do?

I had a lot to consider. There's a degree of politics to this process. Feature requests and ideas come from everywhere. Each group thinks their idea will make a significant difference in the customer experience. I wanted to make sure people were heard because you never know where the next big thing will come from. Our associates see and interact with our customers differently. I expect one might propose a solution others never even thought to address. But you also must evaluate how compelling their rationale is. If someone suggests a change that doesn't immediately resonate and make me think that might improve the customer experience, or this would give us an advantage over competitors, it's off the list. We had a lot of those. Rather than having Mike take the heat for rejected requests, I kept track and told him I would send a note to each associate with a thank you and explain why we cannot do everything.

What effect did your follow-up have on associates?

Many thanked me for taking the time to consider their idea. Several said they appreciated the explanation as to why we could not move on with the idea. I think hearing from me makes people feel appreciated and they know their ideas are heard.

How did you proceed to assess the remaining alternatives?

We pared the list of suggestions down to four prospective features we believed represented the most value, and that could be implemented in the time we had left. But we couldn't accommodate all four features.

What were your choices?

We could better integrate with CRM and bulk email services. Our marketing and sales teams believed social media and email marketing had quickly become an important part of every restaurant's operations. Our competitors' products provide better connectivity. Adding a robust set of connectors to major marketing platforms would take less than a week and could be done by a junior developer.

Our new VP of sales, Brandon, wanted us to include more customization options. For example, every screen could be branded with a restaurant's colors, logo, and unique language. The salespeople had seen a product from a new company, UBServed, at a recent tradeshow; this was the prominent feature of their software.

QA wanted to add an AI-powered chatbot—a robot that could chat with customers and handle easy support or route more complex issues to the right people. Integrating the system required practically no time, but the software cost quite a bit—a $250,000 license and a five-cent fee for every chat. The system could handle many easy problems that often take up our support reps' time.

Mike had code for a bar inventory management system his team had made considerable progress in developing. This feature was on our roadmap for version three as part of a complete restaurant inventory system. Besides being a significant new feature, we could bundle this with core components of our POS to create a specialized product for bars and lounges. Mike thought the team could get the feature in and partially tested. We would need a month or two post-launch to finish any bug catching.

Explain your criteria for deciding which features to green-light.

I was most concerned with meeting our launch date and ensuring the release was not a buggy mess. I also thought about how much flexibility I had to invest in initiatives and new business opportunities. With that in mind, I immediately dismissed the idea of customization. I had looked at the UBServed product and researched the company. These guys are barely on the radar. Their POS might be highly customizable, but it doesn't scale. They aren't a competitor we have to worry about.

The AI chatbot was compelling because one of our most significant expenses is customer support. We use a call center service for level-one support, and I would love to reduce those costs. We looked at the supplier's whitepapers and modeled some scenarios against our operations to see the system's potential impact. We thought it could free up potentially eight to ten hours of daily call center time. We were concerned that our customers might perceive a chatbot at the start of the support call as a downgrade in service. At this point, the initial investment plus the transactional cost was more than the cost of those call center reps. As we grow, I can see revisiting such a system.

I decided we would move on to two features—the marketing integrations and the bar inventory system. The competitive analysis was enough to convince me market technology changes over the last twelve months had put us at a disadvantage. We needed to integrate with the CRMs and email systems. The fact the total investment was practically nothing made this an easy decision.

The bar inventory system was a more difficult decision. I believed it would make our product stickier. Our customers would begin using the feature in front of house and be locked in when introducing back-of-house inventory systems. Mike's plan to have the inventory system "almost ready" was not acceptable. I asked if adding another developer would ensure they could stabilize the code and complete field testing. He was optimistic this approach would ensure delivery to our standards. So, we invested $28,000 in a freelancer we reguarly work with—four weeks exclusively on the bar code.

Our team saw the value of this technology as a standalone product. Many wanted to launch the feature as a separate bar and lounge product at the same time as the new POS. We looked at the numbers and saw a substantial horizontal market we could tap into with basically repurposed code. But launching a product is more than the cost of the software. We would have to invest in expanded marketing, bring on additional support staff, and add new salespeople. More importantly, we have our plate full with this software launch and expansion to the central region that is already delayed forty-five days. I was concerned about diluting our capacity and capital. I told the leadership team I agreed this looked like a great new opportunity. But if we launch a new product, we were going to do it right. I suggested we hold off on any new product plans and begin more thorough research. If we still believed this bar and lounge segment was worth the investment, we would adjust for the next fiscal year to properly launch a product.

What kind of results have you seen from your decision?

The bar inventory system and marketing integrations are both feature-locked and are being tested as planned. We are on schedule. Marketing has been doing some teasers of new features this month. We included the bar inventory system in one of the reveals. If our social media feedback is any indicator, that feature will be popular—it has been liked and retweeted more than any other feature in the campaign. The sales team has been getting some positive feedback in the field too.

We have completed more market research and profiled competitive products. We've come to believe this new bar and lounge software represents a significant new market. Our VP of marketing, Denise, and her team just completed a series of focus groups with prospective customers. The feedback was encouraging. In the next ninety days, I would like to be at the point where I can see a long-term plan, evaluate the investment, and get to a go or no-go decision.

Authors' Insights

A former senior product manager for Adobe's flagship Photoshop program told us he often likened the importance of sticking to your product roadmap and timing to a cross-country trip. He reminded his team there was always time to make some stops *but pick them wisely*. If you waste your time on highway sideshows, you will be disappointed. Try to pack in too many detours, and you will ultimately arrive late, lose your reservations, and your long-planned vacation will be less than great (he used a stronger word). Jamie might have heard his advice. She was focused on maximizing the product development cycle while ensuring the launch. But what began as an exercise in restraint resulted in a potential new business opportunity requiring Jamie to consider timing, capacity, and resources.

The software creep was expected. Jamie's CTO knew how to weed out the unachievable projects, but how do you pick the best combination of features? Jamie prioritized her list to ensure delivery of the product to plan and features that represented the most value. Then she said no. Jamie quickly dismissed the option for greater customization by assessing the competitors and determining that although certainly a wow factor, it would not provide any significant competitive advantage. Jamie saw the impact of rapidly changing technology on e-Dine's product and knew the social and email marketing integration was necessary to remain competitive. We suspect that regardless of the cost, this would have been a feature that made it onto the final release candidate. Jamie also advanced code for a bar inventory system that was not planned for another sixteen months. Her team presented compelling data indicating the feature would introduce their current customers to a new service. Once they tried it out in the limited capacity of their bar management, they would naturally transition to the full house inventory system in the future. This was a way to keep customers locked into the e-Dine platform for years to come, or as Jamie would say:

stickiness. These are all great illustrations of Balanced Decision-Making and Data Savvy.

Jamie demonstrated highly effective Financial Awareness. She recognized the improved efficiency the artificial intelligence system represented but could not justify the investment at this stage of the company's growth. The chatbot did not make it into this release. We suspect Jamie has tucked this information away, likely to revisit it when "minutes of service time" becomes an important performance metric. Despite her CTO's willingness to include the bar inventory code with the caveat the release could be prone to a few more bugs than usual, Jamie considered the brand and financial implications of a buggy launch. She chose to invest in a contract developer to ensure the launch went as planned. We noted she was successful in this effort because the extra developer provided a well-defined and discrete deliverable to a development cycle already considered achievable. She was ensuring her results. In our collective experience, leaders are quick to throw more people on an issue to make an unrealistic deadline. Seldom does this work. Time is one finite variable.

We thought it a judicious choice to delay introducing a separate bar and lounge version alongside the new POS release. Yes, the product was basically an extension of the existing IP. Some could argue she was too conservative and may have missed an opportunity. She could have used the current marketing budget to feature both products at launch, and the salespeople would have had more prospects to whom they could sell on day one. Jamie chose to reserve jumping on an opportunity she had not yet defined. Her approach showed strategic thinking—suggesting the company make appropriate investments once they could determine the opportunity and plan a proper long-term strategy.

We saw some things on the People Judgment side worth noting. First, Jamie was aware of the genuine investment associates across e-Dine had in the upcoming release. She knew ideas submitted to Mike were driven by a desire to see the company succeed.

We were impressed Jamie chose to reach out to those whose feature ideas did not make the cut. That degree of honesty and direct communication likely reinforced those associates' affinity for e-Dine. We thought these actions were excellent examples of Engagement. Jamie also had to disappoint some of her key associates when she agreed to develop the bar inventory system but held off launching a separate product. Jamie acknowledged the potential. She challenged the team to work together to create more comprehensive research from which they could build a plan and most successfully execute. This was effective Team Development.

The impact of Jamie's leadership on e-Dine's results is already appearing in the market; feedback on social media and from the field relating to the bar inventory feature has been overwhelmingly positive. For the short term, the new features stand out among other competitive offerings. Her associates are engaged and appear excited about how the next version of e-Dine's POS will shape the marketplace. It was necessary to invest additional funds into the development cycle to ensure a high-quality and timely release. This short-term cost impacted fiscal results, but this investment appears to have kept the day-to-day operations on task. We saw no notable impact operationally.

Scorecard

Business Judgment			People Judgment		
(1) — (2) — ▼ (3)			(1) — (2) — ▼ (3)		
Data Savvy		2	Engagement		3
Strategic Mindset		3	Relationship Building		NO
Customer Focus		NO	Team Development		2
Financial Awareness		3	Individual Development		NO
Balanced Decision-Making		3	Decisiveness		NO
Results					
↑ Market	↑ People		↓ Financial	↔ Operations	

How did you assess Jamie's leadership in this situation? Where do we agree? How do we differ? Why?

How have you dealt with your industry's version of feature creep?

What were your best feature adds?

What would you have done differently?

Q3: Terry

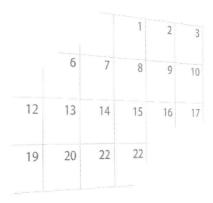

Chapter 25

Holes in the Cheese

In the past few years, the Eat Fresh cheese department has grown in size and popularity. The cheese shop is practically a destination within the store. The variety of fine cheeses and charcuterie, while impressive, has become unwieldy and many of the products are not profitable. Terry must evaluate the offering and decide the value and focus high-end cheeses should be within his business.

Tell me about a business challenge you dealt with this quarter.

Ever since my parents started the store, we have had a small area or counter dedicated to cheeses. We did this because we saw similar stores abroad, and my uncle's store all had large cheese sections. The cheese area, we felt, gave us an international touch and made the stores feel more exclusive. This is an integral part of making the customer feel special since a high-end image is key for our pricing structure—organic foods are still more expensive than non-organic.

We decided to expand the cheese area in the stores during a leadership meeting at the beginning of the year. We went from an unmanned counter to a large counter with a dedicated person. We went from pre-cut pieces to custom-cutting cheese, so you can get any cheese in any size you want. We went from roughly thirty kinds of cheese at the start of the year to offering almost one hundred different cheeses. It's been quite the hit. Some of our customers come to Eat Fresh just to buy a particular cheese.

How was this a business challenge?

241

You would think anything that increases traffic to the store is a great thing. However, George, my head of finance, and I saw our cheese revenues continued to grow steadily, but our profits did not. We thought it was important to address this since our acquisition costs were higher than planned. I wanted to focus on improving profits and cash, or we would be in a lot of trouble. An area that grows in revenue and doesn't grow in profits usually burns cash.

What did you do?

We did a thorough analysis of all the cheeses. We looked at their margin and turnover velocity. We found that about 20 percent of the cheeses generated 80 percent of the profits.

Of course, that created the big question: what do we do now? Do we reduce the number of cheeses and focus on the ones giving us the highest profits, or do we keep the current assortment, as it is an important part of our image and creates pull to the stores? Our problem was, we didn't know how many customers came to the stores for our cheeses. We knew from anecdotal evidence some customers came primarily to buy cheese, but not how many. We could naturally do a survey, but that would take months, and I didn't feel we had the time for that.

How did you decide what to do?

We looked at basket size (for how many dollars) when cheese was included in the purchase. We looked mainly at the baskets that did not have our bestselling cheeses—the ones we knew weren't as popular or profitable. We were trying to figure out if the people coming in were mainly coming to buy our not-as-profitable cheeses and how much we would potentially stand to lose. On average, we saw that their purchases were smaller than our average basket size in both the number of items and total of the purchase for the customers who bought the less-popular cheeses.

Knowing these facts, we could either raise the not-so-profitable and popular cheeses' prices or just take them out of our assortment. As the baskets were generally smaller for these customers, we decided to reduce the variety, as we felt it would reduce revenues more than profits. It would improve our balance sheet of capital tied up in inventory which meant freed-up cash.

We decided to keep fifty-four cheeses because they were high-volume cheeses or had decent volume and a reasonable profit margin.

Who was involved in the decision other than you and George?

When George and I presented this at our weekly leadership meeting, Paul, our head of sales, thought it was a terrible idea. He said many people appreciate Eat Fresh for, among other things, its large cheese assortment. They might not always come here to buy cheese; they come to Eat Fresh for an experience of great products, mostly healthy, that they couldn't find elsewhere. Paul insisted that looking at the basket size and not-so-popular cheeses alone was a flawed analysis. Our approach did not consider a possible loss of customers who might not feel Eat Fresh was so unique.

Your reaction to Paul's objections?

I thought Paul had some good points, but George and I were fairly convinced we needed to do this, even if it meant taking a hit on how customers perceive us. Right now, it was more important to preserve cash and get profits up. I let Paul know he could very well be correct, but we needed to focus on the short term.

What effect has your decision had on the business?

Frankly, it's too early to tell. We know we haven't seen a drop in sales or profits, but we don't know the long-term impact on customers or the ultimate financial impact. I firmly believe we will see it has freed up cash, which will help keep our credit line at a reasonable level. It will also free up resources to be utilized more productively. Dealing with this situation has given me a greater insight into how the number of SKUs we carry impacts our financial performance and everyone in the logistics chain— finding the right balance is important. I think we hit the optimal balance with the cheeses.

Authors' Insights

In the 1990s, the *Boston Consulting Group* introduced a strategic framework called *Portfolio Analysis*—it remains a popular tool for developing business strategy. Despite the foreboding name, the approach is logical and extremely valuable. The analysis asks you to look at your products and services in four categories: *Stars, Problem Children, Cash Cows, and Dogs.* The meanings of the category titles are self-explanatory. If you know what your mix of products and services looks like, you can better decide where to invest your resources and efforts. Terry's cheese bar was part of the Eat Fresh portfolio. He quickly determined several kinds of cheese (SKUs) were "Dogs" and took quick action. Below, we will take a look at the effectiveness and implications of his actions. In the meantime, remember that regularly reviewing your products and services via whatever process makes sense is one of your keys to success.

Terry's financial acumen is on full display in this scenario, as evidenced by his quick identification of increasing revenue from the cheese counter but not a commensurate increase in profit. The authors had differing opinions on the strength of Business Judgment demonstrated by Terry. One perspective recognizes him for quickly identifying the issue, doing some analysis to validate his initial assessment, and taking timely action. As a result, he reduced the SKUs, reassigned resources, and potentially maintained his cash flow and profitability. Overall, strong Business Judgment through Balanced Decision-Making and Financial Awareness, as well as a modicum of Data Savvy. Also, Terry learned an important lesson related to controlling the number of SKUs, which is a valid and equally important lesson for most business leaders, not just those in the retail space—any company can fall into the trap of creating too many product or service variations.

That is one perspective, and it's valid. The chairman and CEO of a major insurance company once reacted to an automated forecasting model by saying: "If this thing is so smart, I could fire half my leadership team." We mention this as a reminder—there are no right or wrong answers to how leaders handle complex situations. Their effectiveness is measured by both short- and long-term results and implications for associates and customers. In this case, it is too early to know what the long-term effects and impact may be, but Terry is hopeful.

A second perspective takes a broader and more temporally measured perspective. First, Terry indicated the leadership team decided to increase the cheese selection and specify a manned counter for display and sales at the beginning of the year. It was a continuation of the high-end image that supported Eat Fresh's pricing structure. They had grown from thirty kinds of cheese to a selection of well over a hundred. Interesting to note that just six to nine months later, Terry has reduced the selection to 54 cheeses and done away with the dedicated employee assistance at the counter.

One might question the speed or the reactionary nature of Terry's decision. He was very concerned with "burning cash," but did he accurately assess the burn rate's amount or timing? Was his analysis of market basket size for nonprofitable cheeses as in-depth and comprehensive as it could have been for a decision of this magnitude? He knew a customer survey would provide him more information from which to make his decision, but he said it would take too long. As a result, he went ahead with his decision summarized above—reduced SKUs and reallocated resources. Authors on this side of Terry's performance saw a leader who committed to maintaining his high-end image fewer than nine months ago reverse course. Terry's reversal was based on short-term, less-than-clear financial information; shallow and less-than-comprehensive analysis of customer impact; no customer input; and a deep concern with burning cash. This viewpoint yields a less-than-effective evaluation for Terry in Business Judgment predicated on ineffective Data Savvy, a lack of Customer Focus, and Balanced Decision-Making. As a result, Terry tended to be much more reactive than strategic in dealing with this situation. He illustrated a less-than-effective Strategic Mindset given that his decision was inconsistent with his vision for Eat Fresh.

On the People Judgment side of the ledger, Terry presented his and George's decision to his leadership team, who strongly supported the increased cheese initiative less than nine months earlier. Although Terry's head of sales voiced his perspective that the data analysis was inappropriate and shallow, he also provided a customer viewpoint consistent with the initial ideas for creating the specialty cheese area. Terry conceded that Paul might have made some good points, but he was convinced he should move ahead even if it "meant taking a hit on how customers perceive us." Although Terry engaged his team in discussing the cheeses and sought their feedback, his Engagement was less effective. Why? Because he ultimately did not seriously evaluate or consider what his team had to say. Terry was going through the motions knowing he had already committed himself to his plan for reducing the SKUs.

The lessons here are numerous. Recognizing the impact and implications of too many SKUs is an important one for business leaders. Another is the importance of looking at a decision within the context of time and initial rationale. Terry did not appear to consider the impetus and nature of strategic decisions made only nine months earlier. The importance of appropriate, comprehensive analysis of information, particularly customer information, is clear from this scenario, emphasizing the importance of staff input. Finally, leaders need to be aware their strengths may sometimes be a weakness. Terry has consistently demonstrated strong financial acumen. So strong, he may have been overly swayed by his initial analysis of the revenue/profitability ratio for the cheese section.

Consider how Terry's leadership decisions relating to the selection of rare and gourmet cheeses impacted Eat Fresh results. Customers who once came to his store for a high-end cheese experience have been quickly displaced, so market results are down. We can see that the shrinking selection of offerings somewhat disillusioned Paul. Will other store associates react similarly, and the people impact be more broad-reaching and long-term? Fewer SKUs with higher margins are the recipe for immediate financial improvements in the department. However, the long-term effect of this decision is unclear. Operationally, the smaller assortment of cheeses is much easier to manage.

Scorecard

Business Judgment			People Judgment		
(1) ▼	(2)	(3)	(1) ▼	(2)	(3)
Data Savvy		NO	Engagement	2	
Strategic Mindset	1		Relationship Building	1	
Customer Focus	1		Team Development	NO	
Financial Awareness		3	Individual Development	NO	
Balanced Decision-Making	1		Decisiveness	1	
Results					
↓ Market	↓ People		↑ Financial	↑ Operations	

How did you assess Terry's leadership in this situation? Where do we agree? How do we differ? Why?

How many SKUs, products, or the service equivalent do you feature in your brand families?

What works well for you?

What would you do differently?

Chapter 26

Where's the Beef?

Eat Fresh's largest beef supplier announced its cattle tested positive for a rare disease that warrants the animals' immediate removal from the company's inventory. The outbreak's impact is severe—the supply chain has been compromised for upward of six months. Terry must quickly find a replacement for at least six months to stock his stores. Without a backup vendor and forced to seek alternative suppliers, how will Terry answer the question: *Where's the beef?*

Tell us about an operational issue you experienced this quarter.

We have always worked with one fantastic ranch that supplies all our meats. Their animals roam free on pure, chemical-free land. They are grass-fed, free-range, and 100 percent organic. The quality of the meat is awesome. Somehow, the cows contracted a rare disease that took the entire herd out of commission. They called us and let us know that it would be at least six months before they could deliver meats. The farm needed to treat and remove the animals, disinfect the property, and then purchase various cows to begin repopulating their livestock.

What a disaster. This was certainly terrible news, but for us, it was magnified by the fact that we have worked with this supplier since the beginning. We had no backup plan for suppliers. We had to scramble.

How did you find new suppliers?

Lucky for us, several of our butchers knew other ranches. Some were close, and others farther away. We reached out to a selection that we believed could deliver both the quality and quantity of beef we were looking for. Of the eleven ranches we identified, only two were aware of Eat Fresh. Even if they knew us, we had no relationships with any of them. Not a great start.

What criteria did you use to evaluate the top prospects?

We wanted certified organic meat, but not a lot of ranches can provide that. The most important was that they offered high-quality beef with no hormones in the animals or their food. We preferred they be close to our stores, as providing local products is part of our brand.

What were your choices?

The only supplier that could provide the quantity and selection of the meats we needed did not meet all the criteria to be labeled organic. Their meat could be labeled grass-fed and free-roaming, which is almost like organic to many. They were also hormone-free, and their prices were lower than our current supplier. If we wanted to label the meat organic, we would have to work with two different suppliers whose prices were considerably higher than our current vendor's prices.

How did you make your decision?

The leadership team and I had many tough discussions of the pros and cons between the two alternatives. Do we stick to our brand promise of only selling organic even though it would erode our profits and increase operational complexity since we needed to deal with two suppliers? Or, since it was a limited time that our supplier would be unable to deliver, was the "almost" organic a better choice? Especially considering it would eventually allow us to have two main suppliers instead of relying on one. The customer could choose between an "almost" organic at a lower price or the true organic at a somewhat higher price.

What did you decide?

After a lot of back and forth, we finally decided to go with the two suppliers who could deliver true organic despite the expected erosion of our profits. We thought it was most important that we kept our brand promise of organic and healthy foods. I liked the idea of offering our customers flexibility in the choice of lower price and still great quality meat versus the higher-priced organic. However, the leadership team and I felt that if we nudged on such a core company belief, what does it say about everything else we believe in at Eat Fresh?

The results of your decision?

In the long term, I think we'll be fine, but it does and will have a significant impact on our financials for the next six months. Normally, meat affects our profits the most. It is costly and has a short shelf life. The new meats have higher wholesale costs; shipping is more expensive as they are farther away, plus, additional time and personnel are needed to work with two suppliers, both of whom are new to us. Our head of finance and I worked hard to find ways to improve cash flow, like getting better payment terms with our new suppliers, going to forty-five days instead of the normal thirty days. In the end, we had to increase our line of credit at the bank, which wasn't what we needed right now. We are already struggling as we incurred unexpected costs from the acquisition. I do not want to max-out our primary line of credit.

On the positive side, when our original supplier can deliver again, we will have leverage to negotiate prices with the new suppliers we are working with. We will also hold our head high, as we did not give in on delivering on our core belief. I also think it is critical for us going forward that we don't go back and rely on only having one supplier in areas as important as meat.

Authors' Insights

Terry's supplier dilemma represented a real "gut check" for Terry and his team. Do they stick to their brand promise and take a short-term hit to their profitability, or was it better to slightly bend their promise to maintain a financial equilibrium? Although Terry indicated the temptation to go with the "almost organic" option with its lower costs, he and his team decided to work with two organic but more expensive suppliers. Let's take a look at what we observed and what Terry learned.

First, Terry realized one could not depend on a single supplier. This is a basic business tenet every leader should recognize. We were surprised that Terry, with his years of experience, would not have recognized the dangerous position in which he placed his company by aligning with just one meat supplier. However, these situations can easily develop in fast-paced PRG environments. You establish a relationship with a dependable supplier who represents high quality and provides reasonable pricing. Why look for someone else? Terry's dilemma illustrates why you need contingencies. Operations management practitioners will tell you that although it's important to manage your supply chain with an eye on exclusivity (to secure low costs), the critical consideration is redundancy. Supply chain researcher Thomas Choi and former Flex Supply Chain executive Tom Linton warned businesspeople to stop the decades-long practice of delegating any part of your supply chain to a handful of top suppliers. They demonstrated competition and changing market conditions produce a degree of business volatility executives should now expect throughout an operating cycle—it's risky to be exclusive. To evaluate Terry's leadership behavior in this situation, we will leave the single-supplier issue as a lesson learned and focus instead on how Terry dealt with the problem.

Terry's first actions were to get input from his butchers as to potential suppliers and to meet with his leadership team to discuss the situation and solutions. Terry liked the option of a lower-cost, "almost organic" meat offering, but his team felt strongly about adhering to the Eat Fresh brand promise. Although he recognized the financial implications of choosing the two separate suppliers of organic meats, Terry agreed with his team—the brand was all about delivering the best organic foods, not *almost the best*. Terry's behavior leading to the decision strengthened his team to promote respect and accountability for achieving shared goals. His behavior made a powerful impact on their commitment to the Eat Fresh vision and mission. As a result, Terry demonstrated excellent People Judgment.

From the Business Judgment view, Terry continues to demonstrate strong financial acumen—he knew exactly what the short- and long-term economic impacts of the decision were to go organic and do so with two vendors. In contrast to some other situations where Terry may have over-weighed potentially negative financial implications of a decision, he did not let his Financial Awareness overshadow the importance of staying on brand. Terry put his promise to customers first, illustrating both Strategic Mindset and Customer Focus.

Terry's decision to maintain the quality commitment will not impact market results as the organic meats supply and prices remain the same. However, we immediately recognize a positive effect on people due to the strengthened teamwork and relationships developed within the leadership group. That positive experience will flow through to lower levels of the organization. His decision will have a negative short-term impact on cash flow and profits, thus lowered financial results. There will also likely be some operational challenges resulting from the mix of two new suppliers for several quarters.

Scorecard

Business Judgment			People Judgment		
① ——— ② ▼ ③			① ——— ② ▼ ③		
Data Savvy		NO	Engagement		NO
Strategic Mindset		3	Relationship Building		2
Customer Focus		3	Team Development		3
Financial Awareness		2	Individual Development		NO
Balanced Decision-Making		3	Decisiveness		NO
Results					
↔ Market	↑ People		↓ Financial	↓ Operations	

How did you assess Terry's leadership in this situation? Where do we agree? How do we differ? Why?

What supply chain strategy has been most effective for you operationally and financially?

What parts of your supply chain are less than optimal?

How will you address this situation?

Chapter 27

Culture Clash

Organic Dangle is now part of the Eat Fresh family, but something is wrong. Before the acquisition, the two companies appeared to have similar cultures and shared the same business values. As Terry begins working with his new associates, he sees stark differences between the two organizations. Now, he must find a way to bring two different cultures together.

Tell me about a people challenge you faced this quarter.

The acquisition of the three Organic Dangle stores is complete, but I see some major cultural misalignments I did not identify during the due diligence process. I'm finding it difficult getting the two company cultures aligned. When we looked at Organic Dangle during the acquisition process, they seemed so much like us. They cared about healthy living, organic products, carried high-end quality foods, and we carried many of the same brands. Their employees seemed to believe in Organic Dangle's vision, just like ours at Eat Fresh.

However, now that we have been together for a little while, I notice differences between the two cultures—and they are problematic. I feel it all starts with leadership. At Organic Dangle, they were much more rigid and formally structured. People did what the leaders said and did things according to processes and procedures. At Eat Fresh, we are more informal and encourage our employees to find solutions that solve the problems.

Give me an example.

Sure. Last week we had a sale on a family-sized pack of granola. The sale was so successful that we soon ran out of the item. At Eat Fresh, if a customer came into the store looking for that product and we were out of stock, our people would go out of their way to provide the customer with a fair alternative—like offering them two of the smaller packages for the same price as the family pack. If the same thing happened at the "old" Organic Dangle stores, an associate would just say, "Sorry, we are out of it." If the customer went to a store manager, the manager was likely to make the same offer. But the store manager is not always around to field these types of customer concerns.

We can debate if selling two smaller packages for the price of a large family pack is a good business decision, but it certainly shows that we value our customers and will go out of our way to make them happy.

Other examples?

Yes. Both organizations say they value teamwork. Well, what people mean by teamwork varies quite a bit between the two companies. At Eat Fresh, anybody will jump in and help out, regardless of title, role, or level, if they thought it was needed. At Organic Dangle, teamwork means you can rely on your associates to do their jobs well, and you won't be let down by your peers. They feel teamwork means others' work never lets the team down. People don't expect to jump in and do others' work because they should never need to.

How did you recognize these differences?

I first began to think there was an issue when I was reviewing store staffing hours. The department managers and supervisors at the "old" Organic Dangle stores were working much longer hours. I was also hearing complaints that they seemed to never have enough time to accomplish their daily goals. I started to wonder why. When we rotated people between stores for one reason or another, they would talk to their colleagues about how things were different in the other store. The conversations were always negative—Organic Dangle associates felt like they did a lot more work with little support and direction.

I started to see an "us versus them" mentality instead of one Eat Fresh. If we didn't address it soon, we would get finger-pointing, and the customer experience would be negatively affected.

How did you address the issue?

The first thing I did was sit down with Helen, our head of human resources, and her team. We needed to crystalize the values and culture each organization had. Helen had managed to keep most senior human resource leaders from Organic Dangle on, which was helpful. They brought a distinct insight. The group quickly outlined where the similarities and differences were and what we should look like in the future.

Once we had really defined our values and the culture we wanted, we had the challenge of aligning around and communicating it. I thought it was important that all the employees in both organizations understood and believed in how we act and do things at Eat Fresh. We called it the New Eat Fresh initiative. Still, the human resources head from Organic Dangle said it felt like only the Organic Dangle people had to change. We wanted a combined new culture and way of working.

What was the New Eat Fresh initiative?

We were able to capture the essence of the New Eat Fresh initiative in four simple statements. First, everyone will understand and buy into what Eat Fresh is, how we work, and what the customer experience should be in all our stores. Next, we are open to change to drive efficiency and deliver quality in everything we do for our customers, colleagues, and suppliers. We also need to act as owners, focused on long-term success and always willing to pitch in. Finally, we all share and live the same values.

How did you plan to communicate it?

The human resources team and I came up with three alternatives for communicating the New Eat Fresh initiative and creating the culture around it.

What were they?

The first choice was that I bring all the store managers and heads of our main office groups together. I would review our findings from working with the human resources team. I wanted to make sure they understood where this was coming from. Then we would design a communication plan and material each leader could then bring to their part of the organization and explain what the New Eat Fresh initiative means.

The second choice was to hold two town halls in person (to cover all employees) and launch the New Eat Fresh initiative. I would start by going through the importance of being one Eat Fresh for all stakeholders, employees, customers, and suppliers. Then, I would present the initiative.

The last alternative was to do a series of half-day offsites, starting with the combined leaders, to explain the New Eat Fresh initiative. Then the leaders and I would hold half-day offsites with the employees to refine the outcome from the work we did as leaders.

What did you decide to do?

I thought with the first alternative, where the leaders roll it out, there was a risk the employees wouldn't take it seriously enough to change behavior. I liked the third option, where the employees help craft how we would do things going forward. However, I thought it was too time-consuming and maybe a bit over the top.

I decided on a version of the two town halls. I liked this alternative as this was an important initiative, so it should come from me in person. But I wanted to be more open and have a conversation, so I condensed presenting both the findings and the New Eat Fresh initiative and allowed for a longer, "ask anything you like" question and answer session. I encouraged everyone to ask questions and make comments. I felt this approach worked well. People were connected and happy we addressed this rising tension. Many also said they looked forward to working together more smoothly.

Have you seen changes?

It's early. However, there are some good signs because people are aware and making an effort to figure out how to solve situations as part of the New Eat Fresh.

What type of follow-up are you planning?

None really. I think the sessions we had should be enough. I mean, it allowed the employees to buy into the New Eat Fresh.

Authors' Insights
Study after study has shown the failure rate of mergers and acquisitions is between 70 and 90 percent. Two important factors underlying failure are a clash of cultures and poor communication. Pfeffer and Sutton's bestselling leadership book, *Hard Facts, Dangerous Half-Truths, and Total Nonsense,*

revealed that mergers of equal-size organizations are more likely to fail or have difficulty succeeding. They suggested the acquiring company's culture should dominate.

With that as our backdrop, we can talk about how effectively Terry dealt with his organization's most critical situation. First, when you think about the High Impact Leadership model's[SM] Motivators, Building a Unique Culture is a characteristic of a Success-Driven leader. So, our first question is: *Is Terry highly motivated to build a culture that takes both Eat Fresh and Organic Dangle to a new level based on shared values and expectations?* We think it's fair to say he is highly motivated to create a unique culture for his growing company. He was quick to recognize differences in behavior patterns evidencing themselves in the two organizations. For example, how associates from the two chains thought about teamwork. He also recognized the distinct differences in associate autonomy. The Organic Dangle associates were used to operating within well-defined procedures, whereas Eat Fresh employees had a degree of flexibility and took the initiative to address customer issues. Terry also quickly met with the combined HR team and began to delineate the similarities and differences between the two organizations, define expectations, and plan communication. Those expectations focused on the customer experience, commitment to shared values, and teamwork.

Given the above behaviors, we feel comfortable giving Terry high marks for his inspiration to build an organization of consequence with a unique set of values to which all managers and associates subscribe. The equally important question is: *Did Terry demonstrate the leadership capabilities to bring his motivation and good intentions to fruition?* In other words, was he able to create a sustainable culture, reflecting the best of both organizations and instilling those values into his associates to the degree those values are demonstrated on a day-to-day basis?

We know from the interview what Terry did to facilitate

culture change; however, we will have to look at the opportunities he missed to ensure we have his effectiveness in proper perspective. The first thing he did was work with the combined HR groups to delineate the organizations' similarities and differences. Then, they began to define the expectations for the New Eat Fresh initiative. He and the HR group considered various approaches for communicating the initiative. Terry chose a series of town hall meetings he hosted, during which he answered any questions. Sounds good, right? Well, we will see.

Going to the HR group was fine to begin putting parameters around the initiative, but HR has a limited perspective. He missed the opportunity to involve his managers and leaders in defining expectations and helping design the rollout. As a result, he lost the chance to build better relations with his managers, develop his team, and empower them. From a People Judgment perspective, these were significant overlooked opportunities. When determining how to roll out the New Eat Fresh initiative, Terry and the HR team considered three options: engage the managers to define and communicate expectations; hold two town hall events; or conduct half-day offsites with the managers, who would, in turn, hold half-day options with their associates. Although Terry said he liked the third option, he thought this approach too time-consuming (in other words, too expensive) and over-the-top. As a result, he chose the town halls and made it a one-and-done initiative with no follow-up.

Given the difficulties organizations face in achieving successful mergers, Terry did not demonstrate the leadership capabilities required to ensure the Eat Fresh and Organic Dangle merger's success. His actions did not leverage both companies' best into a New Eat Fresh that will surpass financial and cultural expectations. Although he was quick and resolute, the quality of his decisions was flawed. As a result, we would score him low in Decisiveness and Balanced Decision-Making because his decisions were of a people and business nature. We will give

Terry credit for being Engaged via the town hall meetings, though the lasting impact of those meetings might be minimal. Culture change requires constant attention, reinforcement, and validation, which Terry's approach did not provide.

Some might wonder if Terry should have been more proactive and done something about the culture at the start of the acquisition. He may have been better off had he taken the time to talk with his new and current associates about the "Eat Fresh approach," including the values on which he built the company. The importance of culture may have become more natural and readily understandable than potentially being seen as artificial and contrived.

In the short term, Terry's impact on people may be positive but short-lived at best. His leadership performance in this situation will have a negligible financial or operational impact.

Scorecard

Business Judgment			People Judgment		
① ▼ ② ③			① ▼ ② ③		
Data Savvy		NO	Engagement		2
Strategic Mindset		2	Relationship Building		1
Customer Focus		NO	Team Development		1
Financial Awareness		2	Individual Development		NO
Balanced Decision-Making		1	Decisiveness		1
Results					
↔ Market	↑ People		↔ Financial	↔ Operations	

How did you assess Terry's leadership in this situation? Where do we agree? How do we differ? Why?

How effectively can you articulate your company culture and explain how it affects your success?

How do you ensure your associates engender those values and ideals?

What can you do differently to affect company culture?

Q4: Jamie

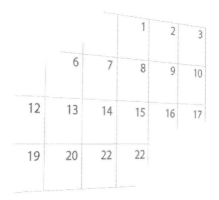

Chapter 28

Social Capital

A prominent and influential prospective customer invites the company to become more involved in a well-known industry charity. Many think e-Dine should be demonstrating more corporate social responsibility (CRS), especially in its industry. But in Jamie's mind, the cost of doing good might be bad for business.

Jamie, looking at this closing quarter, tell me about a unique business issue or opportunity you addressed.

Funny, I recently dealt with a situation involving our company's commitment to social causes. I don't think I ever seriously thought about or planned for a formal corporate social responsibility program at this stage of our company. Honestly, I don't believe I had a CSR component in our long-term strategy. I learned about it in school and read about corporate initiatives in the news almost every day. I guess I just thought that was for bigger companies.

Tell me more about the situation.

Earlier in the quarter, our VP of sales, Brandon, and I attended a fundraising dinner for the Chef's Cooperative, a nationally known charitable organization founded by a famous restaurateur and chef. The Cooperative advocates for healthy eating, delivers fresh foods in urban food deserts, and provides nutrition education worldwide. They do a lot of work to support food service workers. Restaurant workers are more likely to find themselves displaced and in financial need because the industry is often volatile. For example, the 2020 Covid-19 lockdown was particularly hard on restaurants and hospitality workers. The Chef's Cooperative is a great organization. Most of the people who volunteer and support the charity are from our industry.

That evening, we met Ray German. Ray built a small empire of specialty micro-restaurants throughout the East Coast and in the central region where we are about to launch. I wanted to make sure I could do whatever I could to begin building a relationship with the man. We had an instant rapport. Best of all, Ray, not Brandon or I, brought up the topic of e-Dine. He told us he was planning a new chain of Italian grills. He was opening ten or twelve locations in the central region as well as the west. Ray said he had heard many good things about our system and wanted to sit down and see it in action. He admitted his other chains had all been using a homegrown POS that was quickly becoming antiquated. He planned to find a partner with a POS that could serve his needs, start with the new chain, and then work backward to retrofit his other operations. To give you an idea, that looks to be about two hundred restaurants. This was a potentially huge customer.

What did you do next?

After that night, things moved along quickly. Over the next few weeks, we found ourselves with a handshake agreement to install in the twelve new restaurants and discussed how we could start looking at Ray's other chains. During our last meeting, Ray asked me how familiar I was with the Chef's Cooperative. I told him I knew it well and respected the work they did. What I did not know was that Ray is a board member. He proceeded to turn the e-Dine sales call into a Chef's Cooperative sales pitch. Ray emphasized how important it was for companies working in our industry to be visible in the community. He talked about the close-knit culture of the restaurant industry and suggested e-Dine work with the Cooperative; being affiliated with them would bring national visibility and recognition that would be good for business. It was a great pitch. I could see the value the company could garner from being affiliated with this charity. I told Ray we would love to work with them and asked him what he thought we could do. He said he would put some literature and ideas together and send them out the next week.

When his letter arrived, I realized Ray and I had two very different views of e-Dine and what working together meant.

What do you mean?

Ray's letter was a formal invitation to become a corporate sponsor for the charity. Other partners were national restaurant chains, an international commercial appliances manufacturer, a national restaurant supply company, and several other big companies. If you take a minute to think about how well-established and large the existing sponsors are, you probably would not be surprised by the three partnering options. One option was to agree to contribute at least half a million dollars to the Cooperative each year. Another option was an agreement that the company advertises and donates a percentage of a product's sales to the charity. Finally, there was an option to pledge a portion of our yearly sales for the next five years.

None of these were reasonable for a company like ours. We're still growing. Much of what we make we reinvest so we can become a national presence. This year's budget for all donations within the community and those pet projects of key customers is $50,000—and I don't think we've ever exhausted that budget.

I was concerned about the next steps.

What did you do?

First, I called Brandon to ask about the status of the contract for Ray's Italian grills. It was sitting on his desk, waiting to go out in the morning. I told him what I had received and suggested he come to my office. I also asked our VPs of finance and marketing, Perrin and Denise, and Matt from HR, to join us.

I read everyone in. I wanted to ascertain two things: the impact of my saying no to the Chef's Cooperative on the customer relationship we'd begun developing with Ray and the value of working with the Cooperative, regardless of the Ray connection.

Brandon thought we might lose the contract with Ray if we did not work with his charity. I did not. I had begun to build a rapport with this guy. He came to us about the POS. Plus, Ray is passionate about the organization. I saw his invite as a sign he thought we were an impressive company and both organizations would benefit from working together.

The entire team was extremely positive about working with the Chef's Cooperative. Denise felt we were at the point where we should be talking about our corporate social responsibility, and what better a group than one so intimately involved with doing good in our industry. She said, "I can't put a number on it, but having our name up there with those leaders in the hospitality industry would not only make us look bigger and better than every one of our competitors, but everyone in the industry would know our name. There would be a lot of goodwill from our affiliation."

Brandon agreed. Honestly, so did I. But we could not afford to commit to any of the programs Ray had sent me. I was going to go back and talk to Ray. I wanted to explain our position and come prepared with a substantial list of things we could do to partner with the Cooperative. But we had to act fast. For the rest of the afternoon, we brainstormed.

Perrin pulled our charitable giving by line items. I challenged everyone to strike everything they thought we could stop and redirect it to the Chef's Cooperative. We found ourselves with about $20,000 in small donations and community sponsorships we felt we could not stop. That left us about $30,000 in the charitable-giving budget.

Matt explained that we could offer employees pre-tax deductions for charitable contributions to the Chef's Cooperative. E-Dine could also match that amount at any level we saw appropriate. He also suggested a volunteer time off program (VTO). He ran some quick numbers and explained, 79 percent of our associates did not use all eighteen to twenty-one of their Personal Time Off (PTO) days each year. The average use was sixteen. We could create a three- or five-day VTO program specifically for supporting the many Cooperative events. It was unlikely we would be absorbing an extra forty hours off for most employees.

What did you decide?

First and foremost, I wanted to maintain our business relationship. I had to handle this personally and be upfront about our capacity and intentions. I knew there was considerable value to having our name associated with the Cooperative. I desperately wanted that affiliation. I wanted Ray to see where we were as a company and understand why I could not commit to his suggestions. But I wanted to counter with a meaningful package that would be seen as a commitment to long-term partnering.

There had to be a monetary donation. I didn't think $30,000 was substantial, so I took $20,000 from our reserves to make a yearly donation of $50,000. By my estimates, that extra $20,000 would buy us a significant amount of visibility and goodwill.

The employee-giving program was not going to work. My concerns were two-fold. First, I could not afford to match any associate's donation. Second, if we promoted this as a major giving effort and few of our employees gave, the optics would be horrible. I didn't think there was much incentive for our people to give without a match.

I thought the VTO program was a home run for us in terms

of cost-effectiveness and visibility. The five-day program would likely never be fully used by my calculations, much like the PTO time. In the worst case, I would be losing two days of office time if most of our people volunteered at Chef's Cooperative events for five days.

The next morning, I let the team know what I planned to do and asked Brandon to let me deliver the contract to Ray. I called him that afternoon and said we had his contract for the stores, but I wanted to deliver the paperwork in person and spend some time talking about the Chef's Cooperative.

How did you explain your decision to Ray?

That day, although I had the contracts, I kept them aside at first. Even though I knew our business and the charity were not related, I felt it important to begin by talking about the Chef's Cooperative. When Ray asked me what sponsorship e-Dine was planning to do, I said I was afraid we could not commit to any of them. I explained how flattered everyone at e-Dine was to be considered in the same company as many national companies sponsoring the charity, but we are just starting to grow; the company cannot afford to make such large, ongoing financial commitments at this time.

Then I told him how much we were committed to supporting the restaurant community and had come to let him know the Chef's Cooperative would be e-Dine's primary partner in our CSR commitments. I explained the donation and volunteer program and told Ray that e-Dine was committed to supporting the Cooperative more and more as we grew.

What happened?

We won all around. Ray admitted he was, at first, disappointed to hear we would not be participating in the proposed programs.

But he quickly recognized he misjudged e-Dine's capacity to give. He told me he appreciated what appeared to be a genuine interest in his cause. By the end of our conversation, Ray was excited about all we could do. I knew he was happy when he said, "We will both have a lot of great stories to tell about working to support our community." Oh, he also let me know that the POS was never in danger. Ray had been sold on our product well before we even sat down with him. So, we signed a contract for twelve licenses, all with premium support. The initial integration has been excellent. Ray is already talking about the plan for putting our POS into his other chains.

Congratulations. Other results?

Denise and the marketing people are thrilled. The Cooperative has been cross-promoting the new partnership across its website and social media. We've received a lot of earned media. There's a feeling that our national reputation in the industry has increased. This is just anecdotal, but our website page views from the central and eastern regions have spiked. Last week, one of our associates ran into a competitor's rep who jokingly said, "You all have hit the big time."

I am hoping the VTO program begins to get some momentum behind it. Several leadership team members have volunteered at some of the Chef's Cooperative events, and associates have begun volunteering.

Authors' Insights

Michael Porter and Mark Kramer once said, "CSR can be much more than just a cost, constraint, or charitable deed. Approached strategically, it generates opportunity ... and competitive advantage for corporations—while solving pressing social problems." We saw Jamie embrace CSR because she recognized the value e-Dine's commitment to the Chef's

Cooperative brought the company; the initiative increases e-Dine's reputation, building awareness and brand affinity—all of which support her strategic plan and propel growth. Jamie was fortunate she was confronted with an opportunity to adopt a major CSR initiative early in her career. Like many leaders in the PRG, she saw corporate social responsibility as something for larger companies.

There were several things to note on the Business Judgment side. The thorough, efficient, and timely way Jamie reacted to the proposal and chose to respond was impressive. A good example of Balanced Decision-Making.

Jamie was aware of Ray's potential to be a major customer. With restaurants opening in her existing regions and locations in the central and eastern regions, she saw an opportunity to ease her planned entry into those territories and continue her growth. Similarly, we are sure she recognized the good in the Chef's Cooperative work, but what drove her to create and invest in a CSR program with the Cooperative? She made it clear she wanted the affiliation. Jamie knew the more people in the industry heard e-Dine's name as part of the Chef's Cooperative, the more her company's national recognition went up. She saw a competitive advantage that would lead to growth. We have come to expect this kind of strategic thinking from Jamie. Despite being a strong strategic thinker, Jamie was not more focused on CSR opportunities. We are not surprised. As mentioned at the outset, this is one of the blind spots we often see in leaders of companies in PRG environments—CSR is not only the domain of the largest of companies.

We also noted Jamie's consideration of the fiscal implications of giving to the Cooperative. She immediately recognized Ray's original proposal was not reasonable because her growth plans would be compromised. Some leaders may have debated the options and justified the intangibles and affinity their company would receive from such a high-profile affiliation with the charity. When looking at alternative proposals, Jamie carefully considered ways to make meaningful contributions without strapping the company in the months and years ahead.

The choices Jamie made with her people illustrated good People Judgment. She brought her team together and told them about the Chef's Cooperative, asking each their thoughts on the situation and the value of working with the charity. The group overwhelmingly expressed interest. Rather than acknowledging their agreement and deciding how she would engage the Cooperative, Jamie asked all to jump in and brainstorm the best approach. The result was a set of choices representing a CSR program her team was excited to see. In our time with Jamie, she has not regularly demonstrated a penchant for Team Development. Today, she showed she could encourage a group to generate great ideas that better the company.

Jamie's interactions with Ray were open, honest, and demonstrated a sincere interest in creating mutually beneficial outcomes for e-Dine, Ray's restaurants, and the Chef's Cooperative. Jamie could have let the sales contract go out to Ray and followed up about the Chef's Cooperative opportunities after the contract was signed. But she did not want to risk the rapport she had begun building between them. Jamie chose to see Ray, relaying the notion that although his business was valued, their professional relationship was most important to her. Her approach to rejecting Ray's proposals, explaining her position, and then making an offer that was substantial for a company like e-Dine, was appreciated. This was exceptional Relationship Building and Decisiveness, which resulted in the best outcomes for them as individuals and their respective organizations.

Jamie's impact was most notable in the market results. Early indicators, including social media, feedback from the field, prospective customer requests, and media coverage, have spiked. Associates feel good about the company's newfound notoriety. The leadership team provided the early buy-in necessary to further engage associates in the VTO and e-Dine's social mission. Although we are sure everyone at e-Dine would like to think the publicity spike has immediately translated into new sales, we all know those revenues are both difficult to correlate and certainly will not show up in the first month.

Scorecard

Business Judgment		People Judgment	
①————②——▼——③		①————②——▼——③	
Data Savvy	2	Engagement	2
Strategic Mindset	2	Relationship Building	3
Customer Focus	3	Team Development	3
Financial Awareness	3	Individual Development	NO
Balanced Decision-Making	3	Decisiveness	3
Results			
↑	↑	↔	↔
Market	People	Financial	Operations

How did you assess Jamie's leadership in this situation? Where do we agree? How do we differ? Why?

How formal are your organization's CSR commitments and efforts?

What do you do, and how much social capital do they generate?

What would you do differently?

Chapter 29

Coaching Challenge

After firing e-Dine's top programmer, Jamie questioned her CTO's effectiveness in leading the technology team. She was committed to helping him build the skills necessary to develop a group of high-performing associates. Can Jamie *walk the talk* and assist a key associate in becoming a more effective leader?

Earlier, you told us you were planning to work with your chief technology officer to help him lead his people better. Tell us about that effort.

Yes. Mike is my CTO. After the incident where we fired Eric, our most talented developer, I wondered how an associate could have become so problematic without anyone speaking to the issue over his time with us. I was concerned this had not been on Mike's radar, nor had he been working to correct the associate's problematic behavior.

What did you do?

Our developers build the software, but Mike's team also supports several departments. I wanted to know if our problem employee was the exception; so, I talked to the heads of quality assurance, customer service, and the field support group. The feedback indicated our developers were not the best team players I had thought them to be—their timeliness and helpfulness were less than reliable. Two associates on the entire team of nine were consistently reliable. In the past, I had heard complaints about the lack of internal customer service from the technology group and brought it up to Mike on several occasions. He assured me his team was on top of things.

I asked our HR manager, Matt, to walk me through the past two years' performance reviews. I found Mike consistently rated every associate acceptable in the external/internal customer focus category. I noticed he did not make notes on developers' skills or create plans to encourage them to improve their skills. Mike had rated every developer's performance and skills between a 4.5 to a 5 on a scale of 5 but gave no indications of where they were strong or weak.

Now that I had confirmed an issue, I wanted to alert Mike to it and help improve his team outcomes.

How did you do that?

I have weekly one-on-ones with everyone on the leadership team. At the start of the quarter, I told Mike I wanted to talk about his team, what I thought might be some opportunities for them, and how he could make those happen. I told him what I had seen and asked if he saw the same. If so, what was he doing about it?

His response?

Mike told me he knew his team could improve their approach to internal support. He had been trying to lead by example. I told him most people throughout the company said he was the number-one problem solver in our technology group. I questioned if this was really what our CTO should be focusing on. He agreed it was not. Mike told me he is proud of how well his group works together—they cover for each other and are committed to the same goals. I agreed, expressing his ability to get projects done on time and to specification was something I had come to trust and rely on. But that was a narrow view of a great team. I wanted him to consider two things. One, was he as successful in building a group that supports their other team members—the various departments relying on support from the technology team? Second, what was he doing to create high-performing individuals who could make the team more successful? For example, now that Eric was gone, who were the people at Eric's level, or those with the potential to write code and solve problems like he did?

Mike could not answer my questions. He told me he did not think like that but recognized these were approaches he needed to adopt. He was not sure how to pivot from what he thought was his natural leadership style.

What did you do to help Mike achieve those development goals within his team?

Mike has been a senior developer and team leader in no less than four successful software companies, but this is his first time leading a company's technology group. I remembered reading an article in the *Harvard Business Review* about how Apple's approach changed the entire software industry. For decades, developers worked on their own, often in separate locations and seldom working with others. Today, developers collaborate with and support associates from every discipline and department within a company. Mike was great on his team's delivery, but his attention to emphasizing relationships throughout the organization and improving individual performance was not there. Then, I needed to help him to build that mindset and develop top-notch skills in his team.

I suggested we work together to figure out what specific goals he wanted to achieve with his team in the short term and the upcoming year. Then, he and I could determine the best approaches for reaching those goals. We agreed we would take time during our weekly one-on-ones to continually revisit his plan and ensure he was successful.

What results have you seen from Mike and his team?

During the first month, we spent a good deal of time talking about his goals and approaches. Mike wanted to immediately set a new standard for how his team dealt with internal customers. We talked about the best way to bring these expectations to the front of each associate's mind. He went right in and addressed the team's issue, brought Matt in to explain communication best practices, and asked representatives from each of the internal customer groups to sit down with him and the developers to talk about how the technology department impacts the customer. He also sat down with each of his people to identify how they met their internal client responsibilities.

Mike implemented a customer feedback form for anyone requesting help from the tech group—it's the same quick feedback form we use with our external customers. Every day, he gets an update and shares how the group is rated. He also speaks with anyone who does not receive 5 out of 5 ratings. I am impressed with the noticeable change in their performance. More importantly, we can track that performance.

What have you been doing to support Mike?

Things have been quite busy the past month, as you can imagine, with the launch and all. We have not talked much about his team lately. I assume his initial momentum will keep things in the right direction. Come to think of it, I just read a great book about leadership that may be helpful for him. I'm going to order him a copy when we get done talking.

Authors' Insights

Jamie recognized her CTO was overly focused on achieving his team deliverables and was not leading his team to achieve optimal results. Mike had failed to build a collective appreciation among his associates of the importance of serving the internal clients. As a result, departments, including QA, customer service, and field support, were less capable of delivering the superior service on which e-Dine built its reputation. Jamie understood that customers (both internal and external) value fast, solution-oriented, and friendly technical support. This was an example of Customer Focus.

Much of what we observed related to Jamie's People Judgment. Her approach was decisive—soliciting insight from various stakeholders, gathering data, and acting quickly to address the issue thoughtfully but firmly with her CTO. The fact that she was able to collect this feedback and understand the gap came, in part, from her availability throughout the organization. She talked with associates about needs and clarified what was going on internally. These are examples of Engagement.

Jamie identified an area where one of her key people needed help to become a more effective leader. To that end, she talked with Mike about his successes and the areas she recognized he could improve his leadership. She challenged him to identify the opportunity to develop his skills and those of his people accordingly. Together, they created a plan and agreed to talk about his progress regularly. Mike took the ball and ran with it. He took several decisive actions to make his team more collaborative. If we had observed just this initial behavior through the first month as she and Mike worked to address his team's commitment to customer service, we would have collectively said that Jamie demonstrated strong Individual Development behaviors. But there is more to the story.

What happened after four-to-six weeks of regular communication and coaching? Jamie shifted her attention to other operational and business matters and appeared to have left Mike to his own devices. Her commitment was to meet regularly and discuss his short- and long-term goals. They had talked about building a highly skilled team of cutting-edge coders. Did she help him to do this and coach him through the process? No, she did not. Jamie dropped the ball, appearing comfortable her early efforts were enough support for Mike to succeed. She needed to invest more time providing feedback and coaching Mike to ensure he was successful. Well, she did say she was going to send him a book. When we look at Jamie's behavior in the aggregate, she demonstrated what we could only discern to be less-than-effective Individual Development.

Another area we need to point out was her effectiveness in developing Mike and potentially other key people. Why did Jamie need to solicit feedback about the customer service the tech group was providing? Similarly, we found it surprising she had to discover the trend in Mike's performance evaluations of his associates. As his supervisor, we would expect Jamie had reviewed and signed off on these. What does this tell us about her accessibility and her ability to build relationships that require open communications? She appears to have missed some glaring issues for someone who is being genuinely involved and aware of the day-to-day operations. Perhaps an important takeaway here is recognizing that leaders have biases. Sometimes you place more importance on certain types of data and act accordingly. Jamie seems to value the quantifiable metrics, tending to ignore the softer, people-performance data.

We rated Jamie's People Judgment less than effective. She attempted to improve performance across e-Dine by helping a key associate to develop his leadership skills. She did not invest the time to help Mike achieve his goals. Had she continued coaching him, they would have strategized ways to build his people's skill sets. Together, they would have thought of the best approaches for building a truly dynamic and innovative team. Jamie's efforts would have resulted in improved results across the development department, or as we say, she would have moved the mean. And with every incremental move toward better performance, organizations recognize exponential results.

A quick note relating to Jamie's motivation. The High Impact Leadership model^{SM} focuses on two Motivators, one being Industry Passion. A frequent practice of leaders with high Industry Passion is that they read voraciously about their industry. We noticed Jamie's recollection of a current article relating to her industry and her application of that information to help her better assess her current situation. That article, "How Apple is Organizing for Innovation: Experts Leading Experts," was all about the changing role of technology experts in the industry.

As for the impact of Jamie's leadership results? She told us that Mike had achieved noticeable results. His efforts led to improved internal customer service, which, in the short term, equates to increased people and operational results. Long term, we are not confident Mike will achieve his goals without her support.

Scorecard

Business Judgment		People Judgment	
① — ② — ③		① — ② — ③	
Data Savvy	2	Engagement	1
Strategic Mindset	NO	Relationship Building	NO
Customer Focus	2	Team Development	NO
Financial Awareness	NO	Individual Development	1
Balanced Decision-Making	NO	Decisiveness	2
Results			
↔ Market	↑ People	↔ Financial	↑ Operations

How did you assess Jamie's leadership in this situation? Where do we agree? How do we differ? Why?

How do you develop your top people?

What do you do?

What kinds of results are you getting?

What could you do differently?

Chapter 30

Tempted by Growth

As the e-Dine team readies to execute the business plan — releasing the next generation POS system, transitioning to a new pricing model, and expanding to the central region, Jamie sees an opportunity to advance her strategic plan and quickly become a national presence. Can she achieve exponential market growth? Jamie thinks the answer lies in funding. Is there more to the story?

Jamie, tell us about a business strategy challenge you faced this quarter.

This team has done an incredible job of staying focused on implementing our plans. So much so that when I looked at where we were in terms of exposure, market acceptance, and new product rollouts, I thought we might be well-positioned to enter the eastern region sooner than initially thought. I considered accelerating our growth plan.

What did you do?

My goal has been for e-Dine to be a leader in the restaurant support industry. I knew the best approach to growing the brand was to start by region, build a solid reputation, and develop a broad base of loyal customers within each area. Our plan has always been to reinvest our profits into growth. When we started, e-Dine sold in the northwest region, which was rich with our target customers. Our success fueled our expansion to the southwest region in a little more than two and a half years. Now, we are right on schedule to expand from the western region to the central region.

About a month into this quarter, I began to think we might be looking at an opportunity to become a national provider now. Our affiliation with the Chef's Cooperative has given us a lot of exposure, especially in the East. We do not target any advertising to that part of the country and have never had much inquiry from prospective clients. Yet, our web inquiries from restaurant owners in the East have spiked in the past few months. Our name is out there. I thought about how we had planned to enter the eastern region in the future—grow the central region, hit a critical mass of customers, and use a future release of the POS as the entry vehicle. The approach is systematic; gain traction, continue establishing our name, and generate the capital to fund entry into a new market. By that logic, I thought we could reach the eastern region now with additional investment. But that investment was millions, and I would have to find an outside source for the money.

How did you analyze this opportunity?

I knew I had to figure this out quickly. I worked with Perrin, my VP of finance, and my Uncle Bob, who owns a shipping company. He had provided a significant piece of the seed funding I used to start the company. We confirmed the amount of additional investment we needed and began investigating the available funding sources.

What were your options?

Boy, it was tough. A company like e-Dine, despite being successful and growing each day, still finds our plans scrutinized. We do not have the easy access to capital that large companies do and can't raise money in the market. We had several options.

Our bank could issue a loan. It took a lot of handholding,

and the branch VP's advocacy certainly helped us get them on board. The interest rate was on the high side of competitive, but we could service the debt. We also qualified for a government-sponsored, low-interest loan for minority-owned businesses. There were a lot of standards and regulations that went along with the loan.

We looked at some of these new financial technology (fintech) offerings that provide privately backed business loans or crowdsourced funding. The interest rates were well over market. In the case of the crowdsourced services, the funding amount could not be guaranteed—it's like going to an auction and seeing where the bidding ends up.

I reached out to a friend who works in private equity. He was extremely interested. His initial review of our numbers, plans, and the market was incredibly positive. He told me he was willing to take this to his partners and assured me they would agree to do due diligence. If all went to plan, we could not only expect to have the money we needed to fund this effort, but we would also have a partner to help us grow exponentially.

As a last resort, I could put more of my own money into the company. I could not cover the entire amount, though. My uncle told me he would invest if I asked, but he would prefer I look at other sources.

What feedback did you receive from your team?

Perrin was comfortable with the bank loan. She was interested in the government program and thought the lower interest rate gave us more room to manage the debt. If we hit our projections, we could service the loan early. My uncle thought both were reasonable.

No one believed the fintech offerings were feasible. Perrin thought the loans were only suitable for cash-strapped companies with a backlog of receivables. None of us saw e-Dine as the kind of company that could garner large crowdsource backing.

The venture capital option was polarizing. Perrin had worked for two companies that had received VC investments. She noted larger companies had acquired both. She felt we would grow quickly because the nature of VC money is to look for high-growth markets, get in early, and get out with ten times their investment. She said, "It is not patient money."

Bob thought differently. He saw an institutional investor's interest in e-Dine as a sign we were well-positioned to take off. E-Dine would have access to resources, people, and partners within the investors' portfolio. He also pointed out that although this investment was convertible debt, we would look at it like a stock investment—this was not a debt we needed to begin servicing in the short to mid-term. Also, having VC investors meant we had access to additional investment when and if we needed it.

How did you assess the options?

I almost immediately dismissed the fintech options. Despite the low interest rate, I was not inclined to consider the government loan. The oversight and standards made me uncomfortable. The bank was a reasonable choice. We have an excellent relationship with the banking team. I think there is an advantage to keeping your financial services close.

I struggled with the venture capital opportunity. I saw their interest as validation of everything I have worked to do here at e-Dine. I believe they could help us grow quickly. I did have reservations about losing control of my company. My uncle was pushing me to go with them. He called me the night after our meeting and told me I was nuts to turn away from this opportunity. The fact that most companies would not even get a response from an institutional investor told him our industry was high-growth, and we were underestimating just how much impact we could have. I really value his opinion.

What did you decide?

I never had to choose a direction for funding because I decided that trying to reach the East now was too aggressive a move, even with the money.

Why the sudden change?

You know the saying, getting your nose out over your skis? I was doing that. That night, as I was thinking about the financial options, I began focusing on the specifics of simultaneously entering the eastern region. I had allowed myself to get caught up in the opportunity and lost focus on the implementation. I realized—this growth might be achievable financially, but operationally, I was pushing it. The risk of scaling up our operations and staffing to support the growth was incredibly high. I decided this was not an opportunity to invest time and resources into at this time.

How has your business strategy changed as a result of that decision?

For now, we will stay on plan. The new year will kick off with our new POS. Our software will be sold exclusively as a subscription, and e-Dine will officially expand our presence to the central region. But we are not going to wait a year and a half to get to the East.

Market conditions have changed. The opportunity to be a national presence looks different today than it did just nine months ago. After I decided to abandon the immediate expansion, I recognized we could and should work to get there sooner. I brought the leadership team together the following week. I told them what I had been considering and why I abandoned the idea. Now I wanted us to take the next quarter to revisit our current plans and decide when and how we grow to be a national provider.

Bob and I do plan to have another meeting with the venture capital partners. I want to see how they might fit with our revised plans. I think they represent ongoing access to cash that might be helpful to us.

Reaction from your team?

Very positive. We all think e-Dine has the potential to be an industry leader. Everyone is excited that we are at a stage where we can talk about growing earlier than we expected. I think this is a better approach too. I want to keep the team invested.

Authors' Insights

Jamie saw an opportunity to become a national presence in the industry. Her immediate reaction was: *all I need is a source of capital, and we can grow faster than ever expected*. We could not help thinking of a conversation we once had with a national consumer and business bank executive. He opined the biggest problem in the business lending division was business leaders coming in and talking about hyperbolic growth opportunities. Yet, they never could clearly say what happens next and how they planned to support and sustain that growth. PRG leaders are, rightfully, focused on growing their businesses. Jamie's experience is an excellent reminder of how leaders should think about growth—it must be well-planned, measured, and sustainable. With this observation in mind, let's take a closer look at Jamie's approach.

We saw Jamie continually monitoring her business milestones, noting changes across the marketplace and within e-Dine that might represent an opportunity. She believed the company's profile was rising in the East and was wondering how to advance her strategic plan to reach a national audience now. She identified the primary obstacle to this growth— funding. But the catalyst for questioning e-Dine's growth was, from our view, flawed. What other data did she consider beyond the uptick in web traffic from the East? Her sources of data were limited and anecdotal. She did not take the time to thoroughly assess an appropriate range of information to build a compelling case there was a surge in demand and interest. Equally problematic was the impulsiveness that led Jamie to abandon her well-planned approach to building the business. She failed to recognize the impact of such rapid growth on resources, including people and infrastructure. Her thinking was limited to the financial implications. Less-than-effective Data Savvy compromised Jamie's Business Judgment.

Jamie sought out several sources for investment, considering the short- and long-term financial implications of each on the organization. She consulted her VP of finance to ensure she understood the practicality and risk of the choices. Her uncle, an accomplished businessperson and early investor in the company, also provided a perspective. As a result, Jamie could comfortably rank or dismiss the options most appropriate for her and the company. We have come to expect that Jamie would show us this type of Financial Awareness.

Everything Jamie did in this situation was about evaluating a business change, weighing the implications, and making a timely decision that balanced risk and reward. Was there an opportunity to grow? Perhaps. But that opportunity was never validated. Jamie failed to consider resource implications or recognize the impact of time on the growth plan. Instead, she focused on a single factor—how to finance the growth. She did not demonstrate a high degree of Balanced Decision-Making. Jamie was lucky. She recognized she was "over her skis" and chose not to move forward with exploring an expedited launch to the eastern region. By her own account, the feasibility of successfully making that happen was relatively low.

Let's turn to People Judgment. When considering investment opportunities, Jamie went to the appropriate individuals and asked them to advise her. Perrin and her uncle were key stakeholders to consult and expect to have frank debates about the merits of the various funding options. Although we did not see Jamie unduly swayed by her Uncle Bob, we might want to keep an eye out for his potential to be a Derailer as an Informal Influencer. Bob was extremely interested in seeing e-Dine work with venture capital investors. He called Jamie that night to reinforce his opinion. Although Jamie chose to hold on any immediate growth plans, we noticed she and her uncle plan to continue talking with the VC partners.

Jamie shared the change in strategy she had considered over the past few weeks with her key people. She explained the experience convinced her a new possibility lay ahead and challenged them to find the best way to make it happen. Quite frankly, a decision of this magnitude required the input of her leadership team from the outset. Jamie may think the group got excited by the new challenge, but we question if many of her associates wonder how Jamie came to this challenge without any input from her team. For Jamie, effective Team Development would have looked like this: bring people in earlier, trust them to be part of the decision-making process, and create a shared vision for this new growth.

The impact of Jamie's leadership throughout her organization? In the short term, the effect is on people. Key associates like her VP of finance feel trusted and know she values their contributions. Her leadership team has been given a challenge that, collectively, they are ready to make happen. We expect that when news spreads of their intentions to speed up the company's national reach, associates throughout e-Dine will feel charged up about the year that lies ahead. Jamie's decision began with her leadership team. It is likely to spark growth across all the results categories soon.

Scorecard

Business Judgment		People Judgment	
①——②——③		①——▼——②——③	
Data Savvy	1	Engagement	NO
Strategic Mindset	2	Relationship Building	2
Customer Focus	NO	Team Development	1
Financial Awareness	3	Individual Development	NO
Balanced Decision-Making	2	Decisiveness	NO

Results			
↔	↑	↔	↔
Market	People	Financial	Operations

How did you assess Jamie's leadership in this situation? Where do we agree? How do we differ? Why?

Have you experienced a situation like Jamie's, where you might have impulsively reacted to an opportunity?

How did it work out?

What would you do differently?

Q4: Terry

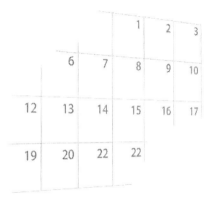

Chapter 31

Change Is Tough

Months after acquiring the Organic Dangle stores, Terry and his team have fully merged the two companies, addressed key cultural differences, and begun streamlining operations. Terry thinks he finally has things in order. But the numbers tell a different story. Although the stores look alike, the former Organic Dangle locations are not as profitable. Why does this acquisition continue to be so challenging?

Tell us about an operational issue you had to address over the last quarter.

As you may recall, during the acquisition process, we saw the Organic Dangle stores were operating at about a 5 percent lower margin than the Eat Fresh stores. We believed if we changed some of the processes, such as purchasing, inventory management, and pricing, so they were like Eat Fresh, our margins would be the same at all locations.

As for shifting the Organic Dangle stores' processes to be similar to the ones at Eat Fresh, it has been difficult to get the employees to change the way they did things. They resisted making the change and always had reasons why the old way was better. You would think they would do what you ask of them after all the training and explaining we did. But no—it was like pulling teeth.

Give us an example.

Sure. Let me give you a simplified explanation of how we manage the purchasing and inventory of beverages.

At Eat Fresh, we work with our main beverage suppliers by committing to spending a specific amount each quarter across all three stores. Store managers have the freedom to forecast and order when and what they need during the quarter. They don't have to consider commitment volumes. Purchasing centrally will reconcile after a quarter if we were over or under the commitment and adjust for the coming quarter. If we are over the commitment amount, it means we lost a little profit, as we could maybe have gotten a higher volume discount. If we end up buying less than the amount we committed to, we pay a minor penalty.

At Organic Dangle, central purchasing always ordered beverages, and they did it on a fixed basis for a quarter. If one store sold more than planned, they wouldn't have enough product at the end of the quarter. If they sold less, they had excess inventory. Purchasing would adjust the future quarter for what they believed would happen. Everything was driven from corporate.

Organic Dangle was centrally controlled, and Eat Fresh allows for more autonomy. How did this become a challenge?

Exactly. The two approaches are so different, and the Organic Dangle employees were stuck in the old way of thinking. For example, Charlie is the store manager at one of the previous Organic Dangle stores. Under our approach to purchasing, he has to forecast and make a judgment call, which made him uncomfortable. He was worried about what it would look like if he had ordered either too much or too little product compared to the commitment. Also, he was not used to speaking to suppliers. He was used to letting purchasing deal and talk to the suppliers. He believed central purchasing had all the numbers and were most qualified to make decisions that would optimize inventory and pricing.

What did you do?

First, I needed him to understand he was closer to what was happening in the stores, and better positioned to make ordering decisions. Charlie could better see what beverages were selling and what was needed.

It was crucial for him to understand that I wasn't so concerned if we went over or under our commitment. It was more important we had the right amount of product in the store. We spent a half-day explaining our approach to purchasing at Eat Fresh, along with training how to do the ordering, and he still had a hard time — not only understanding the numbers but also getting comfortable making the calls.

So, I started letting Charlie spend a few days a week in one of the original Eat Fresh stores working alongside the store manager. I hoped that he could see that what the store manager did wasn't scary or difficult, but different. The store-tag-along's purpose was not only about beverages but also how the stores operated differently. I used beverages as one example of the many things that were different.

Next, he and I spent three to four hours where I asked him questions, like, "How much do you think we lose in revenue and profit if purchasing misses the forecast by 10 percent?" and, "What do you think the impact is on revenue and profit if we sell 10 percent more than planned?" I didn't want him to guess; I wanted him to calculate the results.

It wasn't until he went through the exercise himself that he started to understand why we did it this way at Eat Fresh.

How did your work with Charlie affect his performance?

Once Charlie understood and truly believed in how we did things, he was all in. He has started to build great relationships with several suppliers. More importantly, he has become an advocate among his fellow managers who joined us from Organic Dangle. One of those managers, Jake, emailed me to ask if he could work with an original Eat Fresh store manager in a similar tag-along. I know that request came at Charlie's urging.

Authors' Insights

Profits and people are two of the most significant variables a PRG leader must address to be successful. Add "change" to the equation, and you readily see the complexity of Terry's situation and the potential implications for the success of the new Eat Fresh.

We believe Terry handled this situation effectively, but the more important questions are *why* and *how*—answering the *why* takes us to consider motivation. We know Terry is Success Driven, and his accomplishments are achieved, in part, by his need to build a unique culture. Terry consistently communicates his values. His associates readily see how much he promotes autonomy and their ability to take the initiative (i.e., acting like an owner).

Our point—to engage associates, leaders need to demonstrate their motivation through their behavior. Terry illustrated his belief in the importance of autonomous decision-making as a foundation for Eat Fresh's success. He did so by sticking with Charlie, getting him training, having Charlie spend time with other store managers, and finally, spending a half-day with him. Many less-motivated leaders would have given up and maintained the highly centralized system in the former Organic Dangle stores. Of course, the people impact in both the original Eat Fresh and Organic Dangle stores would have been negative. A "we versus them" culture would certainly develop, and it would ultimately impact the entire company's profits.

The answer to the *why* question is found in one key capability. We know from our history with Terry that he demonstrates and depends on his Financial Awareness as a basis for many decisions. Terry is more than financially aware; he presents a depth of financial acumen. In this scenario, the lagging profitability in the former Organic Dangle stores was the impetus for identifying differences in culture and processes within the newly acquired stores. Terry also demonstrated a sensitivity to customer needs in the beverage example. However, this scenario is more about Terry's People Judgment and motivation than Business Judgment.

First and foremost, Terry made a personally motivated, timely decision from which he did not waver (Decisiveness). He decided all stores would assume the operational and decision-making processes consistent with those of the original Eat Fresh stores. This approach reflected the values that Terry believed made Eat Fresh a great place to work and shop. Although the beverage situation was only one example, it was significant and sufficiently complex to illustrate the depth to which Terry had to go to get one store manager on board.

As illustrated above, the investment in Charlie's development was significant in time and resources, including Terry's time. Charlie needed the focused development Terry provided to enable a shift in mindset and capability relating to autonomous decisions. Terry demonstrated a consistent degree of Engagement throughout the situation. He was there for Charlie to help him internalize the shift. He was also direct and honest in his pursuit of getting the Organic Dangle stores on board. Terry knew it was important for everyone to recognize the value autonomy brought them, and ultimately, their customers.

It is important to note Terry's decision to devote the resources to Charlie's development was a strategic one. Charlie was one of three store managers, each of whom had significant responsibilities and impact on Eat Fresh's success as a whole. As a result, it was a prudent decision for Terry to invest in Charlie. Remember, you as a leader have only so much time in your day. How you invest that time is critical to your success. Pick and choose where and with whom to devote your time and effort. A PRG leader should look to maximize his or her return on investment for their time as well as money. Terry's return? It appears that Charlie has become a pretty good cheerleader for being open to the Eat Fresh operational approaches—perhaps Jake will be the next.

The most significant takeaway from Terry's experience is likely to have impacted him, and perhaps you, the reader. That lesson is: *change is tough.* The need for change comes from the motivation and capability of the leader. Successful transformation requires a steadfast commitment, coupled with patience in helping people lean in and make the change. To successfully introduce change in any organization, a leader must ensure the company's transition is internalized. Individual associates and the mechanisms for achieving this internalization may require varied approaches. But well-considered, business-relevant change is worth the effort.

The results of Terry's leadership are easy to recognize in operational results. As Charlie begins embracing autonomy, processes and day-to-day decisions become more streamlined and efficient. Similarly, when people think like business owners, they typically make decisions supporting customer relationships and saving the company money. Thus, Terry's leadership positively impacts financial results. His effect on people results begins with Charlie, but his commitment to culture change will quickly spread to the newer Eat Fresh store associates, resulting in improved store experiences for the long term.

Scorecard

Business Judgment		People Judgment	
Data Savvy	NO	Engagement	3
Strategic Mindset	3	Relationship Building	NO
Customer Focus	NO	Team Development	NO
Financial Awareness	3	Individual Development	3
Balanced Decision-Making	2	Decisiveness	3

Results

Market	People	Financial	Operations
↔	↑	↑	↑

How did you assess Terry's leadership in this situation? Where do we agree? How do we differ? Why?

What types of significant change issues have you had to institute within your organization?

What worked? Why?

What didn't? Why?

Chapter 32

Know Your Customer

Terry quickly raised prices in the former Organic Dangle stores to match those at the original Eat Fresh locations. Customers have reacted negatively, and many either have stopped coming or buy a lot less. How does Terry get them back?

You mentioned challenges with pricing at the former Organic Dangle stores. Tell us about that.

To get to the same profitability as the original Eat Fresh stores, we not only had to change processes, but we needed to raise the prices. The pricing in our Organic Dangle locations needed to be in line with our other stores — pricing had to be consistent across the brand. Can you imagine what the reaction would be if our long-time customers happened into those newly converted Eat Fresh locations and saw products priced differently? We couldn't have that happen. Also, price is the single biggest driver of profitability and half of my stores were selling high-volume items at a lower margin.

What did you do?

The customers who come to our stores are there mainly for organic, healthy, and quality food. They understand the cost will be more than the alternative, non-organic and bulk-produced foods. So, we raised prices in the Organic Dangle locations to match our original stores. We didn't have to raise all prices — just those of the products carried in all locations.

What consideration did you give to how this change might impact customer traffic and sales?

None. Since the customers in our original Eat Fresh stores seemed to have no problem with our pricing, we thought the Organic Dangle customers would be okay.

What happened?

In all three of the former Organic Dangle stores, we quickly got complaints. There was a notable drop in volume, both in the number of customers and the amount they buy. Customers from the Organic Dangle stores were more sensitive to price than we realized.

What did you do?

Paul, our sales manager, George, head of finance, and I decided we needed to do a more in-depth analysis of the customers in the former Organic Dangle stores. We quickly noticed that the demographics of the customer who came to the Organic Dangle stores were quite different from those of the original Eat Fresh locations—they were generally older, many retired, and with more limited budgets. Both sets of stores' customers cared about eating right, but the Organic Dangle customers couldn't afford to spend the same amount.

What did you consider to address this issue?

We considered a couple of things, but we were not going to lower prices again. That was a non-starter. We couldn't have Eat Fresh in two different but still somewhat close regions with different prices. It would confuse our brand image and it would be impossible to manage two additional cost and profit structures.

We could either figure out how to get back the customers we had lost through targeted marketing and discount incentives on the products we knew they most commonly bought from us, or we could build a new customer base from the people in the area we knew had the resources to shop at Eat Fresh prices. However, before we went there, we needed to take an even more in-depth look at the customer demographics in the areas where the Organic Dangles stores were located. We researched gender, age, ethnic background, etc., and looked at things like health and wellness data and compared them to the Eat Fresh region.

Fortunately, at its core, the demographics and the overall health and wellness of the local region were similar to the one we had in the original Eat Fresh stores. The difference was the Organic Dangle area contained a large segment of senior citizens—and that was the customer Organic Dangle had been targeting. There are plenty of our potential customers matching our key customer profile over there. Actually, the market potential in that region is significantly larger than our original region.

We felt that shifting our focus to attract customers with the same demographic profile we currently serve was the only viable alternative if we wanted to continue to grow Eat Fresh. Otherwise, it would be like us managing several Eat Fresh brands: each with different prices and products. That was going to be too complex, and we were not ready for that.

What did you decide?

First, we don't want to ignore the needs of the older population. We just don't want to do it at our expense. One of the actions we are taking to help satisfy the "older" customers is expanding our product line to include items that are not quite premium quality and offer more affordable price points. We are doing this across all six stores, so hopefully, this will attract more price-sensitive customers to the original Eat Fresh stores. However, our main efforts had to be shifting to the demographic we wanted.

How did you do that?

We knew what channels to leverage to reach the typical Eat Fresh customer. Richard, our marketing head, has been using a focused online marketing approach in our original stores. We found this was the best way of reaching our key demographic. In contrast, the Organic Dangle stores used mostly print and radio commercials, which is more consistent with an older population and exactly why they were more successful. So, we changed our marketing approach.

Why did you continue to stratify your marketing approach after the acquisition?

This has to do with Richard. He really wanted to respect Anne, who oversaw marketing at Organic Dangle. She stayed on with us after the acquisition, which I think was a good call. She knew what worked well in the Organic Dangle region. The thing they did not consider enough was how to begin transitioning the marketing mix to address the company's key customer.

Has the change in marketing strategy reversed the losses you experienced?

It is still too early to tell. It will take time, effort, and money to reach our key demographic. But we identified the customer and now have a solid plan to target them.

Authors' Insights

Harvard business professor Robert Simons urged business leaders to choose the right customer. Doing so requires a focused analysis of a myriad of demographic and market data. Identifying the right or primary customer preferences and values determines what capabilities and resources are necessary to address the customer's needs. Unfortunately, in his haste and enthusiasm to grow via acquisition, Terry did what so many leaders do in the same situation—he failed to analyze and consider a range of data and let his gut lead him to accept faulty assumptions. During the initial due diligence on the acquisition, Terry not only failed to understand the customers he was potentially acquiring, but he also failed to do an analysis of the demographics of the region from which Organic Dangle drew customers. As a result, he and his team were confronted with a profitability issue, which was much more difficult to remedy than they had initially anticipated. It wasn't until he and his team identified the primary and secondary customers that he could directly and effectively address the problem. We will leave this as a lesson learned for Terry, and hopefully, many of you. We will focus our insights and assessment on what he did in this situation some months after the acquisition had been finalized.

This scenario required Terry to make a number of decisions, all of which reflected on his Business Judgment and its associated dimensions. The first issue confronting Terry was identifying the difference in profitability between the former Organic Dangle stores and the Eat Fresh stores. He illustrated a high degree of Financial Awareness by identifying the issue and the cause—pricing. His quick and less-than-measured reaction was to increase the former Organic Dangle stores' prices to the same level as those in the original Eat Fresh stores. The result was a rapid decrease in customers and market basket size. Based on both his haste and the resultant financials, the decision to raise prices across the board was less than judicious.

After recognizing the negative implication of raising prices, Terry began a more measured, analytic approach to addressing his now compounded problem—lower profitability and decreasing customer demand. He started his analysis with a look at his customer base. He found the former Organic Dangle stores had a higher proportion of older retired customers who were more price-sensitive than those in his original stores. Terry considered doing some things to get his former customers back, such as targeted marketing discounts, but decided he needed to expand his analysis to understand the region's demographics better to attract customers. Although he found the older segment of the population was well represented, he also found a much larger population of potential customers whose profile indicated they could well afford to shop at his markets. He quickly decided this was his key market. His challenge was how he would attract them to Eat Fresh. He worked with the head of marketing and his staff to better focus their marketing campaigns. They decided to move away from traditional radio spots and newspaper ads to focus on web and social media (effective Balanced Decision-Making).

Terry made several effective decisions during this scenario. Once he realized the negative financial impact increasing prices across the board was having on the company, he also recognized he could not decrease them. He quickly identified the difficulties in running two different cost and profit structures. He also prioritized the need to find his right customer by doing the regional demographic analysis before expending time and money on attracting back the older customers he had lost. He ultimately made some provisions to get them back by adding less expensive options to high-volume items. It is too soon to tell if that was a good decision. Earlier in the year, he had increased the number of SKUs he had to manage and found it difficult to grow. Then, he decreased the same set of SKUs because of the potential impact on a segment of customers. It will be interesting to see how Terry manages the increase in the number of products (SKUs) to reach the older population while maintaining profitability, so he doesn't end up in the same dilemma as with the cheeses.

What Terry learned from addressing this situation represents important lessons for all of us: recognize price is the single biggest driver of profitability; know both your customers and the demographics of potential customers in your market; complete the depth of analysis required to identify your right customer; bridle your enthusiasm and instincts until you test your assumptions about potential problems; understand the underlying financial, operational, and resource implications of duplicate processes and systems; take nothing for granted, make no assumptions, and ensure your due diligence process is thorough.

Terry's leadership in this situation negatively impacted profitability in the short term. The newer stores lost customers, and that loss is immediately seen in the top-line revenue numbers and customer churn. The changes in pricing and marketing to the key customer will ultimately drive these results up in the future. His recognition of the issue and action is likely to neutralize any further customer loss or negative market results. No significant impacts across the other results categories were observed.

Scorecard

Business Judgment			People Judgment		
(1) ———— (2) —▼— (3)			(1) ———— (2) ———— (3)		
Data Savvy		3	Engagement		NO
Strategic Mindset		2	Relationship Building		NO
Customer Focus		3	Team Development		NO
Financial Awareness		3	Individual Development		NO
Balanced Decision-Making		2	Decisiveness		NO
Results					
↔ Market		↔ People	↓ Financial		↔ Operations

How did you assess Terry's leadership in this situation? Where do we agree? How do we differ? Why?

How well do you know your customers?

What could you do to better understand current and

prospective customers?

How important are the demographics of your market to your business's success? Why?

Chapter 33

Old Dogs, New Tricks

Eat Fresh has experienced several salary and pay issues, as well as a harassment suit. Helen and the human resources team are overloaded. Implementing the people-management system that Terry previously dismissed as bureaucratic and costly is now considered an imperative. Even though everyone agrees Eat Fresh needs the system, Terry finds himself struggling to get his leaders to adopt and use it. How can Terry get leaders to use something they all agreed necessary for the company's continued success?

Tell me about a significant challenge you had to address this quarter.

Several major HR issues came up recently. A new group of hourly employees finished their first week of work. Employees choose the method to be paid—paper check or direct deposit. But because it takes time to set up accounts, everyone's first paycheck is always a paper check. In this case, the new associates either didn't get paid or received the wrong amount. It took us two pay periods to correct the errors. It was embarrassing. This was their first important interaction with their employer, and we screwed it up. Plus, many of these people live paycheck to paycheck, and they can't afford not to get paid.

Another big issue was we have an employee who has filed a harassment lawsuit because of one store manager, Kimberly's, actions. Kimberly had no idea she had done anything wrong. If she had taken our harassment training, she would have known what she did was not appropriate—

and organizationally, we could say that we provided that clear guidance. The thing is, she did not complete the training because she had been too busy, even though it is required for all managerial-level staff.

To what do you attribute these problems?

Helen, our head of human resources, said the HR department is simply understaffed and overwhelmed with work. The mistake with the salaries was human error. The person who does that work is more than capable, but too many things were happening, resulting in his misreporting the new employees' information. As for the lawsuit, HR had invited Kimberly to the training but was unaware she hadn't completed it. Helen said if the people-management system had been in place, the likelihood of these two things happening would have been small. She felt we needed to implement the system as soon as possible.

Your reaction?

Seeing the problems and the reasons each occurred convinced me we needed the people-management system now. I told Helen I had made a mistake regarding the system, and I was sorry for not understanding her better. At the time, I felt that we had too much to do after the acquisition, and the organization was not ready. I still thought we weren't prepared. Helen knows I try to make the best decisions with the facts I have on hand. So, after she poked some fun at me, we began planning how to implement the people-management system.

We met with the rest of the leadership team. Everyone quickly agreed we needed to make this a priority—even the leaders who were against it a few months earlier. They recognized how inefficient our processes had become. They saw we were making needless and costly mistakes. There is nothing like a lawsuit and upset employees to get you to change your mind and put you into high gear.

How did you plan to implement?

Before anything else could be done, a central component needed installing at our corporate offices. While that was happening, our first step was to get the store-level technology in place and ensure the leadership team and store managers knew how to use the system. We began in the former Organic Dangle stores. They had used the system before, so they had all the necessary hardware in place, and all we had to do was update the software. Fortunately, almost all the people in management positions were still there, so there wasn't a lot of training needed.

Next, we installed the software in our original Eat Fresh stores. Technologically, it wasn't too difficult, even though we ran into challenges and had to upgrade some of our hardware. We had pretty extensive training on the system with our store managers and their key people.

As for us in the management team, Helen took us through the training.

When we were ready to launch throughout the company, managers across each store were able to train our associates to use the software.

How successful was the launch and subsequent adoption?

I can't say it has been a home run. Many people were excited to get rid of a lot of the manual record keeping and work they had to do before. Helen's team is certainly pleased and already showing how much more productive they can be now that certain processes have been automated. However, some managers in the original Eat Fresh stores have been slow to adopt. They feel their old way of doing things was easier and didn't require them to enter a bunch of seemingly irrelevant information.

That brings me to my leadership team. They have been terrible, except Helen. They know we must have this, and they agreed that we install it. Yet they find every excuse they can for why they can't use it. They are either too busy; they have more important things to do, etc. Sure, in the beginning, there's a lot of information that needs entering to get the system up and running, but once that is done, it's extremely efficient.

How did you address the issue with your team?

I let them know, we can't agree and invest in things and then not use them. There is enormous value in this system — for everyone in the company. But the software requires a baseline of data before it is fully up and running. If we are going to continue to grow, we need this and other systems in place. What kind of example do they set as leaders if they say others must use it and don't use it themselves? I think a big reason for the store managers not fully using it is that they see that the management team hasn't adopted it.

How did you ensure adoption?

I thought they would come around and use it. However, to speed up the process, Helen and I decided to use the management team and store managers' bonus plans to incentivize system usage. Also, we had the store managers from the former Organic Dangle stores come in and sit down with the management team and the store managers from the original Eat Fresh stores and show us how they use it and talk about the value they get out of it.

How were those decisions received?

They grumbled a bit about the bonus, but they all knew that was probably the best way to force them to use the system.

I think the previous Organic Dangle store managers were influential. Each went through how they had previously used the software. They explained how the system would make things easier and ensure we didn't make big errors. Each was visibly excited to have the people-management system back and running in their stores. That enthusiasm sold a lot of people.

Authors' Insights

From a leadership perspective, this scenario might more aptly be titled: *Better Late than Never, Nothing Like Problems to Change Your Perspective*, or *Hindsight Is 20/20*. You may recall when debating the implementation of a people-management system arose soon after the acquisition of Organic Dangle, Terry was quick to dismiss it for several reasons: too much to do, too early after the acquisition, too bureaucratic, and, most importantly, it diminished the entrepreneurial spirit and culture he was trying to build. Terry's knee-jerk reaction at the time also precluded him from recognizing the long-term value and benefits. His lack of a more strategic perspective led him to reject implementing the system. Let's see what he did to support the system implementation at this point.

This scenario represents a relatively simple situation requiring a straightforward response and set of actions by the PRG leader. Terry's actions represent an effective set of responses to the immediate situation. He quickly recognized the value of implementing the people-management system across all stores. He realized he had to acknowledge his error in judgment by initially minimizing the importance of the system. His apology, coupled with quickly entrusting implementation responsibilities to Helen, did a great deal to improve his relationship with her. Terry's support also demonstrated his commitment to successful implementation. Most importantly, Terry was Decisive by mandating adoption of the people-management system as quickly as possible.

Terry quickly recognized mandating something does not always yield the results you may be looking for. His inclination was to attribute his team's reluctance to adopt the system to old dogs not wanting to learn new tricks. Unwilling managers (old dogs) may have been part of the problem, but perhaps the "lead dog" contributed to the situation. Although Terry stated his commitment to the new system, he never personally and formally communicated the people-management system's value and benefits to his team members, nor was he visible during the implementation process. According to Terry, he and Helen chose to incent utilization by adopting the management bonus. Although team members grumbled, they went along with the bonus idea. Does it sound like Terry missed an opportunity to engage his team in what it would take to maximize their involvement? Could he have demonstrated the value the new system brought the company and each associate? As PRG leaders, you know the importance of clear, frequent, and direct communication of change initiatives; it is critical to organizational adoption and success. The message needs to come regularly from leaders and informal influencers throughout your company. Without such effort, studies from researchers like *The Center for Change Leadership* suggest a little more than half (54 percent) of all major change efforts fail.

Another possible issue with the "lead dog" was the sequence and prioritization of implementation and learning during execution. Terry stated they started with the former Organic Dangle stores supported by a lot of training and then came to the original Eat Fresh stores. It was not clear to us if the implementation took place one store at a time, two at a time, etc. Also, we heard nothing about the incremental learning and best practices Terry's team developed as they implemented the system from one store to the next. Although the former Organic Dangle store managers were asked to help train the Eat Fresh managers, this sounded like an ad-hoc move resulting from the Eat Fresh managers' difficulties. Terry's leadership effectiveness and impact in this scenario represent some strong positives, particularly his Decisiveness. But some missed opportunities would have helped the implementation move more quickly and smoothly.

Let's return to the three titles we suggested that may be areas of critical learning for Terry: *Better Late than Never, Nothing Like Problems to Change Your Perspective,* or *Hindsight Is 20/20.*

We think it is fair to say that Terry's initial meeting with Helen demonstrated he was ready to go and recognized that adopting the people-management system was better late than never. He also stated there was nothing like a lawsuit and employee issues to get one's attention; so, problems were an impetus to his new perspective on the need for the system. Finally, did Terry look at this situation in retrospect to gain some 20/20 hindsight? We think not. Although he apologized to Helen for not initially implementing the system, he restated his rationale for not doing so—it originally was too much to do after the acquisition, the organization was not ready. He also commented during his conversation that Helen "knew he made decisions based on the facts at the time." Such statements indicated Terry did not think of the missed opportunities to solicit more information about the benefits of implementation, weigh the financial implications of implementation, recognize the operational burdens he placed on HR, nor think about the long-term impact on his vision for the company. Terry did not appear to reap the benefits of hindsight nor change his tendency to overreact to a particular issue rather than step back, collect information, and think about the long- and short-term implications of his decisions.

The impacts of Terry's leadership in this situation were largely negative. Store associates are learning a new process, and few have been sold on the value. This change is affecting organizational morale and, thus, driving down people results.

In the short term, operations are also negatively impacted as the Eat Fresh employees master the new systems and processes. Financially, there was an immediate cost relating to phasing out the old system's investment and inefficiencies.

Scorecard

Business Judgment		People Judgment	
①————②————③		①————②————③	
Data Savvy	NO	Engagement	2
Strategic Mindset	NO	Relationship Building	2
Customer Focus	NO	Team Development	1
Financial Awareness	NO	Individual Development	NO
Balanced Decision-Making	NO	Decisiveness	3
Results			
↔	↓	↓	↓
Market	People	Financial	Operations

How did you assess Terry's leadership in this situation? Where do we agree? How do we differ? Why?

How have you dealt with comparable change initiatives?

What did you learn?

What would you do differently?

Year End
Insights and Results

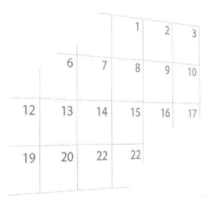

Chapter 34

Summary Insights

We have been on an interesting journey with Terry and Jamie. We observed them addressing various issues, opportunities, problems, and challenges for a year. After each scenario, we provided our insights into what capabilities a leader demonstrated, the degree of effectiveness they exhibited, and the impact of their leadership on organizational results (as best we could forecast such an impact). We invited you to compare your insights and assessments with ours and evaluate your effectiveness in comparable situations. Hopefully, this process has helped you understand the High Impact Leadership model[SM] better. The model provides both a structure for thinking about leadership effectiveness and a process for evaluating and developing the capabilities you need to lead in the PRG environment successfully.

After a year of one-on-one interviews and evaluations, we wanted to end our time with Jamie and Terry, summarizing our perspective more quantitatively. We will aggregate our assessments from the year, illustrate overall levels of effectiveness per capability, and develop a profile for each leader. The profile will highlight relative strengths and areas where our leaders should focus their development if they hope to achieve maximum impact on the success of their respective organizations. We will also identify and discuss areas that may represent a Derailer to a leader's success, if not tempered appropriately. Finally, we will link Terry's and Jamie's effectiveness with the results achieved across their respective organizations for the year.

Frequency Data

Let's discuss the frequency with which our leaders demonstrated the capabilities underlying Business and People Judgment. We observed Terry and Jamie address thirteen and fifteen scenarios, respectively. Although some of the scenarios were more Business Judgment-focused, our leaders could expand the scope and be more cognizant of the people implications of the issue, thus demonstrating some People Judgment behaviors. The opposite was also true. Some scenarios were People Judgment-focused while allowing the leader to interject Business Judgment behavior on the situation. Our point is that *leaders have the flexibility to deal with comparable situations in different ways*, applying different capabilities to the problem. A leader's ability to solve a problem depends on how each evaluates the situation and the leader's confidence in applying the most appropriate behavior to achieve a positive outcome. Remember, there is seldom a right or wrong answer to how a leader addresses a situation. But there are positive and negative implications as well as impacts stemming from their behaviors. Also important is that leaders are often not cognizant of the capabilities they need to address a situation. They simply evaluate the set of circumstances and choose a course of action they believe will produce the best outcome.

We've used the model to identify and evaluate the capabilities Jamie or Terry demonstrated. Our objective has been to make you more aware of the capabilities required of a leader, ensuring you are more aware of those capabilities and selecting the most appropriate behavior to make key critical decisions. Think of it as developing *muscle memory* but between your ears.

We are going to initially look at the frequency with which each leader demonstrated the capabilities for Business and People Judgment. We can identify trends and link the behavioral frequency to Jamie's and Terry's leadership effectiveness from these data. Ultimately, we will use the frequency and effectiveness data to create leadership profiles for each.

Terry

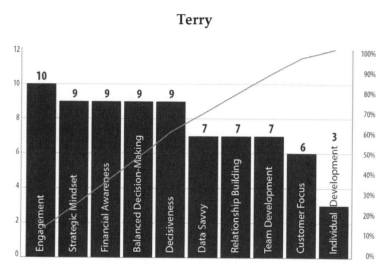

Figure 1:
Pareto chart describing Terry's capabilities observed over the year

Figure 1 illustrates the frequency with which Terry demonstrated the capabilities that define Business and People Judgment throughout thirteen scenarios we observed over the year. Terry's frequency profile tells us quite a bit about how he approaches challenges. Terry is consistent. He regularly relies on an assortment of capabilities with which he is comfortable and capable. For example, he demonstrated Engagement in ten of the thirteen scenarios (77 percent of the time). This should be no surprise since nearly all the events in which we observed Terry required a degree of awareness and responsiveness to associates.

The next most demonstrated capabilities were Strategic Mindset, Financial Awareness, Balanced Decision-Making, and Decisiveness (70 percent of the time). The frequency of behaviors is somewhat predictable. Each scenario required either a Business or People decision heavily reliant on Balanced Decision-Making and Decisiveness, respectively. We have come to expect Terry to depend on his financial acumen as either the basis for deciding or the impetus for identifying a situation that needs a decision.

In the five less frequently used capabilities, Terry used Data Savvy, Relationship Building, and Team Development in seven out of thirteen instances, with Customer Focus slightly less at six (all at or above 50 percent). The glaring deficit in frequency was Terry's demonstration of the Individual Development capability—three occurrences observed over the year. However, the opportunities to work with his staff on development opportunities presented themselves on a number of occasions. For example, all three store managers would have benefited from Terry's coaching. He also could have begun developing his head of finance for greater responsibilities.

Three of the five lower frequency capabilities are related to People Judgment and two to Business Judgment. Interestingly, Customer Focus was only observed in six of the thirteen scenarios. This critical fact stood out to us due to the nature of Terry's business, retail grocery. Terry had opportunities to be more mindful of customer demographics and needs during the acquisition process, the inconsistency in pricing issues between the original Eat Fresh and Organic Dangle stores, and several other situations. He missed those opportunities to be Customer Focused. Was this due to his lack of confidence in his capability or a lesser priority? We will get more insight into the answer when we begin looking at his effectiveness ratings.

Jamie

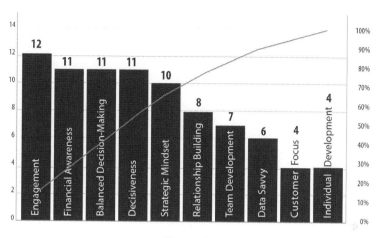

Figure 2:
Pareto chart describing Jamie's capabilities observed over the year

As we turn our attention to Jamie's frequency data, we see a comparable ordering of the capabilities. Jamie's five most frequently demonstrated capabilities are the same as Terry's (see Figure 2). The most frequent distribution is also three Business and two People Judgment; however, the relative order is different. Engagement was the most frequently occurring capability (80 percent), followed by Financial Awareness, Balanced Decision-Making, Decisiveness (73 percent), and Strategic Mindset (66 percent). Given our insights on the effectiveness of Jamie's strategic thinking in several scenarios, we may have expected Strategic Mindset to have been relatively higher, particularly relative to Financial Awareness. We will see shortly how effectiveness impacts our perceptions.

Interestingly, Customer Focus and Individual Development were observed least frequently (26 percent). We know the scenarios provided more opportunities than Jamie demonstrated in both of these capabilities. Jamie had strong tendencies to look at the aggregate of her customers and potential customers by understanding the market she was in; however, her focus on individual customers and their individual needs was seldom seen as a priority for Jamie. Nor was her inclination to focus on the unique needs of her direct reports. As we move onto effectiveness ratings, we will see the link between effectiveness and frequency, particularly at the low end of the frequency count.

Effectiveness

The frequency data is an excellent starting point, providing a macro-view of the capabilities leaders appear to rely on most often in addressing opportunities and challenges. Now, let's consider the data we have relating to leader effectiveness. There is a relationship between frequency and effectiveness, and you will see the critical performance insights we can glean from the juxtaposition of data.

Terry

Business Judgment						People Judgment					
Capability	Rating			Total	Weighted Effectiveness Rating	Capability	Rating			Total	Weighted Effectiveness Rating
	1	2	3				1	2	3		
Data Savvy	3	3	1	7	12	Engagement	2	5	3	10	21
Strategic Mindset	3	4	2	9	17	Relationship Building	2	4	1	7	13
Customer Focus	3	1	2	11	11	Team Development	2	2	3	7	15
Financial Awareness	1	2	6	9	23	Individual Development	0	1	2	3	8
Balanced Decision-Making	5	3	1	9	14	Decisiveness	5	0	4	9	17
Total Business Judgment	15	13	12	40	77	Total People Judgment	11	12	13	36	74

Figure 3:
Effectiveness Data — Terry

The data found in Figure 3 provides a summary of Terry's effectiveness ratings and the observed frequency of each capability for thirteen scenarios. Each row has five columns. The first three represent how the authors rated a particular capability:

1 = Ineffective
2 = Effective
3 = Highly Effective

The fourth column shows the total number of times each capability was rated. Let's look at Data Savvy as an example. We observed the capability during our interviews and rated Terry "Ineffective" three times. He was "Effective" three times, and "Highly Effective" once, for a total of seven ratings (the frequency count).

The final column represents the weighted effectiveness rating. This rating is calculated by multiplying the different ratings of a dimension (1, 2 and 3) by the total times it was observed (frequency). Continuing the Data Savvy example—Terry was rated a "1" three times (3 x 1) and also three times as a "2" (3 x 2). He was rated a "3" once (3 x 1). The total of each rating multiplied by the frequency count is twelve, the weighted effectiveness rating.

Figure 3 summarizes Terry's effectiveness ratings for each capability of the High Impact Leadership model℠. This data is presented as a ranked order of Terry's weighted effectiveness in each of the underlying capabilities of Business and People Judgment in Figure 4.

Business Judgment		People Judgment	
Financial Awareness	23	Engagement	21
Strategic Mindset	17	Decisiveness	17
Balanced Decision-Making	14	Team Development	15
Data Savvy	12	Relationship Building	13
Customer Focus	11	Individual Development	8

Figure 4:
Weighted Effectiveness Ranking — Terry

Terry's most effective and most frequently used Business Judgment capability is Financial Awareness. Terry must be cautioned about being overly dependent on his financial acumen. Although his Strategic Mindset and Balanced Decision-Making appear relatively strong, Terry needs to look more closely at his effectiveness on these two capabilities. In the nine scenarios in which Terry demonstrated Strategic Mindset, he was rated ineffective three times (33 percent). The scenario in which Terry decided to sell the potentially tainted baby food was an example of ignoring the implications of his decision on his brand and his strategy for short-term earnings. The same mixed bag is true for Balanced Decision-Making. Of the nine opportunities in which Terry exhibited decision-making behavior, five were rated ineffective (more than 50 percent).

A critical point to remember — the weighted effectiveness scores are relative to the individual leader, not a comparison of leaders' effectiveness. As a result, Terry must look at the relative ranking and dig into the frequency with which he was rated ineffective. By identifying inconsistencies, such as what we see in Balanced Decision-Making and Strategic Mindset, Terry can learn from analyzing how he's been effective versus ineffective.

Business Judgment capabilities in which Terry must increase his effectiveness and frequency are Data Savvy and Customer Focus. In both cases, Terry was rated ineffective in nearly 50 percent of the scenarios where he demonstrated these two capabilities. More focus on his customers and data may have helped him avoid the significant issues he had with his Organic Dangle acquisition. If Terry hopes to continue to grow his business, he can ill afford to ignore the needs and input of his customers nor ignore the availability of relevant information as he makes critical organizational decisions. The financials are important but not the sole factor on which all decisions should be predicated.

Continuing to look at Figure 4, we see Terry's significant strength in People Judgment was his Engagement. He continually exhibited a high degree of availability, open communication, and responsiveness to associates' needs. He also demonstrated considerable effectiveness in Decisiveness with his quick, resolute decision-making regarding people issues. Terry's Individual Development effectiveness ranking was ranked last; however, when he decided to foster the development of a colleague, he was effective or highly effective. The issue was his frequency. Whether he is not confident in his effectiveness, he doesn't see it as a priority, or he has not made the time to develop his staff, we don't know. We know how critical helping associates improve their performance is to the long-term viability of an organization and its leader.

Jamie

Business Judgment					People Judgment				
Capability	Rating			Total	Weighted Effectiveness Rating	Capability	Rating			Total	Weighted Effectiveness Rating
	1	2	3				1	2	3		
Data Savvy	3	3	2	8	13	Engagement	4	7	2	13	24
Strategic Mindset	1	6	4	11	24	Relationship Building	4	3	1	8	13
Customer Focus	2	1	1	4	7	Team Development	2	3	2	7	14
Financial Awareness	2	6	4	12	25	Individual Development	3	1	0	4	5
Balanced Decision-Making	1	4	7	12	29	Decisiveness	4	3	11	18	22
Total Business Judgment	9	20	18	47	98	**Total People Judgment**	17	17	16	50	78

Figure 5:

Effectiveness Data—Jamie

Let's look at Figure 5, which represents the same frequency and effectiveness data for Jamie as we discussed in Figure 3 for Terry. Note in the total Business Judgment row that Jamie was rated as ineffective on only nine occasions of forty-seven opportunities. In contrast, Jamie was rated ineffective in seventeen out of fifty events calling for People Judgment. We will dig into the implications of those inconsistencies in Figure 6.

Business Judgment		People Judgment	
Balanced Decision-Making	29	Engagement	24
Financial Awareness	25	Decisiveness	22
Strategic Mindset	24	Team Development	14
Data Savvy	13	Relationship Building	13
Customer Focus	7	Individual Development	5

Figure 6:

Weighted Effectiveness Ranking—Jamie

Figure 6 illustrates Jamie's significant strengths in Business Judgment: Balanced Decision-Making, Financial Awareness, and Strategic Mindset. These three capabilities were demonstrated at a high frequency (twelve, twelve, and eleven, respectively) and were rated as either effective or highly effective. In only one scenario of the thirty-five in which these three capabilities were demonstrated, we had an ineffective rating. Jamie received this rating for Financial Awareness when she refused to give a discount to a large, long-term customer and lost his business.

Data Savvy and Customer Focus were both low, but Customer Focus was significantly lower than any other capability, including Data Savvy. The low overall rating for Customer Focus results from being demonstrated in only four of fifteen scenarios. In two of the four, Jamie was rated as ineffective. Those ineffective ratings came in the new pricing model scenario in which she and her team did not pay much attention to the customer perspective that might arise from the change. The other ineffective rating was in the discounting scenario in which she would not consider any special treatment for a long-term, large customer.

As we look at Jamie's People Judgement combined effectiveness ratings via Figure 6, we see Engagement and Decisiveness as rated significantly higher than other capabilities. We would assume these to be strengths. They are strengths relative to other People Judgment capabilities. Still, they represent a mixed bag of effectiveness Jamie cannot ignore if she expects to continue to grow as a leader. Four of the thirteen scenarios where Jamie exhibited Engagement behavior were rated as Ineffective. This was typically when she failed to consult individuals from whom she should have solicited input and possibly moved too fast.

An example was when she unilaterally decided on the need to collect sales force data and didn't get the head of sales or any other sales perspectives. This is a good example of no behavior is behavior. She had the opportunity to demonstrate Engagement but didn't, and it had negative implications for her leadership effectiveness.

The same mixed bag is true for Decisiveness. She demonstrated Decisiveness in eleven out of fifteen scenarios; however, she was rated ineffective in four of those eleven situations. Decisiveness may be the most important People Judgment capability. People-related decision effectiveness is highly visible throughout an organization. Jamie can obviously make effective people decisions, as demonstrated in seven of eleven scenarios, such as how she sensitively addressed the departure of her sales VP or resolutely handled her top developer who failed to display the organization's values. This is an inconsistency Jamie cannot overlook. She should think of what effective Decisiveness means by definition; then, look at where she's demonstrated it effectively. For example, in the social capital scenario. She decided that it positively impacted the customer and the organization. Jamie has the capability; she just needs to demonstrate it more consistently.

Comparing Our Leaders

Figure 7 allows us to compare the summary effectiveness scores of our leaders, Terry and Jamie.

Business Judgment	Terry	Jamie	People Judgment	Terry	Jamie
Data Savvy	12	13	Engagement	21	24
Strategic Mindset	17	24	Relationship Building	13	13
Customer Focus	11	7	Team Development	15	14
Financial Awareness	23	25	Individual Development	8	5
Balanced Decision-Making	14	29	Decisiveness	17	22
Total	**77**	**98**	**Total**	**74**	**78**

Figure 7:

Total Effectiveness Scores Comparison

In comparing their weighted effectiveness scores for Business Judgment, Jamie's effectiveness is significantly stronger than Terry's (98 versus 77). Jamie not only tended to use her Business

Judgment capabilities more frequently, but she also used them more effectively. For example, of the forty-seven times Jamie demonstrated Business Judgment behavior, nine were ineffective versus fifteen out of forty opportunities for Terry (see Figures 3 and 4 for frequencies). Both our leaders were low in Data Savvy and Customer Focus. Jamie demonstrated Customer Focus in only four of fifteen scenarios and was rated ineffective in two of those four situations.

Overall, Jamie is a stronger business leader than Terry and more consistent in the effectiveness and frequency of her Business Judgment behavior. She is also more balanced in the application of her Business Judgment capabilities, while Terry is inconsistent. He's stronger in Financial Awareness, and the depth of his financial acumen can be both a blessing and curse for his leadership effectiveness.

In People Judgment, the rank ordering of their capabilities is the same, and their summary effectiveness scores are comparable. Both of our leaders demonstrated considerable inconsistency in demonstrating effective or highly effective behavior in the People Judgment capabilities. Of the thirty-six opportunities Terry took to demonstrate People Judgment, he was rated ineffective 31 percent of the time (see Figure 3). Jamie was rated Ineffective in seventeen of fifty opportunities, or 34 percent. Both leaders have significant opportunities to improve their People Judgment.

Derailers

Our summary insights relative to Jamie and Terry have focused on the comparative effectiveness of leadership capabilities. Our objective has been to focus on strengthening their capabilities to make them more successful as leaders. On the other hand, Derailers get in the way of a leader's progress, inhibiting them from reaching their potential. Derailers typically lead to the quick demise and failure of a leader.

In Chapter 2, we presented the results of our research on Derailers in the PRG environment. We discovered four derailers unique to small business leaders:

- *Formality-Structure Disconnect*: Minimizes the importance of structure, process, and performance standards within the company
- *In the Weeds*: Becomes immersed in day-to-day activities resulting in a sharp decline in personal productivity and company performance
- *Informal Influencers*: Routinely consults a group of advisors or confidants who are not direct reports but whose opinions may be less informed and overly weighted
- *Over-Simplified Decision-Making*: Rushes to make complex decisions while relying on incomplete information and gut feelings

Let's discuss the potential derailers our leaders may have demonstrated throughout the year.

Terry

Terry demonstrated Derailer tendencies in several areas. Although Terry used performance standards and key metrics to measure success, he tended to minimize the importance of structure and process. On several occasions, Terry balked at the effective use of the process. In selecting the first set of store managers, Terry went through a rigorous process but decided to override the resulting decision and promoted an assistant manager who ultimately failed. He also rejected implementing a people-management system to help in the assimilation process of Organic Dangle and manage a growing employee roster. After some problem situations and a possible lawsuit, he saw the benefit of the process. These are all examples of the Formality-Structure Disconnect Derailer.

Terry tended to get In the Weeds on some occasions. Engagement is a strong capability for Terry, but he would benefit from being more focused and discriminating in how he communicates and spends his time with associates. By that we mean, Terry should focus on high-impact opportunities for engagement. In the "adding the last 10 percent" scenario, Terry spent considerable time helping his associate implement her idea. On the other hand, he limited his involvement in establishing a common culture and values between the original Eat Fresh and Organic Dangle stores. The potential benefits and impact of his increasing his engagement in the culture alignment process were much more significant than getting into too much detail on an individual situation, especially when the individual was quite capable of successfully completing the assignment.

Finally, Terry tends to show Over-Simplified Decision-Making. We have discussed the number of times Terry reacts to a situation based on a financial metric being out of line with his expectations. His over-reliance on his financial acumen leads to this over-simplification and is exacerbated by his tendency not to acquire and analyze other data (Data Savvy).

We have consistently used the word "tendency" as we described Terry's potential Derailers. None of his behaviors have reached a point where they represent a significant problem. On the other hand, all three Derailer tendencies we discussed for Terry limit his potential as a leader. He must address each to reach his full potential to lead Eat Fresh to the level of success to which he aspires.

Jamie

Jamie demonstrated a strong tendency for demonstrating derailing behavior for Informal Influencers. She routinely consulted her husband on people-related decisions, much to the frustration of her HR manager and others who observed her. The "remote work" and "paying the bonus" scenarios were examples where she solicited her husband's opinion and let it override those of her staff. She also requested and overly weighted the view of her uncle instead of her CFO when considering the offer of a venture capital group to fund her expansion plans.

Jamie also tended to get In the Weeds more often than appropriate. She was decisive to a fault on some occasions in that she did not take time to get the input and feedback of her staff before she announced a decision. The "skyrocketing benefits" and "paying the bonus" scenarios illustrated this tendency. As was the case with Terry, Jamie's Derailer tendencies limit her potential and must be addressed. Fortunately, the Derailers we identified do not appear hardwired but are learned over time. As a result, Terry and Jamie need to be aware of their Derailer tendencies, then establish a feedback mechanism to help reduce the frequency. Our research indicates that the In the Weeds Derailer is perhaps the most significant issue for PRG leaders.

Leader Scorecards

In conclusion to this chapter, we have presented a detailed, quantitative perspective of Terry's and Jamie's capabilities and Derailers, and we return to the scorecards. The format is one with which you are familiar—we used it to summarize leadership effectiveness and short-term results in each scenario. The scorecards for Terry and Jamie appear below. Each contains the average rating for Business and People Judgment and the associated capabilities. The scorecards are followed by a behavioral summary of strengths and areas needing development for each of our leaders.

Terry's Scorecard

Business Judgment		People Judgment	
1.9 ▼		2.1 ▼	
①————②————③		①————②————③	
Data Savvy	1.7	Engagement	2.1
Strategic Mindset	1.9	Relationship Building	1.9
Customer Focus	1.8	Team Development	2.1
Financial Awareness	2.6	Individual Development	2.7
Balanced Decision-Making	1.6	Decisiveness	1.9

When summarizing Terry's Business Judgment, his Financial Awareness is most evident. For every decision, he considers the fiscal impact in both the long and short term. Surprisingly, a leader who manages so much by the numbers does not appear to appreciate or take the time to gather other potentially relevant data more frequently. He just looks at the financial metrics. Terry seems to be In the Weeds often, trying to be involved in every process and decision. We believe he recognizes he has an issue. We are not sure Terry fully sees how his not letting people do their jobs affects his ability to invest his time in more comprehensive and informed decision-making.

As for People Judgment, Terry is in a high-touch, consumer-facing business. He closely interacts with individuals in the store and the community, works with employees who support the customer, and frequently sees the effect of his interactions and relationships. Despite what are strong interpersonal skills, Terry nevertheless experienced several people-related issues over the year. He failed to consider the culture he wanted to create at Eat Fresh before and well after the merger with Organic Dangle. After several false starts and organizational struggles, it appears he is now aware of the culture, and people are beginning to become aligned. As Terry continues to grow the company, he must stay vigilant to his cause. He should work closely with his store managers to continually send a consistent message about the "Eat Fresh way" of doing business.

A final thought about Terry: We have observed this role-shift hesitancy in many leaders who began growing their companies in the PRG. Terry must stop thinking of himself as an entrepreneur and recognize that he is a CEO. His job is not to do everything and ensure each task is completed on time. He needs to delegate and focus his efforts on truly leading the organization.

Jamie's Scorecard

Business Judgment		People Judgment	
2.3		**1.8**	
Data Savvy	2.2	Engagement	1.9
Strategic Mindset	2.4	Relationship Building	1.6
Customer Focus	1.8	Team Development	2.0
Financial Awareness	2.3	Individual Development	1.3
Balanced Decision-Making	2.6	Decisiveness	2.0

Much of Jamie's success as a leader was predicated on solid Business Judgment and her passion for and outstanding knowledge of the industry. She relies on her market insights and uses competitive intelligence to guide the company's product portfolio development, resulting in innovative product and service offerings. Jamie is continuously operating with an eye on the future. This Strategic Mindset, coupled with Financial Awareness, helps her to drive the company to continued success.

On the people side, Jamie tends to make unilateral decisions, failing to solicit insights from people with specific knowledge and experience. This approach undermines her relationships with her direct reports. More importantly, no leader is omnipotent. The best decisions are built on diverse inputs garnered from various multifunctional professionals who bring distinct views to the decision-making process. Jamie often talks about the importance of teams throughout the organization but seldom appears interested in developing the group most critical to her success—the leadership team. Executives in a PRG company must become more than a group who work together. They must become one cohesive entity to achieve through their collective performance, becoming a high-performance team (HPT). Such teams continually succeed and innovate. Jamie must engage her people, trust the autonomy of their roles, and invite them to help shape the organization's future. We observed that Jamie is frequently quick to recognize development needs in her people but fails to follow through and help her associates to improve their professional acumen. As the company continues to grow, Jamie's deficits in People Judgment could impede organizational effectiveness and morale. She needs to focus on more effective Engagement. She must learn to trust and include the leadership team in many of her decisions. Without a trusted team, Jamie will struggle to "know everything," and her execution will be compromised.

Chapter 35

Leadership Results

The High Impact Leadership model[SM] is tied directly to organizational results. The decisions and choices made by a PRG leader impact their company in a litany of ways. Throughout the year, we used the scorecard to identify the immediate effect of our leaders' decisions in four critical results areas: *Market, People, Financial,* and *Operations.* As we discussed possible results for each scenario, we reminded readers that the impact is what we saw at the time—the short term. On occasion, we speculated on the mid-to-long-term impact.

We asked each leader to share year-end financial data and key metrics each used to monitor performance across the four areas. We summarized their results and provided a simple rating, indicating our perspective on performance in each area:

Positive Results: a level of successful performance at or above expectations

Mixed Results: a mixture of success in some metrics but below expectations in others

Negative Results: a trend in performance below expectations

Let's look at Jamie's and Terry's performance impact.

E-Dine: Year-End Summary

We begin by looking at changes in organizational dynamics. At the start of the year, e-Dine employed sixty-one full-time associates. At the close of the year, it had 103 full-time associates and over a dozen contract employees. Much of the growth has been in the sales group and customer service department. In a year, the company has expanded to a new region and is already eying nationwide coverage. The levels of management have begun to grow. The VP of sales now has two regional sales managers supporting the sales effort. E-Dine *looks like* a company in the PRG: rapid growth in associates and increased hierarchy to better manage operations.

When we first spoke with Jamie, we explored the foundations of her Business Judgment. During that interview, she told us several measures and controls she regularly tracks to monitor business performance. The following dashboard contains the year-end metrics for e-Dine:

Market	People	Financial	Operations
Quarterly Subscribers **34%**	Associate Satisfaction **>4**	Quarterly Sales Growth **10%**	Support Ticket Time - Tier 1 **< 8 Minutes** - Tier 2 **< 2 Hours**
Web Traffic **15% Monthly**	Employee Turnover - Tech Staff **4%** - Other Staff **12%**	Churn Rate **2%**	Customer Downtime **1%**

Jamie's Impact on Results

E-Dine experienced significant growth in market share and recognition. The switch to subscriptions lowered the barrier to purchase for a large group of prospective customers. Jamie's decision to invest in partnering with the Chef's Cooperative charity increased the company's recognition. Her marketing team reported increased web traffic, and their web analytics show higher click-throughs across all ad exposures. E-Dine is exceeding in metrics indicating market awareness. For example, the growth in the permission lists suggests customers and potential clients are interested in e-Dine products. So much so that they are signing up for news and company updates. Denise, the VP of marketing, has also been tracking news coverage and recognition factors. Her findings are positive. E-Dine's market penetration strategy appears on track—the brand is growing and attracting new customers.

Market Area Rating: Positive

E-Dine's employee turnover rate was below the industry standard of 16 percent for technology staff, but turnover among e-Dine customer service and sales associates was 12 percent. This is slightly higher than the industry and e-Dine's target of 9 percent. This turnover suggests the workplace environment may be less fulfilling to some associates. Each year, the company HR department conducts an associate satisfaction survey. Every e-Dine associate reports their perceptions of the company mission, its success in achieving goals, customer satisfaction, and happiness in the workplace. Jamie and her team have always looked to earn above-average ratings across these categories. This year was no exception, but two questions stood out. These two questions had average ratings of less than three (on a satisfaction scale of one to five). The first asked how associates' opinions and input are considered and respected by leadership. The other was related to overall employee happiness with their job and the workplace. Jamie's often less-than-effective use of her People Judgment can be attributed to these lower scores. In several scenarios throughout the year, we observed her propensity to act unilaterally rather than consulting with and building consensus with her leadership team. Similarly, she was frequently unaware (or uninterested) in the thoughts of any associates throughout the company.

People Area Rating: Mixed

Financially, the company's top-line revenue grew each quarter by 5 percent or more. User adoptions of the POS product drove this growth. Quarter 4 was particularly strong at 10 percent. Revenue rose, but the user base increased more than 35 percent over previous quarters—*more adoptions but from customers paying a fraction of what a customer previously paid to adopt the e-Dine POS.*

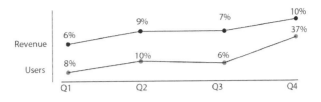

This can be attributed to Jamie's decision to shift to a subscription-pricing model, a plan expected to accelerate user adoption and increase the company's customer base. E-Dine generated less revenue than projected for the year and was less profitable. Quarterly cash from operations dropped dramatically, a result of the new pricing plan. Also, employee growth was significant (almost 70 percent). The organization expanded its salesforce, which helped drive new revenue. E-Dine's customer service and support operations also grew, an investment to ensure customer satisfaction and affinity. Thanks to Jamie's relationship with her primary bank, the company secured a short-term loan at a reasonable interest rate that covered the cash shortage and employee investments.

What is important to recognize are the implications for the year ahead. The timing of revenue forever changes the balance sheet and how e-Dine manages monthly operations. The lowered subscription fees decreased monthly income but represent considerably higher annual reoccurring revenue (ARR). If her organization can hasten adoptions and simultaneously manage new customer churn rates, her yearly P&L will show improved profitability in the year ahead. Churn is a standard industry steering control for subscription products, and Jamie began tracking that rate each month. Early indications are reasonable. Gartner Research suggests the typical churn for a B2B software subscription is between 3 and 7 percent. In the first two months of subscription sales, less than 2 percent of subscribers dropped the POS.

Financial Area Rating: Mixed

Operationally, Jamie tracks several service-related metrics. She explained, "Our service has always been an important differentiator, but with our switch to subscriptions, it's a lot easier for a customer to leave us if they have an unpleasant experience. Our support has to be better than ever." E-Dine continually monitors service and support operations—from the length of time a ticket is open to the levels of support required to resolve an issue. Despite the growth, helpdesk times have remained exceptionally low, and the average customer experience rating continues to score four or greater (on a satisfaction scale of one to five).

Customer downtime is another crucial metric that Jamie monitors. The company goal of 99 percent uptime dropped to 97 percent in the last two months, and this can be directly attributed to a lack of field associates. The field support team found it difficult to scale with the influx of new customers. The developers are effectively managing overrun (the time they miss software updates or release dates) that can drive up costs and result in delays.

Operations Area Rating: Positive

Eat Fresh: Year-End Summary

Early in the year, Terry acquired the Organic Dangle chain, doubling the number of stores in the company. This dramatic growth affected the organizational dynamics—Terry now employs 171 full-time or full-time equivalent employees. In quarter 1, he employed under one hundred associates, and had just begun to transition out of the store manager role in the original three locations. He now has six store managers reporting to him. Although his organization has almost doubled in size, there has been little growth in his leadership team or effort to add management to formalize operations.

Like Jamie, Terry shared the measures and controls he used

to evaluate his business performance. The dashboard contains Eat Fresh's year-end performance metrics:

Market	People	Financial	Operations
Same Store Sales **7%**	Turnover - Hourly FT & PT **107%** - Salaried **4%**	Revenue **60%** - New Revenue **15%** - Acquisition Revenue **45%**	Inventory Turns **15%**
Basket Size **-8%**	Employee Engagement **7.7/10**	Profit **40%**	Waste **-5%**
Loyalty Card Members **48%**		Profit Margin **-10%**	Cash from Operations **55%**

Terry's Impact on Results

A significant portion of Eat Fresh's growth came from the acquisition. Still, Terry and his team also developed a portion of new customers and revenue from their existing markets through organic growth. They identified new customer groups in the former Organic Dangle regions that better fit the demographics of his key customer. This approach came with some expense. Many long-time Organic Dangle customers were lost due to the price increases and shifts in the marketing and promotion mix. He is working to win back a share of those customers. The Eat Fresh loyalty card program experienced some growth throughout the year, indicating customer affinity. Terry focused the program on products and services his target customers care about most. In the future, he plans to use the loyalty card to attract the senior populations in both regions the stores serve. Eat Fresh can be found in more places, and brand recognition is rising. Both factors correlate directly to growth.

Market Area Rating: Mixed

Terry typically demonstrates strong People Judgment. He engages with his associates and tries to build a team environment. Terry appreciates individual contributions and is quick to recognize their efforts. That said, he faced several challenges throughout the acquisition. He was not necessarily aware of the potential conflicts that could arise when combining two distinct business cultures. At times, his tendency to make decisions based solely on financial results may have negatively affected his associates. Each year, the HR department conducts an employee satisfaction and feedback survey. Questions relating to associate happiness and engagement dropped from 8.8 to 7.9 (on a scale of 10). When one considers that this survey was completed within six months of the merger, the downward shift is negligible. Eat Fresh associates appear happy with their work and the company. Terry's leadership has had a considerable impact on his associates.

People Area Rating: Positive

Eat Fresh grew in large part by buying revenue. Late in quarter 2, Organic Dangle's three stores represented a 197 percent increase in monthly revenues. The new stores' lower margins and the challenges with the integration negatively affected fiscal results. In addition to the acquisition, Terry also pursued several significant investments in logistics software and a people-management system. However, these initiatives are not expected to pay off until the mid-to-long term. Their immediate impact was seen in overall profit margin and restricted operational capital. That said, the company was profitable, primarily because of Terry's exceptional financial acumen. He worked diligently to minimize margin loss and maximize inventory turns, which resulted in a reasonably healthy year-end balance sheet. The close of the year was just six months after the acquisition. Many of Terry's programs for improving profitability and increasing the average cart size have yet to be fully implemented across all six stores. It appears he has positioned the company for excellent financial results in the years ahead.

Financial Area Rating: Mixed

Operationally, Eat Fresh encountered several challenges with mixed results. Terry was ill-prepared for the loss of a compromised beef supplier. His removal of, then subsequent reintroduction of the people-management system, introduced confusion and inefficiency throughout the company. Terry successfully brought on new store managers, but his approach to aligning cultures and identifying talent, at times, resulted in less-than-optimal store efficiency. Although the logistics system was a buggy launch, the software has dramatically improved inventory management. Products are less likely to be out of stock, and there is less chance of spoilage issues like the baby food incident Terry encountered early in the year. The fast growth Eat Fresh experienced this year somewhat forced Terry and his team to improve operations quickly. They could not afford a trial-and-error approach to operations. Terry has likely learned that process and structure help maintain control and quality as the company grows.

Operations Area Rating: Mixed

Transitioning from Jamie and Terry to You

Throughout the last two chapters, we summarized our insights into Terry's and Jamie's effectiveness over the year. We provided a quantitative assessment of each leader's Business and People Judgment, highlighting the frequency and effectiveness level they demonstrated in the various dimensions of the Judgments. Subsequently, we illustrated the impact of their leadership effectiveness on the results of their respective organizations. We hope you have enjoyed our journey with Terry and Jamie and have found the insights we have discussed with you helpful to your continued growth as a leader. However, we would be remiss if we left your continued growth to what you gleaned from your reading thus far.

The following section will take you from *reading to action*.

You will hold the proverbial mirror up to yourself via a self-assessment instrument that will result in a leadership profile relative to the High Impact Leadership model[SM]. The profile will highlight strengths you want to leverage and identify capabilities in which you will want to improve your effectiveness. Finally, our chapter on Development will provide the information and approaches you need to act on your development needs in a highly relevant, practical, and effective manner.

At that point, our journey together will be complete. You will be on your way to enhancing your leadership effectiveness and generating strong market, people, financial, and operational results for your organization.

Section IV
Self-Awareness

Our objective in *From 50 to 500* has been to enable you to become a stronger, more confident leader who positively impacts a range of results throughout your organization. To help achieve this objective, we took you on a journey during which you became more aware of what constitutes high-impact leadership and what such leadership looks like in our leaders, Terry and Jamie. At the end of each scenario, we encouraged you to apply the insights you gained to understand your motivations and capabilities better. In other words, we encouraged you to become more self-aware. Self-awareness is a critical attribute for the high-impact leader in the PRG environment. Self-awareness is the capacity to recognize one's strengths and limitations, resulting in behavior change. In other words, the willingness to hold a mirror to yourself and act on what you see.

You may be asking: If self-awareness is such an essential element of successful leadership, why doesn't it appear in the model? Great question! First, we did not want to complicate the model with a psychological construct that was neither a Motivator nor a capability. Second, self-awareness requires a leader to genuinely understand what drives their success and limits their potential. Self-awareness cannot be pursued in an ad-hoc manner. Introducing you to the tools and concepts associated with self-awareness at the end of the book allows you to apply those insights to your leadership behavior immediately. The "mirror effect" and its application will be quicker, more meaningful, and insight-driven.

In Chapter 36, we dissect the definition of self-awareness. Then, you can focus your capacity to recognize strengths and relative weaknesses using a comprehensive self-assessment tool. The tool provides an in-depth, quantitative perspective of your effectiveness across each component of the High Impact Leadership model[SM]: Motivators, Business and People Judgment, and Derailers.

You will learn to complete and score your self-assessment.

Then, we will review and interpret a sample report. We will discuss how to identify strengths—the easy part—and focus improvement efforts to move the mean of one's leadership effectiveness efficiently.

We will continue our focus on self-awareness in Chapter 37 by discussing the secondary piece of its definition: taking action to change. There is little value to a leader knowing where you should improve but failing to take action to change. Behavior change focused on performance improvement is typically referred to as development. Our approach to development enables leaders to act on the results of their self-assessment. We explore the three Development Domains available to small business leaders. Within each, we highlight relevant tools, resources, and approaches for supporting behavior change.

A deep dive into the application of self-awareness is the focus of our final chapters.

Chapter 36

Self-Assessment: Looking in the Mirror

We began this final section talking about self-awareness, the metaphorical mirror you hold up to yourself to begin to understand what motivates you and the capabilities you demonstrate as a leader. This chapter will introduce a self-assessment tool to be used as a vehicle for capturing and communicating your personal evaluation of your leadership profile. *This tool is the Polaroid camera that produces your leadership picture.*

The self-assessment tool is available in two modalities: self-scorable or automated through our online system.

- You can download a full-size, printable copy of the self-scorable instrument from www.from50to500.com/print
- The web-based version of the self-assessment tool is available at www.from 50to500.com/PRG

The content of both formats is the same. We have provided a leader's manual self-assessment in Appendix A. This same leader's report generated from the automated tool is also included. We will highlight portions of those documents throughout this chapter. First, we will explain how to complete either version of the tool, emphasizing the rating scales for Motivators, the Judgments, and Derailers. Then, we will focus on your self-assessment results—how they are calculated and how to interpret them.

Self-Assessment: Leader's Response Survey

The survey structure is consistent with the four components of the High Impact Leadership model^{SM}: Motivators, Business

Judgment, People Judgment, and Derailers. You will be asked to evaluate and rate yourself across a range of illustrative behaviors associated with the model's various dimensions. Let's begin by reviewing how to use the rating system to evaluate different components.

Rating Motivators

Motivators represent the first section of the instrument. You will be reminded of the two Motivators critical to the success of a PRG leader and their definitions. Then, the dimensions of each Motivator and their illustrative behaviors are displayed. Finally, you rate the *frequency* with which you demonstrate the behavior.

Before rating yourself, take a moment to think about the behavior as it applies to you and the frequency with which you demonstrate the behavior. For example, if you rate yourself as Seldom (1), you rarely demonstrate this behavior. If you show it occasionally but inconsistently, rate it Sometimes (2). Finally, suppose you demonstrate the behavior regularly, and it is a significant part of your repertoire of behaviors—then rate it Frequently (3).

Rating Judgments

The rating scale for Business and People Judgment is comparable to the Motivators, except that you are now rating your *effectiveness* relative to each behavior.

Rating yourself as Less Than Effective (1) means the quality and consistency of your behavior is less than one might expect of a leader in your role. An Effective (2) rating represents a solid positive rating in which the quality and consistency of your behavior adequately addresses the situation to which it is applied. In other words, you feel comfortable with your demonstration of the behavior, and the implications are positive. On the other hand, you recognize you could raise your level of quality and consistency. Doing so would serve you well as a leader. This leads us to Highly Effective (3), a rating reserved for behaviors in which you demonstrate consistent quality and reliability. You should feel confident in showing the behavior to a high degree.

Rating Derailers

The last section of both instruments focuses on our four Derailers — each of which can be problematic for PRG leaders. You will again use the three-point scale, but your rating will be based on the *frequency* with which you show a particular behavior.

For each Derailer, you are asked to rate five behaviors that illustrate the Derailer. Like the Motivators, you are evaluating frequency. A Seldom (1) rating indicates it's unusual for you to show this behavior — it is not a part of your typical behavioral pattern. Sometimes (2) indicates an occasional demonstration but not a consistent part of your repertoire. Frequently (3) means this behavior is common. As in all the ratings you make in this instrument, it is important that you try to be as accurate as possible. Only you will see your results, and only you will benefit from a precise assessment relative to each variable in the tool.

Calculating Your Results

Before we dig into interpreting your results, let's look at how the scores are calculated for each survey component. If you choose to use the automated tool via our website, the system calculates your scores. It then creates a customized report of your assessment results and appends your ratings data. The manual instrument provides you with the same summary and performance data, but you will need to complete the calculations. We will highlight portions of a completed manual self-assessment (from Appendix A) to illustrate how to calculate your scores.

We begin explaining the scoring of the manual version with an example of the Motivators. Figure 1 illustrates how a leader scored herself on the Builds a Unique Culture dimension.

1	2	3
Seldom	Sometimes	Frequently

Builds a Unique Culture

Empowers associates to take initiative (act like an owner)	1 2 ③
Creates a personal and professionally rewarding work environment	1 ② 3
Talks regularly about company values	1 2 ③
Models company values (walks the talk)	1 ② 3
Implements values and capability criteria for advancement	1 ② 3

Sum of ratings: 12   Divide by 5 = **M1 Rating:** 2.4

Figure 1–Scoring a dimension of the Motivators

To calculate her rating for this dimension of the Motivator, she would add the individual ratings and divide them by five. In this case, the sum of the ratings was 12, and the average rating was 2.4.

The manual self-assessment requires the user to repeat this process across all four components of the model and their foundational dimensions. Here are examples of how our leader calculated her scores in various dimensions of the four components (Figures 2, 3, and 4):

Financial Awareness

Evaluates short-term and long-term financial requirements to execute plans	1 ② 3
Defines and monitors key financial metrics	1 ② 3
Seeks out expert guidance to identify the financial implications of a decision	① 2 3
Evaluates the financial risks and potential impact of potential decisions	1 ② 3
Demonstrates a comprehensive understanding of how the company makes money	1 2 ③

Sum of ratings: 10   Divide by 5 = **B4 Rating:** 2.0

Figure 2–Scoring a dimension of Business Judgment

Decisiveness

Assesses the situation from the viewpoint of the individual and the organization	1 ② 3
Considers alternative courses of action and implications	1 ② 3
Solicits the perspective of others when appropriate	1 2 ③
Recognizes the importance of making a timely decision	1 2 ③
Delivers the decision in a thoughtful but firm manner, always sticking to his or her decision	1 ② 3

Sum of ratings: 12   Divide by 5 = **P5 Rating:** 2.4

Figure 3–Scoring a dimension of People Judgment

Oversimplified Decision-Making

Rushes decisions	1 ② 3
Fails to collect or purchase critical data	1 2 ③
Places heavy emphasis on "gut" feeling	1 ② 3
Does not rely on a suitably diverse and experienced group to analyze problem or opportunity	① 2 3
Makes unilateral decisions without consultation	① 2 3

Sum of ratings: __9__   Divide by 5 = **D4 Rating:** __1.8__

Figure 4–Scoring a Derailer

After scoring all components of the Motivators, Judgments, and Derailers, you are ready to complete the results section that includes your leadership scorecard. As you can see from the example in Figure 5, our leader has followed the scoring directions and completed her report.

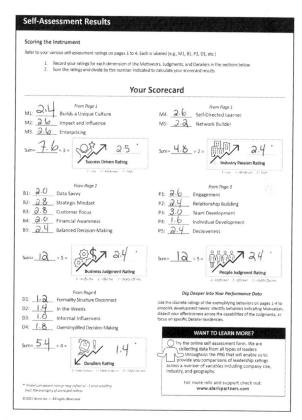

Figure 5–Sample of a leader's manually calculated scorecard

You will transpose the various scores you calculated on pages 1 through 4 into the associated Motivator, Judgment, or Derailer sections of the scorecard. Then, calculate the mean of those scores. For example, notice that each dimension of the Motivators our sample leader scored is labeled M1, M2, M3, M4, and M5. The first step to completing the scorecard is to calculate your Success Driven rating. In Figure 6, our leader has copied her ratings for Builds a Unique Culture (M1), Impact and Influence (M2), and Enterprising (M3). Summing those ratings and dividing that number by three results in a 2.5 Success Driven rating.

Figure 6–Example of scoring a leader's Success Driven rating

Continue this process of transcribing your results and calculating final scores for each of the remaining categories: Industry Passion, Business Judgment, People Judgment, and Derailers. You now have a leadership scorecard and self-assessment data that you can use to evaluate yourself. We will help guide your evaluation process below.

Analyzing Your Results

Regardless of the format (online or manual), you now have a self-assessment report from which you can begin analyzing your leadership performance. This section will use screenshots of both the manual and web reports to illustrate the performance of each capability.

Motivators

So, let's start with the Motivators. Figure 7 shows our sample leader's scorecard for the Motivators in both the manual and online versions.

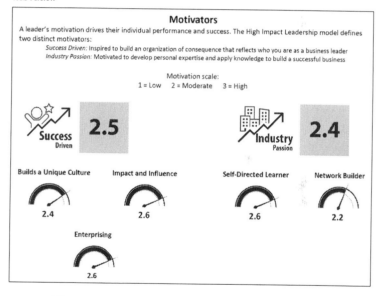

Figure 7–Manual and web versions of Motivators

A quick look at her Success Driven and Industry Passion scores indicates our leader is relatively strong in both Motivators. Her scores for the underlying dimensions of the Motivators are also comparatively strong. Her lowest rating of 2.2 was in Network Builder. Although still in the effective range, a look at the data section of the sample report (or the self-ratings in the manual instrument) will help our leader get a better fix on how she might demonstrate stronger motivation in this dimension. The raw scores for Network Builder indicate a rating of 1 for "Uses social media."

Uses social media 2 3

Given the importance of a social media presence for most PRG businesses, our leader could readily focus on demonstrating more of that behavior.

At this point, you could be asking:

Isn't motivation internally driven?
Are we trying to manipulate my motivation?
Why is it important to anyone but me?

Reasonable questions. Yes, motivation is internally driven, but elements of motivation can be learned. For example, you may be motivated to develop your expertise, which is part of Industry Passion. Still, you may not recognize the importance of a social media presence. As a result, your motivation is not reaching its maximum potential. We are not trying to manipulate your motivation but make you aware of elements you may otherwise not recognize as necessary. A leader must demonstrate the highest motivation because motivation, in turn, inspires and motivates associates and stakeholders.

We hope that helps with your analysis of your Motivator results. Remember to look beyond the summary numbers and use the raw data to identify behaviors you can address to help move the mean of your leadership effectiveness.

Business and People Judgment

Let's switch our focus to Judgments. Below, Figure 8 provides a snapshot of how Judgments are reported in both the manual and web-based reports.

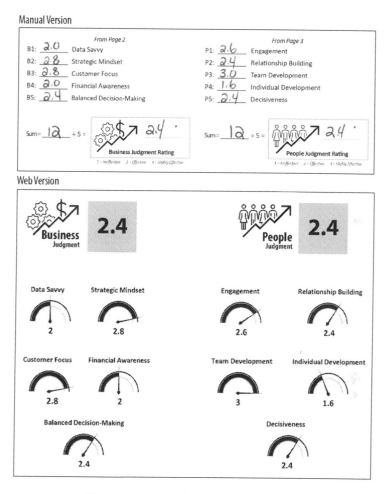

Figure 8– Manual and web versions of Business and People Judgment

The transposed scores or gauges indicate the rating averages for each capability underlying Business and People Judgment. The ratings of 2.4 for Business Judgment and 2.4 for People Judgment appear strong. This leader shows a reasonably high degree of effectiveness in both areas. But, as suggested above, you must look beyond the average rating and identify how you can move the mean of each capability.

In the case of Business Judgment, our sample leader's ratings for Data Savvy and Financial Awareness are 2.0. She could take a deeper dive into these capabilities to discern what is limiting her effectiveness. Using the self-rating pages of the manual tool (or the data section of the web-based report), she will see she rated herself a 1 in "Recognizes patterns in seemingly unrelated data to develop actionable insights."

Recognizes patterns in seemingly unrelated data to develop actionable insights

This behavior is critical to Data Savvy. The leader also assessed herself as a 1 in a component of Financial Awareness.

Seeks out expert guidance to identify the financial implications of a decision

By holding up the mirror, this leader knows where to focus on improving her overall Business Judgment. By taking action to improve her effectiveness, she can readily move those 1s to 2s. As a result, her Data Savvy and Financial Awareness scores would move to 2.2, and her overall Business Judgment would rise to 2.5. This an example of moving the mean of your leadership effectiveness. We are not talking about drastic changes but the incremental improvement that's meaningful in refining your effectiveness as a leader.

Let's look at our sample leader's People Judgment results before we move to Derailers. Again, the overall score of 2.4 is good. But the 1.6 in Individual Development attracts attention. When reviewing the illustrative behaviors associated with this capability, we see two behaviors with a 1 rating.

Invests in the ongoing development of associates   (1) 2 3

Ensures managers demonstrate effective coaching skills   (1) 2 3

Improving her effectiveness in these two important leadership behaviors would not appear difficult; however, moving them up a notch would significantly impact associates. From a rating perspective, it would move the Individual Development score to 2.0, which is solid and gives a better base for moving the mean in People Judgment.

Derailers

As discussed earlier, Derailers can negatively impact your leadership effectiveness by undermining your Business and People Judgment. Figure 9 illustrates our sample leader's Derailer results. Remember, when assessing Derailers, one rates the frequency with which they demonstrate the behaviors characterizing the Derailers. The less frequently one showed these behaviors, the less likely they are to present a given Derailer.

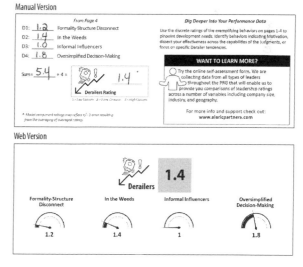

Figure 9 — Manual and web versions of Derailers

At first glance, our leader's Derailer profile looks okay—all dimensions are less than 2. However, Over-Simplified Decision-Making, at a rating of 1.8, is approaching a 2. Let's look at the raw data.

Oversimplified Decision-Making	
Rushes decisions	1 ② 3
Fails to collect or purchase critical data	1 2 ③
Places heavy emphasis on "gut" feeling	1 ② 3

The leader indicated she Frequently (3) "Fails to collect or purchase critical data." Also, she reported that she Sometimes (2) "Rushes decisions" and "Places heavy emphasis on gut feeling." These ratings represent a strong tendency toward Over-Simplified Decision-Making. The implications of not dealing with these tendencies are considerable. Over-Simplified Decision-Making often leads to diminished Business Judgment and, either directly or indirectly, has a deleterious impact on associates and stakeholders. Therefore, our collective recommendation is to look closely at the behaviors underlying each Derailer. Any behavior rated as 1.6 or above should be noted and monitored to ensure it does not detract from your leadership effectiveness.

Putting Your Self-Assessment to Use

Hopefully, these examples will help you dig deeper into your report results. Holding up the mirror is a simple process, highly intuitive, and an excellent investment in yourself as a leader. Think of it as a form of honest feedback to yourself. Feedback is a gift, and no one better than you to provide it. If you have been introspective during the self-assessment, you now have an excellent picture of what your leadership looks like. The next step is to commit to making change. We will explore the many approaches to making change happen in the next chapter.

Chapter 37

Development: Taking Action to Change

In the previous chapter, we talked about self-awareness, the metaphorical mirror you hold up to yourself to *see* and better understand how you perform as a PRG leader. The self-assessment tool (online or paper version) provides you with what is basically a leadership profile to summarize your effectiveness across the various capabilities of the High Impact Leadership model^{SM}. Earlier, we talked about taking a picture of a leader. The image comes slowly into focus like a Polaroid. Your assessment results are that photo—a snapshot in which your strengths and areas for development can be readily seen.

What are you going to do with that photo?
How do you want that image to change over time?
Can you improve the picture?

The answers to those questions represent the other side of self-awareness—the ability to affect professional growth.

Development: How PRG Leaders Learn

Let's put this out there: *By merit of your success in building a company within the PRG, you are unlikely ineffective in any component of the model.* In our experience, executives like you often demonstrate a degree of effectiveness across the various capabilities engendered within the High Impact Leadership model^{SM}. We would be surprised if any reader's scorecard was riddled with Less Than Effective ratings. But we would be more surprised to find a leader rated Highly Effective across the board. The model illustrates the perfect leader. It is the ideal that can never be fully achieved. No one is or needs to be perfect. Outstanding leadership is about understanding your capabilities and striving to become more effective every day. As a PRG leader, the continued growth and success of your company depends on your ability to gauge your performance and ask:

Where are my strengths and areas I can improve?
How can I change my behavior?
Who can help me to facilitate this learning?

The answers to those questions are found in your approach to development, the continuing actions you take to improve your effectiveness. As a PRG leader, there are many opportunities to learn and enhance capabilities. Each type of development has benefits and associated costs or limitations.

The United States Military has been responsible for some of the most comprehensive and meaningful leadership research. The 2013 US Army Leadership Development Strategy suggests that development occurs in three distinct domains. We have refined the army's categories for PRG leaders. Small business leaders learn and grow through three overlapping development domains: *Professional Development, On-the-Job Development,* and, finally, *Self-Development.*

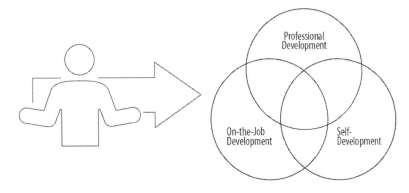

Professional Development is found outside of your company. It consists of training organizations, practitioners, and subject matter experts specializing in identifying leadership capabilities and offering highly relevant tools that support executive learning.

On-the-Job Development encompasses the opportunities a leader has to learn and improve their performance within the boundaries of their day-to-day work.

Self-Development is how a leader engages and learns outside the routine of their role. The learning is self-initiated and prescriptive; a leader proactively seeks to fill performance gaps and expand capabilities.

Each domain represents different opportunities and approaches, some more readily accessed by PRG leaders than others. The fields overlap, as one's experience in any domain is frequently informed by other development activities. Let's briefly explore the forms of training and learning you may consider within each domain.

Professional Development

Leadership directly affects results across an organization. Today's growth-oriented companies look for every competitive advantage—why not start with the people driving the organization? Corporate investments in leadership consulting typically support current executives or identify and develop the next generation of corporate leaders. Leadership assessment and training and development are a worldwide industry. These consulting firms and practitioners offer a range of products and services to support a leader's development.

Leadership assessment firms often emphasize talent development. These practices identify high performers within an organization and focus on cultivating their leadership skills. These methods might include what are called 180s and 360s, which allow for analysis of feedback from a leader and other stakeholders, like direct reports, expert observers, and supervisors. Some companies use academic and industry research to build competency models—inventories of skills, abilities, and knowledge specific to a job or role that suggest success. Others make use of behavioral frameworks or psychological and psychometric models. Assessment practices help leaders to understand their capabilities and prescribe approaches for improving performance.

Training and development firms provide an array of opportunities for executives to learn and grow. In many organizations, leaders identify problems then look for specific solutions to help them navigate the situation and become better executives. Some consulting firms offer specialized, hands-on training that enables leaders to practice their decision-making skills via simulations. A simulation can be incredibly intricate, offering leaders the opportunity to make choices on pricing, "go-no-go" decisions, or react to competitor actions.

Captain Chesley "Sully" Sullenberger famously executed a casualty-free emergency landing of his commercial plane into the Hudson River. We asked him if he had ever experienced that challenge before or trained for such an event. He told us he had not, but much time in the flight simulator made him more than prepared for the challenge. That is the power of a leadership simulation—leaders can practice decision-making in a range of scenarios. Training companies provide services that help executives improve business acumens, like strategic planning or global expansion. Some specialize in helping develop sales leadership or assisting executives in facilitating organizational change. We are comfortable saying there is a robust training tool or program for every distinct leadership capability. Here is the problem: *Not a single organization we know of currently offers a product or service developed explicitly for leaders like you.*

To be perfectly frank, the world of leadership assessment and development is outside the reach of most PRG leaders. We began this book by arguing that *size matters*. It does. A company with fifty, one hundred, two hundred, or more employees has structure. The business is sustainable. To some, it may look like a large company, but we all know it is not. The professional development market is about big, enterprise companies— everything from the research grounding the approaches to the client experiences and outcomes validating the methods. Many of the tools these firms offer do not scale to a small company. In a large firm, the board of directors and CEO are typically driving executive development. They are endeavoring to assess and improve the skills and abilities of the C-suite and GMs of divisions with billions in revenue responsibility.

In a small company, you are the leader of consequence. As you progress through the PRG, your team, with your help, will become leaders. But the leadership pool will never look like a large company. By its nature, the consulting industry is not built for the PRG. Even if you could find a program or tool to further your professional development, the cost would likely be astronomical.

Smaller firms and management consultants may have the capacity to assist you. Again, our concern is the perspective that grounds their support. Unless the consultants have been working with small or perhaps mid-sized companies, they bring a square peg to a round hole.

If you do find a firm with the proper credentials, we suspect the next hurdle will be the costs of customizing the work. This is not to say you should not pursue practitioner support. As a PRG leader, you must prioritize investments in your strategy, your people, and you. What kind of return might a professional engagement bring you? Perhaps a full-on engagement is out of reach. Still, there are seminars and online courses offered by leadership consultants, universities, and professional organizations. Take the time to investigate what is available.

Beyond the leadership assessment firms and the training

and development consultants are executive coaches. Executive coaching is usually for leaders in large companies. Since 2010, there has been a surge of interest in coaching for leaders in high-growth early-stage companies. This trend was spurred by venture capitalist investors trying to focus on brilliant entrepreneurs and help them transition to become leaders of their companies. Many coaches have been executives in large companies and high-growth startups. This combined perspective can apply to the PRG. An executive coach can help you identify where you want to focus your development efforts and facilitate your learning plan. If you have ever played a sport, think about what the coach did—*they helped you play your best game possible.* How? Giving you feedback, offering suggestions, and helping you practice, so a skill almost became second nature. That is what you should expect from an executive coach. They are not there to second-guess your business plan. They are not your therapist but an objective third party who understands your role and can work with you to improve your capabilities. To be valuable, you and your coach need to meet every two to four weeks for at least a year. Although not as costly as a client engagement, executive coaching requires a commitment of time and money.

Professional assessment and development tools should be more targeted and accessible to PRG leaders. As of this writing, the market is heavily skewed toward large companies. But we think that is going to change in the years to come. Small business leaders looking to invest in professional development can be well-served by an executive coach. There are also workshops and seminars explicitly organized to address business acumen and leadership. Investing in any of these forms of professional development can result in exceptional dividends for you as a leader.

On-the-Job Development
Believe it or not, the process of showing up and being actively engaged presents leaders with powerful development

opportunities. The day-to-day work experience is an opportunity to monitor and improve your performance continuously. PRG leaders have access to experts from whom they can elicit knowledge and insight. Great leaders seek feedback on their performance and use it to focus their development better. This array of development opportunities is found on the job.

Reflective Learning

Children learn by repetition. When a child recites the alphabet each day, they eventually memorize the letters. This recognition is the foundation for reading and writing. Adults take repetition to the next level—they cursorily analyze reoccurring events to understand what went on better. Take that natural curiosity a step further, and you have a powerful form of continuous development. Leaders can learn from what they did the day before, good or bad, by using self-awareness—recognizing what they did and the implications of their actions.

Suppose you regularly assess your decisions concerning the capabilities of the High Impact Leadership model℠. By doing this, you set yourself up to make more effective choices the next time around. Each day you go to work, you are presented with opportunities to understand and refine your leadership. How would your leadership effectiveness change if, each night, you reviewed the critical decisions made during the day and asked yourself four specific questions:

How effectively did that demonstrate Business or People Judgment?
When faced with a comparable situation, what would I do the same?
What would I do differently?
How did my decision have an impact on my organization?

This process is reflective learning. Daily self-assessment will

365

dramatically improve your effectiveness. You will be acutely aware of the positive change in your capabilities as you encounter the same decision situations throughout the weeks and months ahead.

The Experts in the Building

The opportunity to regularly assess one's leadership capabilities and adjust performance is, by itself, a valuable aspect of On-the-Job Development. But there are several other ways a leader can grow and learn using resources within their company. Consider this: Where could a leader go to gain specialized knowledge or guidance to support their development? Think of the capabilities representing the Judgments; those skills, behaviors, and knowledge span many disciplines—finance, accounting, strategy, operation, marketing, economics, human resources, big data, sales, and more. Armed with their self-assessment, a leader will aim to improve their performance across several capabilities. Who might be a resource to help them develop a specific skill or ability?

The answer is right in front of you. The people you work with every day, especially the leadership team, are valuable and easy-to-access resources who can help you become a better leader. If you recognize you could improve your Data Savvy, talk to the direct report you know understands big data. Maybe that is your VP of marketing or the CFO. Whoever holds the knowledge, speak to them. Get them to teach you ways to better understand and execute in that area. There is no shame in asking your team to help make you a better leader. This approach can improve your leadership across several dimensions of the model. As you are working to develop a specific capability, you are also engaging your associates. You are demonstrating trust and building professional relationships—behaviors that are indicative of strong People Judgment.

Feedback

Your leadership team represents more than discipline and industry knowledge. Each works closely with you. They *see* your leadership in action and are affected by your decisions and how you execute those choices. Within your direct reports lies a critical development tool—*feedback*.

Feedback from subordinates can provide a leader with additional assessments of their capabilities. These new views of Business and People Judgment validate a leader's self-assessment. They may uncover development areas of which a leader is less conscious. You can use internal feedback to evaluate and improve your leadership performance.

You want to ensure the feedback you are receiving is honest. Sometimes, even the most confident direct reports may fear criticizing you. Some could be afraid of retaliation or fear internal politics. Hopefully, you have built a culture of trust and transparency, making your request little more than a reminder of the value critiques can play in improving everyone's performance. Make sure your team knows—you are open to feedback, and there are no repercussions for sharing their opinions.

There is a process to asking for, receiving, and evaluating feedback. Several popular models define feedback as a loop or a cycle. We would suggest you think of feedback as a more self-directed procedure. A leader needs to solicit observations from their direct reports, interpret what they report, reflect on the findings, then act to make changes in leadership performance.

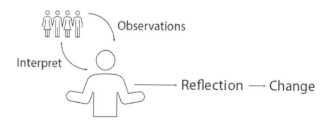

When seeking internal feedback, make sure you ask for the correct information. Do not ask general questions like: "How do you think I am doing?" or "Do you like the way I have been leading the company?" Be specific. Focus on your behavior—what did you do and what were the results? What happened because of your decisions or actions? Ask your associates to tell you what they saw and how they gauged the outcomes. You may want to explore a particular Judgment or set of capabilities from the High Impact Leadership model^SM. In which case, describe the various dimensions and ask them how they saw you demonstrate each on the job. You could give team members a copy of the self-assessment form and ask them to rate you on the various dimensions of the model using the effectiveness rating scale. However you gather feedback, you must clarify what you hear.

To ensure the feedback you collected is meaningful, a discussion must occur, one in which your subordinate feels comfortable sharing their observations. At the same time, you must confidently determine the validity of their evaluation without being defensive. Make sure to ask probing questions to help you understand what an associate is communicating and ensure you interpret the correct meaning of their feedback. For example, suppose you were talking with your VP about a recent decision to change their budget. In that case, they might initially observe you made a poor decision. Ask them to elaborate as to why. What were the implications for them? For others? You want to clarify what aspects of the decisions were effective and ineffective.

Inviting feedback from your team will result in rich, detailed assessments of your leadership capabilities. Much like you held up the mirror to yourself with your self-assessment, you must now use self-awareness and reflect on these additional views of your performance. What does your leadership profile look like now? Using this new snapshot, how will you change your performance moving forward?

The opportunities for improving your leadership capabilities within the boundaries of your day-to-day work are varied and significant. Unlike Professional Development, the approaches are easy to access and require little to any investment. But committing to any combination of these On-the-Job Development activities will bring you closer to high-impact leadership.

Self-Development

The final type of development is the most pervasive and accessible form of leadership development. It is outside your organization (excluding Professional Development) and limited only by one's engagement and interest. In other words: *How committed are you to becoming a great PRG leader?* Your answer is likely reflected in your assessment of the Motivators. Success-Driven leaders are typically focused on building a company that reflects who they are as a business leader.

Self-Development requires you to explore beyond the routine of your role. It is self-initiated and prescriptive. We have found a barrier to even the most motivated, performance-focused leader is simply their ability to navigate the Self-Development domain. Many are not familiar with the appropriate learning resources nor recognize the most practical approaches for improving different leadership capabilities.

If a leader asked us the best ways they could create Self-Development opportunities, our response would be:

- Seek out trusted peers and stakeholders
- Read books and research that address a particular development need
- Look to specialized resources and communities

Yes, it's common sense. But ask yourself: How often do you regularly endeavor to improve your leadership skills using these suggested approaches and resources? We suspect your answer is not a resounding, "Every day, using several approaches." Nonetheless, the most powerful Self-Development techniques are often within your grasp; you just need the roadmap to seek them out.

Trusted Peers and Stakeholders

Did you know Harry Truman and Herbert Hoover came together to support then-President Dwight Eisenhower in what has gone on to be called *The Presidents Club*? Nancy Gibbs reported, since 1953, US Presidents have come together to support each other (regardless of party or public quarrel) as an informal network of advisors. As leadership roles go, one can imagine being the leader of the free world comes with some particularly distinct challenges. Imagine the perspective and clarity a current president gains from hashing out ideas and gathering feedback from the handful of leaders who have also held the job of President of the United States.

We mention The Presidents Club because it is an easy-to-understand example of Self-Development through peers—people who hold the same role and, thus, collective knowledge. This entire book is about the unique role of the small business leader. Like the US Presidents, who better understands the challenges you face each day than other PRG leaders? Within your network, you are likely connected to similar executives. Outside a direct competitor, is it unreasonable to think about sitting down with someone who demonstrates exceptional People or Business Judgment to discuss how they approach leadership challenges?

What if Jamie and Terry were connected? Terry might identify Strategic Mindset as a capability he wished to strengthen and recognizes Jamie as an excellent strategic thinker. What would happen if Terry asked her to talk with him about strategy and long-term business planning? How would that conversation go? We can tell you—Jamie would talk about her experiences, how she approaches strategic issues, and why she has been successful. Terry could take her perspective and apply it to his unique situation.

You might also look at your network as an informal leader support group. What value might you and your peers gain from regularly connecting and talking about the challenges you face? Like The Presidents Club, a PRG leaders club could support each other in ways few other professionals could.

You can further refine your leadership profile by talking to key stakeholders. The powerful insights and focus on your leadership effectiveness gained by seeking feedback from your direct reports are also available outside your organization— but the view is different. How do your board members "see" your leadership? Suppose you do not have an active board of directors. In that case, there are likely several professionals with whom you regularly work who have observed your leadership. What insights might you solicit from your banker, a key supplier, manufacturing or sales partner, or employment recruiter? The process for requesting, clarifying, evaluating, and acting on stakeholder feedback is the same as asking direct reports for their feedback within On-the-Job Development. If you invest in this form of Self-Development, your leadership effectiveness will be significantly enhanced.

Books and Research

Reading is one of the most used and effective forms of Self-Development. It seems almost silly to tell a group that our research indicates "reads voraciously" to read more, but that is precisely what we are telling you. The key to reading for Self-Development is identifying the knowledge and information that best speaks to a particular need. Most PRG leaders regularly read business, financial, local, and world news. In our experience, they keep up with industry and trade periodicals and consume a range of business books. This is what good business savvy looks like. Your breadth of information provides you with a vibrant macro view of the economy and your industry. Daily reading is a critical first step in Self-Development. When focusing on your leadership effectiveness, the goal is to improve your performance in Business or People Judgment and associated dimensions.

The volume of discipline-specific knowledge available to businesspeople can make one's head spin. We could point you to literature that supports your leadership needs. But this is Self-Development. We are not in the room with you each day. For reading to become a valuable component of your learning, you must identify and evaluate the books and research that most effectively and efficiently address a particular leadership capability. For simplicity's sake, we describe three categories of business knowledge, each differing in empirical approaches, detail, theory versus application, and intended audiences. It is important you understand how you can put each type of knowledge to use to strengthen your leadership capabilities.

Seminal Works: Sometimes called pivotal works or landmark studies, these articles and books initially presented an idea of great importance or influence within a discipline. Most, but not all, stand the test of time. A seminal work almost always provides a foundational explanation of most leadership capabilities. For example, Michael Porter is the recognized researcher of strategy. If you wanted to develop your Strategic Mindset, his competitive advantage and generic strategy models are timeless. Drucker earned the title Father of Management. Technology and processes have dated some of his narratives. Admittedly, the "men as leaders" tone of the 1970s now feels chauvinistic. Yet, his seminal book *How to Be a Manager* presented five key behaviors a leader must demonstrate to succeed. Others, including us, have refined and built on his work, but the five behaviors remain sacrosanct to effective leadership. We provided these examples to illustrate the enduring value of seminal works. Their fundamental nature suggests these works should be a starting point for understanding any specific business discipline. There are likely things you intuitively do well as a leader—these works will crystallize your understanding of those highly effective behaviors. Just take each with a grain of salt and recognize how time may impact the proposed theory or framework. We have provided a list of seminal works that we believe represent a solid introduction to business leadership in Appendix B.

Academic Research: Academics are responsible for a surplus of knowledge across disciplines that collectively represent the business world. Millions of researchers regularly study organizations, industries, and business processes. Applying the scientific method, they collect and analyze data and report their findings. Most importantly, these experts interpret the findings and propose theories, models, and frameworks to help businesspeople to improve results and outcomes. Those findings inform other academics, government agencies, and practitioners. Academic research can be beneficial to leaders who have targeted an already effective capability for additional development. The most accessible and relevant academic research can be found at Harvard Business Review (HBR.org). The initial search is conveniently broken into the most referenced business disciplines, and the article summaries are comprehensive. Although HBR charges for most content, the nature of academic research is to share knowledge freely. The site academia.com is a popular open-source repository boasting studies from over 159 million academics and researchers. The collection is expansive and timely. Unlike HBR, the content spans every imaginable discipline. You should plan meaningful keywords and phrases that relate to a topic you are interested in exploring.

General Audience Business Books: Books like *From 50 to 500* and other leadership titles are just one category of general business books. Like us, you have probably spent time with whatever business book has become trendy every few years. The value of these titles must always be judged individually.

When looking to the commercial presses for Self-Development, remember you are not reading to be entertained. Instead, you are reading to learn. Therefore, you must scrutinize the content, approach, and relevance of a title to your specific learning goal. Closely examine titles that take a mindset shift approach. They are difficult to implement and may not be appropriate to you. Again, you are looking for books that correlate to improving one of the leadership capabilities.

Books and research can play a critical role in your Self-Development plan. Although we wholeheartedly endorse them, we would be remiss not to remind you again: *the context will not perfectly align with you and your organization.* Although 99 percent of all companies throughout North America and Europe are small companies, most of these titles are written about or for executives and managers in large companies. To maximize your learning, you need to "filter" the knowledge in these works through the lens of the PRG.

Specialized Resources and Communities
The success of your Self-Development is predicated on your ability to identify significant and valuable learning resources. Trusted peers, stakeholders, and reading can significantly advance you on your journey. Still, you will inevitably find yourself looking for other, more specialized sources to help you better demonstrate various leadership capabilities. The gaps in your development plan are likely discrete and correlate to a particular dimension of Business or People Judgment. You may have identified a development need. Maybe you want to drive up your effectiveness in a specific capability. Shifting your performance, in either case, requires targeted learning material. Jamie recognized that her Team Development capabilities needed work. So, she planned several On-the-Job and Self-Development activities. But Jamie knew that she needed more focused training and support. She turned to the Society for

HR Management (SHRM) and found an affordable web-based training class on building teams.

Sometimes, leaders improve a capability by gaining a greater depth of expertise in a functional area. For example, you might develop Data Savvy, in part, by better understanding the structure and capabilities of relational databases. A Self-Development approach to achieve this growth might be to invest in a video training course through LinkedIn Learning. On the People Judgment side, the Association for Talent Development (ATD) provides blogs, user forums, and online seminars a leader could use to support capability-specific learning. In the US, you can find Small Business Development Centers (SBDCs) in every state. SBDCs provide free business consulting services and seminars that could be particularly relevant to your development plan. These are just a few examples of the many specialized resources and communities a PRG leader might investigate as part of their self-development plan. As you focus on improving your effectiveness within individual capabilities, try to seek out more narrowly defined and specific tools and material to supplement your learning.

Your Development Plan

In this chapter, we explored how PRG leaders can improve their performance through leadership development. Many learning opportunities are available across the three domains of development. We hope you now have a clear idea of the resources, information, and approaches, as well as the benefits, costs, and potential hurdles to these learning resources. Now, you will want to create and manage your development plan.

It may sound formal, but a clearly defined, outcome-oriented approach to your development is easy to create and will ensure you achieve optimal results. We have created a personal development planning tool you can easily use to map, track, and assess your progress toward strengthening your leadership capabilities. We have included a copy of the planning tool in Appendix C and provided you with a free printable version of the tool at www.from50to500.com/devplan.

As you begin to consider a personal development plan, start with your self-assessment. Identify the one or two capabilities you most want to improve. You can dissect the capabilities too. Consider the illustrative behaviors to identify discrete learning that might improve an overarching capability. You cannot address everything at the same time; development must be measured and focused. Your development plan should be predicated on answering the following questions:

What capabilities have I identified as needing development?
Which of these capabilities have the highest priority for me?
What approach from the three Development Domains would work best to help me strengthen a particular capability?
What results do I anticipate or what changes am I looking for?
How will I know?
What time frame should I consider?

We used these questions to create the planning tool—the six columns represent the development process. Each row is a separate or distinct effort to address a capability targeted for development.

Capability	Approach	Desired Outcome	Time Frame	Outcome Achieved	Follow-Up
Priority #	☐ Professional Development ☐ On-the-Job Development ☐ Self-Development Plan				

To use the tool, think of each column as a stage in your development process. You have identified and prioritized specific capabilities you wish to strengthen—write the first and most pressing in the "Capability" column. Now, consider your "Approach" to developing that capability. From which of the three Development Domains will you draw? What specific activities or resources will best support your learning or growth? Note what you plan to do. Next, in the "Desired Outcome" column, write down what you want to happen after investing time and effort in this specific development. Estimate the "Time Frame" required to complete the tasks, and when you are done—write down what happened, noting the "Outcome Achieved." At the end of each development process (row), evaluate changes in your capability. Have you achieved the level of effectiveness to which you were aiming? Do you need additional development opportunities? Your answers will determine what you write in the "Follow-Up" column.

Here is an example of how a PRG leader used the planning tool to create components of their personal development plan. After reviewing their self-assessment, this leader's top priority was to strengthen Data Savvy. They wanted to become more confident and comfortable with the rapidly changing digital data space and then improve their data analysis skills to make more effective decisions. They created the following plan.

Capability	Approach	Desired Outcome	Time Frame	Outcome Achieved	Follow-Up
Priority # 1 Data Savvy	☐ Professional Development ☐ On-the-Job Development ☒ Self-Development Plan Read "Big Data 2.0" and enroll in online video training course about analyzing business data	- Improve my comfort and confidence in current terms and approaches to data acquisition & analysis - Establish broader base for data analysis	Book - 4 wks Course - 6 weeks after I finish book	- I am comfortable with relational databases - Understand how web and technology create new sources of data - More comfortable with types of predictions that can be made	Look for and read new articles and blog posts that talk about data acquisition and analysis
Priority # 1 Data Savvy	☐ Professional Development ☒ On-the-Job Development ☐ Self-Development Plan Identify new data sources, analyze, and present to my team for feedback	Identify at least one unique new variables to provide insight for company growth	6 weeks post completing book and course	Provided several new insights to my direct reports after discovering and analyzing a new data source connected to our industry	Commit to regularly attending the quarterly analysis meetings of various groups so I can provide more feedback and continue building insight

Recognizing the first step toward strengthening Data Savvy began with a greater understanding of the subject area, the leader chose to read a highly relevant book and then enroll in an online training course. Both are Self-Development opportunities that build individual knowledge. Note the time frame—they knew the amount of time necessary to complete this plan and committed. The result? Their understanding of data analytics improved considerably, which resulted in greater confidence.

But this was not the degree of growth to which they aspired. To reach that level of Data Savvy, the leader recognized they needed additional development. The next step in their plan made use of On-the-Job Development to apply their skills at work and seek feedback from those data experts we know are right there in the building.

This leader also wanted to strengthen Individual Development. Their plan reflects multiple phases of development drawing from resources within the different Development Domains.

Capability	Approach	Desired Outcome	Time Frame	Outcome Achieved	Follow-Up
Priority # 2 Individual Development	☐ Professional Development ☐ On-the-Job Development ☑ Self-Development **Plan** Contact Rich at RJR- he's really good at growing his people. Ask for help in improving my feedback and coaching	I want to be able to give more timely and actionable feedback to associates	4 weeks to meet and create a plan to begin working with my people	Rich provided resources and examples of how he develops his people. We created an action plan to help me practice my approach with one of my people	- Select associate - Spend next 2 months working with them and evaluating results
Priority # 2 Individual Development	☐ Professional Development ☑ On-the-Job Development ☐ Self-Development **Plan** Select an associate to coach using my new action plan and practice new approaches	1. See meaningful improvement in my associate's work 2. Become more confident in my ability to develop my people	2 months with employee Another 4 weeks to get their feedback, look at results and evaluate my growth	Associate has been extremely successful this quarter. They reported that my feedback helped them be a better producer. I am becoming more comfortable with this role	Upcoming quarter— work with 3 associates in some capacity to continue refining my abilities in this area

The leader began Self-Development by consulting a trusted peer with a reputation for developing his people. After several meetings, they were able to create an action plan—a personalized training program for coaching associates. Now, after working with an employee for two months, then assessing the impact of their feedback and guidance, the leader plans to continue strengthening Individual Development by coaching more associates.

Use the tool to create a personal development plan that maximizes the time and effort you invest in strengthening your leadership capabilities. The key to any development plan is to continually monitor your progress to determine when you have achieved the effectiveness level to which you aspired. If you find you do not realize the planned results, revisit your development approaches and adjust the plan. Development should be responsive and flexible. When you recognize your goals, review your self-assessment and identify new capabilities. Great leaders will recognize this method for what it is — *a recipe for highly effective leadership.*

Keep in mind that leadership development is a process of continuous improvement. High impact leaders are always learning, continually striving to be more effective, and using self-awareness to pinpoint ways to move the mean and drive their organizational results through the PRG.

We have given you the playbook. The ball is now in your hands.

Closing Thoughts

We hope *From 50 to 500* was not only a great read but a valuable guide to help you grow your small company through high impact leadership. At the outset, we said that we wanted to provide you with an easy-to-understand, relevant, and actionable model you could use immediately to affect your leadership performance. Now, at the end of our journey, let's look at how we achieved those goals.

First, we introduced the concept of the PRG to help all understand that small businesses are distinct. Growing companies like yours require a particular set of capabilities.

Then, we introduced the High Impact Leadership model^{SM}. Together, we saw it in action through Jamie and Terry, over a year of their lives running their businesses. The model is the picture of perfect PRG leadership—a collection of behaviors one can look to, emulate, and become a more effective leader.

After experiencing the model through other leaders, you held up the mirror to see your leadership using self-awareness. The self-assessment tool resulted in a leadership profile summarizing your effectiveness across the various capabilities—Motivators, Business Judgment, People Judgment, and Derailers.

Finally, we explained how you could take action on what you see in your self-assessment through various types of development: Professional Development, On-the-Job Development, and Self-Development.

You now have the insight, tools, and access to the information and resources you need to be a high impact leader. Remember, even if today you score as highly effective, it is essential you continuously evaluate and modify your leadership to remain highly effective and impact the growth of your business. Use the model and assessment tool; build a continuous development plan. Remember, with every incremental change in performance, you will see exponential results across your organization and propel every kind of growth—people, revenue, and market share.

We are excited to hear how your leadership positively changes your company in the short and long term. Please send us an email and share your experiences and stories at leaders@ from50to500.com. If you have a few moments, please feel free to add your review of the book to your favorite online sites.

Best,

Richard Jones

Partners to the World's Small Businesses

We wrote this book because we saw a giant hole in the leadership consulting market. We are pleased to announce the launch of our new company, *Alaric,* a worldwide leadership development and strategy enhancement firm for leaders of small companies.

What's in a name?

Long ago the Goths were a small but driven people under the leadership of King Alaric. They quickly grew to become the Visigoths, dominating Moesia, then Athens, and eventually Rome—a small group that rapidly grew to compete with the biggest and most powerful warrior states.

In many ways, Alaric is the story of the very best small business leaders—you have a vision for your company and work to hone your leadership abilities so you can build a company of consequence that grows quickly and makes its mark in the marketplace.

We eat, sleep, and dream small business! To us, being a small company does not mean you are limited to anything less than big leadership and even bigger results. At Alaric, we partner with clients to provide expert insight and services, including:

- Assessing leadership capabilities and creating development plans for leaders and their teams
- Connecting PRG leaders with similarly enterprising executives in a virtual peer-coaching network
- Supporting your and your team's success through one-on-one, team coaching, or both
- Improving Business and People Judgment through simulation-based online programs and live workshops
- Helping to transform your successful business plan into a viable long-term strategy

We have big plans for the small business community. Our experiences and small company-specific research make us uniquely qualified to partner with PRG leaders throughout the world. Check out our blog at www.alaricpartners.com/blog and reach out to us and see how we can help you and your company achieve greater impact and growth.

Partners to the world's small business leaders

🌐 www.alaricpartners.com

in @alaricpartners 🐦 @alaricpartners f @alaricpartners

About the Authors

Our varied backgrounds and tenures represent a combined one hundred years plus of insight into challenges and needs of small to mid-sized leaders. We have founded and grown small companies, built market-leading firms that grew to employ hundreds of high-performing employees. We have worked as executives in large corporations. Also, we have seen both sides of the institutional investment world, having a first-hand view of companies that both succeeded and failed to grow. Our work has been across the business, practitioner, and academic fields. These distinct experiences, combined with a comprehensive collection of small business-specific research, provide what we think is a credible view of small business leadership.

We are Jonathan and Richard Dapra and Jonas Akerman. We have known each other personally and professionally for many years (Rich has known Jonathan for his entire life—he is his father). We three share a similar perspective on leadership and the approaches one can take to develop their capabilities. *Small business leadership is a new and distinct focus for us.* The prospect of supporting a long-overlooked group of leaders was appealing. But we were drawn to this area for distinct reasons. Rather than provide a trio of boring biographies, we thought we would tell you a bit more about our backgrounds and why we were inspired to research and develop solutions specific to leaders like you.

Jonathan has spent most of his professional life working in, leading, investing in, or consulting with growing companies. He has started companies in the tech and gaming industry and helped build the Photoshop special effects plugins company

AutoFX. He was part of the leadership team at *Dynamic Graphic* (DG), a creative solutions company that produced royalty-free photos, provided illustrations to most of the country's newspapers, offered professional training, sold graphic design software, and published three nationally-known magazines. "People used to ask me what it was like working at such a big company. I never knew how to answer. I was hung up on people thinking DG was a large company. It didn't feel big—around two hundred employees, an office in the UK, the president and five officers. Were we a small business? A mid-sized firm?"

This question and the implications for myself and others working in similar companies led Jonathan to focus his doctoral research on small business leader success factors. As a professor at Plymouth State University, he continues this research and applies it; consulting with business leaders and partnering with small companies across the state.

Jonas has been a lifelong entrepreneur. In 1992, he came to the United States to build a US presence for the Swedish leadership and development firm *BTS Group*. During his twenty-four-year tenure, he grew *BTS USA* from just himself to over two hundred professionals, working with executives or leadership teams in over two hundred of the Global Fortune-500 companies. Today, BTS is publicly traded and employs over seven hundred professionals across the globe. After leaving BTS, he returned to his native Sweden to become the CEO of a housing development company with nearly one hundred employees and contractors.

"When Rich first sent me some of Jonathan's research and shared his views on the need for more role-specific assessment and development materials, it was like a lightbulb went off." Having spent much of his professional life growing small companies and developing leaders in large, global organizations, Jonas instinctively knew most business tools, simulations, and leadership development materials were not the right fit for executives growing small companies. He quickly came to realize how many leaders throughout the world are flying without a handbook, let alone a good set of tools to help them better prepare for their experiences. "I knew I wanted to be a part of this effort to support a large but neglected group of businesspeople."

Rich's introduction to leadership began as an officer in one of the world's largest organizations noted for its legendary leaders and highly effective leadership development, the US Marine Corps. His first post-doctoral job was at a fledgling assessment and development company, of which he was one of just four early associates. Three years later, that company, *Development Dimensions International* (DDI), had grown to upward of fifty people. DDI currently employs over 1,100 associates and is noted for its assessment and development solutions. Subsequent to DDI, he began and grew his own assessment company, Resource Analysis and Development. He led RAD Inc. until one of his clients, Pitney Bowes, lured him away. The next thirty years plus of Rich's career were spent in Fortune-100 companies including *Pitney Bowes, Aetna*, and *Liberty Mutual*, where he worked closely with CEOs and business unit heads on the acquisition, assessment, and development of talent. These experiences provided first-hand observations of leadership challenges and the capabilities required to meet them. At the end of his career, he joined Jonas' growing and already successful leadership development company, BTS USA, where he built what is now BTS's global assessment practice.

Several years ago, Rich began working with Jonathan and Jonas to generate targeted research and build a practical, actionable, and valuable approach to leadership assessment and development for the small business leader.

Our collective experiences and expertise give us a broad and complete view of the leadership landscape. *We see the holes,* the large groups of executives and business owners underserved by the existing theory. We recognize the shortcomings of the professional development frameworks and systems available to executives who wish to develop their leadership skills. This book is our first step toward educating and supporting small business leaders.

Work Vessels for Veterans

A portion of the proceeds from sales of *From 50 to 500* will be donated to *Work Vessels for Veterans, Inc.*

Mission: To equip America's injured veterans with the tools they need to start a business or pursue career education.

Work Vessels for Vets is a unique national charity. No other nonprofit is solely dedicated to awarding equipment to America's injured veterans to start a business. Since 2008, the awards ranged from commercial fishing boats to farm tractors, skid loaders, hay balers, trucks, trailers, UTVs, drones, electronics, carpentry tools, machinery and even a therapy horse! To date, more than 2,400 veterans across all 50 states have received equipment valued at over $3.5 million. Work Vessels for Vets provides critical equipment and direct services to injured veterans who see self-employment as a way forward to accommodate combat injuries, frequent medical appointments and "bad days." This charity's commitment to helping vets succeed is recognized with the highest national ratings including *GuideStar*'s highest "Platinum Status" for Efficiency & Transparency, the annual Top-Rated Nonprofit Award from the *Great Nonprofits* rating agency, and "Best Accredited Charity" by the *Better Business Bureau*.

A recent survey of 500 Work Vessels for Vets past awardees revealed that more than $16 million in economic activity per year is being generated by the hundreds of new veteran-owned businesses that have created over 2000 new jobs.

Through this journey, Work Vessels for Vets has remained a small but mighty, all-volunteer organization, maintaining a low 2% administrative overhead!

Information, success stories and veteran applications are found on the website, www.WVFV.org.

Work Vessels for Vets, Inc. is a 501-c-3 Public Charity. Donations and in-kind contributions are fully tax-deductible.

Appendices

Appendix A

Self-Assessment Reports

A PRG leader completed the self-assessment using both forms of the tool. The leader's self-ratings and results are shown first in the printable, self-scoring version available as a download from www.from50to500.com/print.

The same ratings were entered in the web-based self-assessment tool at www.from50to500.com/prg. After completing the online version, a customized report was generated for the leader. That report is also shown in this appendix.

Self-Assessment

Motivators
The Motivators that define the High Impact Leadership model are:
1. *Success Driven:* You are inspired to build an organization of consequence that reflects who you are as a business leader.
2. *Industry Passion:* You are motivated to develop personal expertise and apply knowledge to build a successful business.

Review the behaviors that define the Motivators. Consider the frequency with which you demonstrate each and rate yourself using the following scale:

	1	2	3
	Seldom	Sometimes	Frequently

Builds a Unique Culture

Empowers associates to take initiative (act like an owner)	1 2 ③
Creates a personal and professionally rewarding work environment	1 ② 3
Talks regularly about company values	1 2 ③
Models company values (walks the talk)	1 ② 3
Implements values and capability criteria for advancement	1 ② 3

Sum of ratings: 12   *Divide by 5 =* **M1 Rating:** 2.4

Impact and Influence

Paints a compelling picture of a future	1 2 ③
Listens carefully without bias	1 ② 3
Evangelizes company efforts in industry and community	1 2 ③
Conveys confidence in the company mission and strategy	1 2 ③
Communicates thoughts and ideas clearly	1 ② 3

Sum of ratings: 13   *Divide by 5 =* **M2 Rating:** 2.6

Enterprising

Articulates new and significant opportunities	1 ② 3
Formulates tactics to quickly advance from concept to product or service	1 ② 3
Takes measured risk	1 2 ③
Deploys existing assets in support of new opportunities	1 2 ③
Fails fast	1 2 ③

Sum of ratings: 13   *Divide by 5 =* **M3 Rating:** 2.6

Self-Directed Learner

Evaluates personal strengths and weaknesses	1 ② 3
Creates a personal growth plan	1 ② 3
Reads voraciously	1 2 ③
Seeks new knowledge and insights from varied sources	1 2 ③
Reviews daily decisions, asking: What would I have done differently?	1 2 ③

Sum of ratings: 13   *Divide by 5 =* **M4 Rating:** 2.6

Network Builder

Uses social media	① 2 3
Looks for contacts everywhere	1 2 ③
Participates in industry events	1 ② 3
Identifies the right people with whom to establish relations	1 ② 3
Treats network as relationships, not connections	1 2 ③

Sum of ratings: 11   *Divide by 5 =* **M5 Rating:** 2.2

-1-

Sample Self-Assessment Page 1 of 5

Business Judgment

The quality of decisions you make to execute strategy, overcome obstacles, and recognize opportunities to innovate and grow.

Dimensions of Business Judgment:
- Data Savvy
- Customer Focus
- Balanced Decision-Making
- Strategic Mindset
- Financial Awareness

Review the five capabilities of Business Judgment and rate your effectiveness in the associated behavioral dimensions using the following scale:

1	2	3
Less Than Effective	Effective	Highly Effective

Data Savvy

References different types of qualitative and quantitative resources	1 (2) 3
Recognizes patterns in seemingly unrelated data to develop actionable insights	(1) 2 3
Uses analytical tools to manipulate and visualize information	1 (2) 3
Asks incisive questions to get to core issue	1 2 (3)
Seeks multiple opinions	1 (2) 3

Sum of ratings: 10   Divide by 5 = **B1 Rating:** 2.0

Strategic Mindset

Explains how a potential business plan is likely to play-out	1 2 (3)
Identifies opportunities to create increased value through innovation	1 (2) 3
Monitors industry, societal, and governmental environment to identify opportunities or threats	1 2 (3)
Seeks new markets within existing industries	1 2 (3)
Recognizes organizational core competency	1 2 (3)

Sum of ratings: 14   Divide by 5 = **B2 Rating:** 2.8

Customer Focus

Demonstrates thorough knowledge of one's own products and services	1 2 (3)
Engages with customers to solve problems and understand their needs	1 2 (3)
Knowledge of the most important factors/metrics driving success in the client's business	1 2 (3)
Identifies the growth potential (or limitations) of customers	1 (2) 3
Monitors competitors' actions	1 2 (3)

Sum of ratings: 14   Divide by 5 = **B3 Rating:** 2.8

Financial Awareness

Evaluates short-term and long-term financial requirements to execute plans	1 (2) 3
Defines and monitors key financial metrics	1 (2) 3
Seeks out expert guidance to identify the financial implications of a decision	(1) 2 3
Evaluates the financial risks and potential impact of potential decisions	1 (2) 3
Demonstrates a comprehensive understanding of how the company makes money	1 2 (3)

Sum of ratings: 10   Divide by 5 = **B4 Rating:** 2.0

Balanced Decision-Making

Develops cost-effective solutions to overcome obstacles to meet plan milestones	1 (2) 3
Involves appropriate associates in decisions	(1) 2 3
Recognizes operational capacity and resource implications of decisions	1 2 (3)
Develops "what if" scenarios to better evaluate the short-term and long-term outcomes of a business decision	1 2 (3)
Balances short-term risk and reward	1 2 (3)

Sum of ratings: 12   Divide by 5 = **B5 Rating:** 2.4

Sample Self-Assessment Page 2 of 5

People Judgment

The quality of decisions you make to build and lead a team of driven, thoughtful, and company-centric associates.

Dimensions of People Judgment:
- Engagement
- Relationship Building
- Team Development
- Individual Development
- Decisiveness

Review the five capabilities of People Judgment and rate your effectiveness in the behavioral dimensions using the following scale:

1	2	3
Less Than Effective	Effective	Highly Effective

Engagement

Available to associates on a regular basis	1 2 (3)
Encourages open communication and candid feedback	1 (2) 3
Employs a direct and honest communication style	1 (2) 3
Discusses organizational needs and direction	1 2 (3)
Explains the rationale for decisions	1 2 (3)

Sum of ratings: 13 Divide by 5 = **P1 Rating:** 2.6

Relationship Building

Develops professional relationships in a variety of contexts	1 (2) 3
Communicates regularly with external partners and customers	1 (2) 3
Engages associates from all areas of the organization	1 (2) 3
Handles interactions judiciously and empathetically	1 2 (3)
Personalizes conversations/interactions	1 2 (3)

Sum of ratings: 12 Divide by 5 = **P2 Rating:** 2.4

Team Development

Participates in setting clear individual and team goals	1 2 (3)
Coaches associates to think beyond personal achievement	1 2 (3)
Promotes respect and relationships within teams	1 2 (3)
Values diversity in experience and backgrounds	1 2 (3)
Encourages team generated ideas and accomplishments	1 2 (3)

Sum of ratings: 15 Divide by 5 = **P3 Rating:** 3.0

Individual Development

Establishes consistent processes and procedures for development and advancement	1 (2) 3
Invests in the ongoing development of associates	(1) 2 3
Identifies and fosters the development of potential leaders	1 (2) 3
Provides regular performance feedback and coaching	1 (2) 3
Ensures managers demonstrate effective coaching skills	(1) 2 3

Sum of ratings: 8 Divide by 5 = **P4 Rating:** 1.6

Decisiveness

Assesses the situation from the viewpoint of the individual and the organization	1 (2) 3
Considers alternative courses of action and implications	1 (2) 3
Solicits the perspective of others when appropriate	1 2 (3)
Recognizes the importance of making a timely decision	1 2 (3)
Delivers the decision in a thoughtful but firm manner, always sticking to his or her decision	1 (2) 3

Sum of ratings: 12 Divide by 5 = **P5 Rating:** 2.4

Sample Self-Assessment Page 3 of 5

Small Business Leadership Derailers

Derailers are the actions and approaches a PRG leader can take that lead to organizational dysfunction and ineffectiveness.

Derailers include:

- Formality-Structure Disconnect
- In the Weeds
- Informal Influencers
- Oversimplified Decision-Making

Review the behaviors associated with each Derailer. Consider the frequency with which you demonstrate each and rate yourself using the following scale:

1	2	3
Seldom	Sometimes	Frequently

Formality-Structure Disconnect

Builds a relatively flat organization	(1)	2	3
Rejects operating procedures or support systems	(1)	2	3
Rejects vertical integration	(1)	2	3
Fails to plan for leadership succession	1	(2)	3
Rejects concerns for company's long-term viability	(1)	2	3

Sum of ratings: 6   Divide by 5 = **D1 Rating:** 1.2

In the Weeds

Micromanages lower-level decision-making processes	1	2	(3)
Adopts vanity projects	(1)	2	3
Disrupts the decision-making of subordinate leaders and managers	(1)	2	3
Inability to prioritize	(1)	2	3
Unwilling to abandon a failing product or service	(1)	2	3

Sum of ratings: 7   Divide by 5 = **D2 Rating:** 1.4

Informal Influencers

Consults "experts" whose expertise is not related to the issue/problem at hand	(1)	2	3
Conveys lack of confidence in direct reports	(1)	2	3
Allows family members to have undue influence	(1)	2	3
Establishes informal advisory boards with vague charters	(1)	2	3
Unduly influenced by personal coach	(1)	2	3

Sum of ratings: 5   Divide by 5 = **D3 Rating:** 1.0

Oversimplified Decision-Making

Rushes decisions	1	(2)	3
Fails to collect or purchase critical data	1	2	(3)
Places heavy emphasis on "gut" feeling	1	(2)	3
Does not rely on a suitably diverse and experienced group to analyze problem or opportunity	(1)	2	3
Makes unilateral decisions without consultation	(1)	2	3

Sum of ratings: 9   Divide by 5 = **D4 Rating:** 1.8

-4-

Sample Self-Assessment Page 4 of 5

Self-Assessment Results

Scoring the Instrument

Refer to your various self-assessment ratings on pages 1 to 4. Each is labeled (e.g., M1, B1, P1, D1, etc.)

1. Record your ratings for each dimension of the Motivators, Judgments, and Derailers in the sections below
2. Sum the ratings and divide by the number indicated to calculate your scorecard results

Your Scorecard

From Page 1

M1: 2.4 Builds a Unique Culture
M2: 2.6 Impact and Influence
M3: 2.6 Enterprising

Sum = 7.6 ÷ 3 = 2.5
Success Driven Rating
1=Low 2=Moderate 3=High

From Page 1

M4: 2.6 Self-Directed Learner
M5: 2.2 Network Builder

Sum = 4.8 ÷ 2 = 2.4
Industry Passion Rating
1=Low 2=Moderate 3=High

From Page 2

B1: 2.0 Data Savvy
B2: 2.8 Strategic Mindset
B3: 2.8 Customer Focus
B4: 2.0 Financial Awareness
B5: 2.4 Balanced Decision-Making

Sum = 12 ÷ 5 = 2.4
Business Judgment Rating
1=Ineffective 2=Effective 3=Highly Effective

From Page 3

P1: 2.6 Engagement
P2: 2.4 Relationship Building
P3: 3.0 Team Development
P4: 1.6 Individual Development
P5: 2.4 Decisiveness

Sum = 12 ÷ 5 = 2.4
People Judgment Rating
1=Ineffective 2=Effective 3=Highly Effective

From Page 4

D1: 1.2 Formality-Structure Disconnect
D2: 1.4 In the Weeds
D3: 1.0 Informal Influencers
D4: 1.8 Oversimplified Decision-Making

Sum = 5.4 ÷ 4 = 1.4
Derailers Rating
1=Low Concern 2=Some Concern 3=High Concern

Dig Deeper Into Your Performance Data

Use the discrete ratings of the exemplifying behaviors on pages 1-4 to pinpoint development needs: Identify behaviors indicating Motivation, dissect your effectiveness across the capabilities of the Judgments, or focus on specific Derailer tendencies.

WANT TO LEARN MORE?

Try the online self-assessment form. We are collecting data from all types of leaders throughout the PRG that will enable us to provide you comparisons of leadership ratings across a number of variables including company size, industry, and geography.

For more info and support check out:
www.alaricpartners.com

* Model component ratings may reflect +/- 1 error resulting from the averaging of averaged ratings

© Copyright 2021 Alaric Inc. All International Rights Reserved.

-5-

Sample Self-Assessment Page 5 of 5

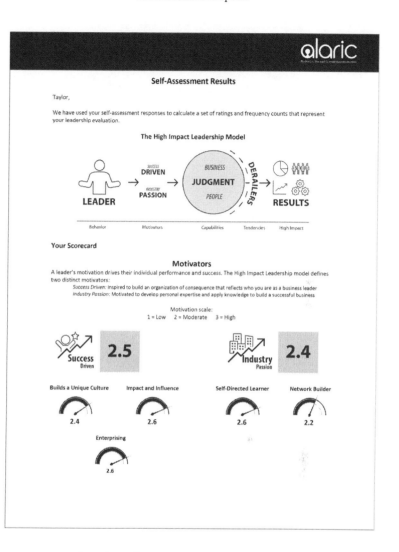

Sample Web Report and Data Page 1 of 7

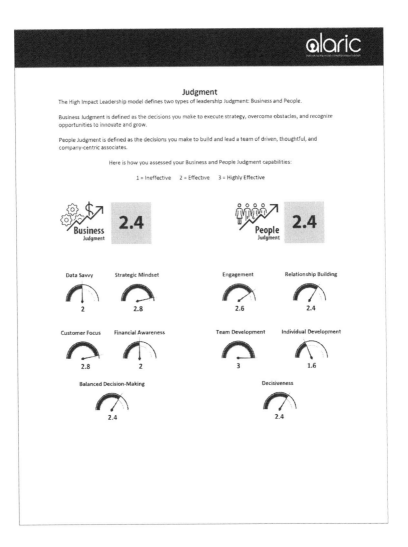

Sample Web Report and Data Page 2 of 7

Derailers

Derailer tendencies can negatively affect your leadership effectiveness. Our research uncovered four significant Derailers that influence PRG leaders: Formality-Structure Disconnect, In the Weeds, Informal Influencers, and Oversimplified Decision-Making.

The following self-assessment scores indicate your tendency to exhibit a Derailer:

1 = Low Concern   2 = Some Concern   3 = High Concern

Derailers   **1.4**

Formality-Structure Disconnect	In the Weeds	Informal Influencers	Oversimplified Decision-Making

| 1.2 | 1.4 | 1 | 1.8 |

Want to learn more?

We are collecting data from all types of leaders throughout the PRG that will enable us to provide you comparisons of leadership ratings across a number of variables including company size, industry, and geography.

For more information and support, check out **www.alaricpartners.com**

Sample Web Report and Data Page 3 of 7

alaric

Business Judgment	Rating
Data Savvy	**2**
References different types of qualitative and quantitative resources	2
Recognizes patterns in seemingly unrelated data to develop actionable insights	1
Uses analytical tools to manipulate and visualize information	2
Asks incisive questions to get to core issue	3
Seeks multiple opinions	2
Strategic Mindset	**2.8**
Explains how a potential business plan is likely to play-out	3
Identifies opportunities to create increased value through innovation	2
Monitors industry, societal, and governmental environment to identify opportunities or threats	3
Seeks new markets within existing industries	3
Recognizes organizational core competency	3
Customer Focus	**2.8**
Demonstrates thorough knowledge of one's own products and services	3
Engages with customers to solve problems and understand their needs	3
Knowledge of the most important factors/metrics driving success in the client's business	3
Identifies the growth potential (or limitations) of customers	2
Monitors competitors' actions	3
Financial Awareness	**2**
Evaluates short-term and long-term financial requirements required to execute plans	2
Defines and monitors key financial metrics	2
Seeks out expert guidance to identify the financial implications of a decision	1
Evaluates the financial risks and potential impact of potential decisions	2
Demonstrates a comprehensive understanding of how the company makes money	3
Balanced Decision-Making	**2.4**
Develops cost-effective solutions to overcome obstacles to meet plan milestones	2
Involves appropriate associates in decisions	1
Recognizes operational capacity and resource implications of decisions	3
Develops "what if" scenarios to better evaluate the short-term and long-term outcomes of a business decision	3
Balances short-term risk and reward	3

Sample Web Report and Data Page 5 of 7

People Judgment	Rating
Engagement	**2.6**
Available to associates on a regular basis	3
Encourages open communication and candid feedback	2
Employs a direct and honest communication style	2
Discusses organizational needs and direction	3
Explains the rationale for decisions	3
Relationship Building	**2.4**
Develops professional relationships in a variety of contexts	2
Communicates regularly with external partners and customers	2
Engages associates from all areas of the organization	2
Handles interactions judiciously and empathetically	3
Personalizes conversations/interactions	3
Team Development	**3**
Participates in setting clear individual and team goals	3
Coaches associates to think beyond personal achievement	3
Promotes respect and relationships within teams	3
Values diversity in experience and backgrounds	3
Encourages team-generated ideas and accomplishments	3
Individual Development	**1.6**
Establishes consistent processes and procedures for development and advancement	2
Invests in the ongoing development of associates	1
Identifies and fosters the development of potential leaders	2
Provides regular performance feedback and coaching	2
Ensures managers demonstrate effective coaching skills	1
Decisiveness	**2.4**
Assesses the situation from the viewpoint of the individual and the organization	2
Considers alternative courses of action and implications	2
Solicits the perspective of others when appropriate	3
Recognizes the importance of making a timely decision	3
Delivers the decision in a thoughtful but firm manner, always sticking to his or her decision	2

Sample Web Report and Data Page 6 of 7

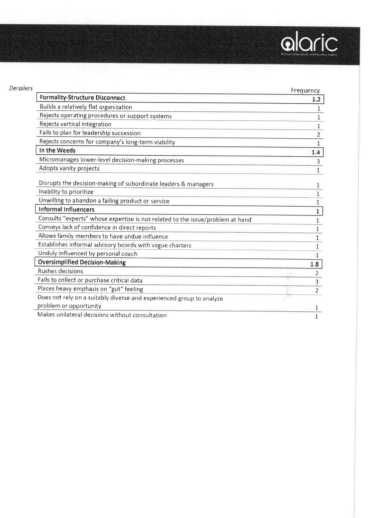

Derailers	Frequency
Formality-Structure Disconnect	**1.2**
Builds a relatively flat organization	1
Rejects operating procedures or support systems	1
Rejects vertical integration	1
Fails to plan for leadership succession	2
Rejects concerns for company's long-term viability	1
In the Weeds	**1.4**
Micromanages lower-level decision-making processes	3
Adopts vanity projects	1
Disrupts the decision-making of subordinate leaders & managers	1
Inability to prioritize	1
Unwilling to abandon a failing product or service	1
Informal Influencers	**1**
Consults "experts" whose expertise is not related to the issue/problem at hand	1
Conveys lack of confidence in direct reports	1
Allows family members to have undue influence	1
Establishes informal advisory boards with vague charters	1
Unduly influenced by personal coach	1
Oversimplified Decision-Making	**1.8**
Rushes decisions	2
Fails to collect or purchase critical data	3
Places heavy emphasis on "gut" feeling	2
Does not rely on a suitably diverse and experienced group to analyze problem or opportunity	1
Makes unilateral decisions without consultation	1

Sample Web Report and Data Page 7 of 7

Appendix B

Seminal Works in Leadership

A seminal work almost always provides a foundational explanation of most leadership capabilities. We have provided an overview of pivotal works and landmark studies that we believe represent a solid introduction to business leadership.

Among the hundreds of seminal works, almost everyone has a favorite theorist or researcher to whom they regularly refer. This is our list of influential experts in the various disciplines speaking to leadership. We encourage you to spend time with these books and articles. As Business Judgment and People Judgment typically overlap, it is not surprising that many of these titles speak to both capabilities. We have provided several leadership-specific resources and works representing business and people-oriented performance.

Foundational Works in Leadership

Peter Drucker's enduring work *The Practice of Management* (1954) examined organizations by structure and function to help businesspeople understand how managers influence productivity and achieve improved results. Drucker introduced the term *knowledge workers,* suggesting that employees use their ideas and efforts to better themselves and organizations. He declared management a practice rather than a science, and his five behaviors remain foundational to many leadership theories.

Behaviorists Blake and Mouton's leadership styles remain an essential topic in introductory management textbooks. *The Managerial Grid: Key Orientations for Achieving Production through People* explored conflicts managers face when endeavoring to motivate people and simultaneously achieving organizational results. The grid explored distinctive behavior styles to achieve success with their people and reach business goals. They later updated the research as *Leadership Dilemmas — GRID Solutions.*

We have always been partial to Tannenbaum and Schmidt's 1973 article in the *Harvard Business Review*: "How to Choose a Leadership Pattern." This groundbreaking study documented a range of leadership behaviors. The authors were the first to tell leaders that the greater autonomy you provide to people, the higher the likelihood all would achieve outstanding results.

Transformational leadership theorists focused heavily on inspiring people — help your associates to grow or aspire, and everyone wins. James MacGregor Burns, a historian and political scientist, wrote *Leadership* in 1978. He began profiling several of the country's most famous leaders. But in the process, Burns discovered common themes and behaviors these leaders displayed as they sought to accomplish important things. He suggested great leaders inspire change. Transformational leadership is an enlightened approach that aims to build a relationship of mutual needs fulfillment between leaders and followers. Burns' work inspired Warren Bennis. He wrote *On Becoming a Leader* (1989), which many believe is the modern guide to becoming an inspirational leader.

These are, in our opinion, timeless general management and leadership works. There are many more. A great seminal reference guide is *The Bass Handbook of Leadership: Theory, Research, and Managerial Applications.* Bernard Bass' book has been the bible to leadership students for over three decades. We highly recommend adding the latest edition to your collection.

Business and People Performance-Oriented Works

Some other more discipline-specific works we recommend include *In Search of Excellence: Lessons from America's Best-Run Companies* by Peters and Waterman. This is considered by many to be one of the all-time greatest business books. The authors' research into companies spanning a range of industries provided leaders with eight critical principles of business success (spanning operational effectiveness, strategy, people, and profit-maximation).

Good to Great is another favorite. Jim Collins' research focused on long-term sustainability. He studied companies that failed to make the leap from good to great. His findings provided insights into both business strategy and leadership. We would also point you to Jeff Pfeffer and Robert Sutton's *Hard Facts, Dangerous Half-Truths, and Total Nonsense: Profiting from Evidence-Based Management*. Their research reminded an entire generation of leaders that effective decision-making is driven by facts and data, not gut reactions or "follow the leader" approaches.

With his first book, *Competitive Strategy* (1980), and later *Competitive Advantage* (1985), Michael Porter has answered fundamental questions about competition and achieving competitive success. Porter's work has never been trendy but is always relevant. Seldom are his books and articles *how-to* approaches (e.g., step a, then step b, and eventually you arrive here). Instead, his work is more about *how to think*. We recommend his most influential articles: "What Is Strategy?" (1996) and "The Five Competitive Forces That Shape Strategy" (2008), the update to his original 1979 work.

If you are interested in group dynamics, Bruce Tuckman published some of the first research on how teams develop. His article in the *Psychological Bulletin*, "Developmental Sequence in Small Groups," introduced *forming, norming, storming*, and *performing*. But it was Jon Katzenbach who will be known as the most notable researcher on teaming. He and Douglas Smith first introduced the concept of high-performing teams in an HBR article, "The Discipline of Teams." They highlighted a team's unique potential to deliver exceptional results. Katzenbach expanded on this work a decade later in the book *The Wisdom of Teams: Creating the High-Performance Organization*.

The following seminal research may interest you when looking to understand the people skills and communication inherent in great leadership. Daniel Goleman's well-regarded HBR article "What Makes a Leader?" (1999) applied pieces of his popular emotional intelligence theory to business executives. Goleman's wife, a prominent researcher in her own right, is Carol Dweck. In *Mindset: The New Psychology of Success,* she argued that individuals could develop a growth mindset enabling them to learn, grown, and ultimately be more successful and happier. Leaders can unlock this mindset in their associates.

We can suggest several works to ground you in everything at the organizational level, from culture to change management. You probably know Maslow's hierarchy of needs ("A Theory of Human Motivation," *Psychology Review*). Interesting story. Before his death, Maslow appeared at the University of Utah and announced he never intended his hierarchy as a tool for practitioners or leaders. He said the model was based on mentally ill subjects and was relevant to businesses or employees. Jonathan's dissertation chairman was there—he said people openly wept. Whatever Maslow intended, go ahead and continue considering his theory of needs. Despite its origins, years of on-the-job application validate the hierarchy. Plus, it is a simple and easy-to-understand concept of motivation within the workplace.

Hertzberg's 1987 HBR article "One More Time: How Do You Motivate Employees?" was the first to suggest that employees are motivated by engagement. He suggested executives refrain from punishing people or looking to pay as the answer to performance. Leaders needed to make their associates' jobs more interesting. In 1992, Kotter and Heskett researched more than two hundred US corporations and found a strong relationship between organizational culture and business performance. Their book *Corporate Culture and Performance* is considered primary knowledge into organizational culture.

In 1953, Gordon Allport first addressed issues of minority employees in the workplace. But it was not until the late 1980s that researchers began examining the benefits of diversity on the job. Roosevelt Thomas' HBR article "From Affirmative Action to Affirming Diversity" explored the value of gender, race, and cultural perspectives in the office. His findings are the tenets of today's organizational inclusion and social justice programs. Finally, when thinking about leading organizational change, we would suggest reading Dr. Rosabeth Moss Kanter. In *The Change Masters: Innovation and Entrepreneurship in the American Corporation* (1983), she explained how employees react to change. Kanter promoted building an entrepreneurial culture in which associates help solve problems and implement new strategies.

As promised, a brief sampling of literature that informs Business and People Judgment capabilities. This is just that—a sample. Hundreds of leadership theorists discovered important information relating to becoming a highly effective leader. Just to give you an idea, at least one of us authors is still rambling off names like Adair, Ansoff, Argyris, Barnard, Chemers, Drury, Fiedler, Graen & Uhl-Bien, Heller, Kouzes & Pozner, Likert, McCall, McGregor, Schein, Selznik, Taylor, Vroom, and Zaleznik. Perhaps you can use those names as a breadcrumb trail if you want to go deeper.

Appendix C

Development Planning Tool

The planning tool is a useful way to create a personalized development plan. A copy of the tool is shown in this appendix. A free and printable copy of the tool is available to download from www.from50to500.com/devplan.

PRG™ Leader Development Plan

Capability	Approach	Desired Outcome	Time Frame	Outcome Achieved	Follow-Up
Priority #	☐ Professional Development ☐ On-the-Job Development ☐ Self-Development <u>Plan</u>				
Priority #	☐ Professional Development ☐ On-the-Job Development ☐ Self-Development <u>Plan</u>				
Priority #	☐ Professional Development ☐ On-the-Job Development ☐ Self-Development <u>Plan</u>				
Priority #	☐ Professional Development ☐ On-the-Job Development ☐ Self-Development <u>Plan</u>				

Bibliography

"Army Leader Development Strategy—2013." In *U.S. Department of the Army*. Https://usacac.army.mil/.

Bass, Bernard. *Bass & Stogdill's Handbook of Leadership: Theory, Research, and Managerial Applications*. 3rd ed. New York, NY: Free Press, 1990.

Bentz, Jon. "The Sears Experience in the Investigation, Description, and Prediction of Executive Behavior." *Measuring Executive Effectiveness*, 1967, 147–206.

Bray, Douglas W. "The Management Progress Study." *American Psychologist* 19, no. 6 (1964): 419–20. Https://doi.org/10.1037/h0039579.

Brown, Tom. "The Essence of Strategy." *Management Review*, April 1997, 9.

The Center for Change Management. *The Annual Change Management Impact Study*. S&B Partners, 2014.

Center for Creative Leadership. *Off the Track: Why and How Successful Executives Get Derailed*. By Morgan McCall and Michael Lombardo. Report no. 21. Greensboro, NC: Center for Creative Leadership, 1983.

Chester, Barnard. *The Functions of the Executive*. Cambridge, MA: Harvard University Press, 1938.

"Consumer Price Index Data from 1913 to 2015." *U.S. Department of Labor Statistics*. Last modified 2015. Http://www.usinflationcalculator.com/inflation/consumerprice-index-and-annual-percent-changes-from-1913-to-2008/.

Dapra, Jonathan. "Small Business Leadership Competency Modeling: A Mixed Methods Study to Distinguish Success Factors for High-Performing Leaders of Small Companies." PhD diss., Argosy University, 2017.

Drucker, Peter F., and Joseph A. Maciariello. *Management*. Rev. ed. New York, NY: Collins, 2008.

European Union European Commission. *Final Report: Framework Service Contract for the Procurement of Studies and Other Supporting Services on Commission Impact Assessments and Evaluations Interim, Final and Ex-Post Evaluations of Policies, Programmes and Other Activities Evaluation of the SME Definition.* Accessed 2012. Https://ec.europa.eu/cip/files/cip/ executive_summary_cip_final_report_en.pdf.

— — —. *Report on European SMEs 2016/2017–Focus on Self-Employment.* Accessed 2017. Http://ec.europa.eu/.

— — —. *User Guide to the SME Definition.* Http://ec.europa.eu/.

Eurostat. Small and Medium Sized Enterprises. Last modified 2016. Https://ec.europa.eu/eurostat/web/structural-business statistics/small-and-medium-sized-enterprises.

Gibbs, Nancy, and Michael Duffy. The Presidents Club: Inside the World's Most Exclusive Fraternity. New York, NY: Simon & Schuster, 2012.

Government of Canada Innovation, Science and Economic Development Canada Small Business Branch. *Key Small Business Statistics — 2020.* Report no. ISSN 1718-3456.

Hooper, C. N. "Defining 'Small Business' in Government Programs." *Journal of Small Business* 10, no. 4 (1972): 28–34.

Isaacson, Walter. *Steve Jobs.* New York, NY: Simon & Schuster, 2011.

The Managerial Grid: Key Orientations for Achieving Production through People. Houston, TX: Gulf, 1972.

McCall, Morgan W., Michael M. Lombardo, and Ann M. Morrison. *The Lessons of Experience: How Successful Executives Develop on the Job.* Lexington, MA: Lexington Books, 1988.

"Number of Firms, Number of Establishments, Employment, and Annual Payroll by Enterprise Employment Size for the United States and States, Totals." *U.S. Census Bureau.* Last modified 2017. Http://www.census.gov.

Peters, Thomas J., and Robert H. Waterman. *In Search of Excellence: Lessons from America's Best-Run Companies.* New

York, NY: Harper & Row, 1982.

Pfeffer, Jeffrey, and Robert I. Sutton. *Hard Facts, Dangerous Half-Truths, and Total Nonsense: Profiting from Evidence-Based Management.* Boston, MA: Harvard Business School Press, 2006.

Podolny, Joel, and Morten Hansen. "How Apple Is Organized for Innovation: It's About Experts Leading Experts." *Harvard Business Review,* November/December 2020, 4–11.

Porter, Michael, and Mark Kramer. "Strategy & Society: The Link Between Competitive Advantage and Corporate Social Responsibility." *Harvard Business Review,* November/December 2006, 1–14.

Porter, Michael E. "What Is Strategy?" *Harvard Business Review,* November/December 1996, 10.

Pryor, Mildred Golden, Lisa Pryor Singleton, Sonia Taneja, and Leslie A. Toombs. "Teaming as a Strategic and Tactical Tool: An Analysis with Recommendations." *IEEE Engineering Management Review* 39, no. 1 (2011): 3–13. Http://dx.doi.org/10.1109/EMR.2011.5729967.

Reynoso, Carlos, Moisés Alarcón Osuna, and Luis Figueroa. "Micro, Small and Medium-Sized Businesses in Jalisco: Their Evolution, and Strategic Challenges." *Review of Business & Finance Studies* 26, no. 2 (2009): 320–33.

Ruth Porat on Leading through Crisis and Google's Latest Moonshot: To Rebuild the U.S. Economy—One Small Business at a Time, September 17, 2020. Accessed 2020. Https://www.forbes.com.

Select Government of Mexico. *Number of Companies in Mexico in 2020, by Number of Employees (in 1,000s) [Graph].* 2020. Https://www-statista-com/statistics/1185241/mexico-businesses-workforce/.

Simons, Robert. "Choosing the Right Customer." *Harvard Business Review,* March 2014.

Spencer, Herbert. *The Study of Sociology.* New York, NY:

Appleton, 1873.

"Statistics for All U.S. Firms with Paid Employees by Industry, Gender, and Employment Size of Firm for the U.S. and States: 2012—More Information 2012 Survey of Business Owners." *U.S. Census Bureau*. Last modified 2013. Https://www.census.gov.

Taylor, Frederick Winslow. *The Principles of Scientific Management*. New York, NY: Norton, 1967.

"2012 Survey of Business Owners: Preliminary Data." *U.S. Census Bureau*. Last modified 2015. Https://www.census.gov.

U.S. Small Business Administration. *Annual Report of the United States Small Business Administration*. Washington DC, 1971.

U.S. Small Business Administration SBA Office of Advocacy. *Advocacy: The Voice of the Small Business in Government*. Http://www.sba.gov.

BUSINESS
BOOKS

Business Books

Business Books publishes practical guides and insightful non-fiction for beginners and professionals. Covering aspects from management skills, leadership and organizational change to positive work environments, career coaching and self-care for managers, our books are a valuable addition to those working in the world of business.

15 Ways to Own Your Future
Take Control of Your Destiny in Business and in Life
Michael Khouri
A 15-point blueprint for creating better collaboration,
enjoyment, and success in business and in life.
Paperback: 978-1-78535-300-0 ebook: 978-1-78535-301-7

The Common Excuses of the Comfortable Compromiser
Understanding Why People Oppose Your Great Idea
Matt Crossman
Comfortable compromisers block the way of anyone trying to
change anything. This is your guide to their common excuses.
Paperback: 978-1-78099-595-3 ebook: 978-1-78099-596-0

Mastering the Mommy Track
Juggling Career and Kids in Uncertain Times
Erin Flynn Jay
Mastering the Mommy Track tells the stories of everyday working
mothers, the challenges they have faced, and lessons learned.
Paperback: 978-1-78099-123-8 ebook: 978-1-78099-124-5

**The Most Creative, Escape the Ordinary, Excel at Public
Speaking Book Ever**
All The Help You Will Ever Need in Giving a Speech
Philip Theibert
The 'everything you need to give an outstanding speech' book,
complete with original material written by a professional
speech-writer.
Paperback: 978-1-78099-672-1 ebook: 978-1-78099-673-8

Small Change, Big Deal

Money as if People Mattered
Jennifer Kavanagh
Money is about relationships: between individuals and
between communities. Small is still beautiful, as peer lending
model, micro-credit, shows.
Paperback: 978-1-78099-313-3 ebook: 978-1-78099-314-0

The Failing Logic of Money
Duane Mullin
Money is wasteful and cruel, causes war, crime and
dysfunctional feudalism. Humankind needs happiness, peace
and abundance. So banish money and use technology and
knowledge to rid the world of war, crime and poverty.
Paperback: 978-1-84694-259-4 ebook: 978-1-84694-888-6

Modern Day Selling
Unlocking Your Hidden Potential
Brian Barfield
Learn how to reconnect sales associates with customers and
unlock hidden sales potential.
Paperback: 978-1-78099-457-4 ebook: 978-1-78099-458-1

Readers of ebooks can buy or view any of these bestsellers by
clicking on the live link in the title. Most titles are published
in paperback and as an ebook. Paperbacks are available in
traditional bookshops. Both print and ebook formats
are available online.

Find more titles and sign up to our readers' newsletter at
http://www.jhpbusiness-books.com/
Facebook: https://www.facebook.com/JHPNonFiction/
Twitter: @JHPNonFiction